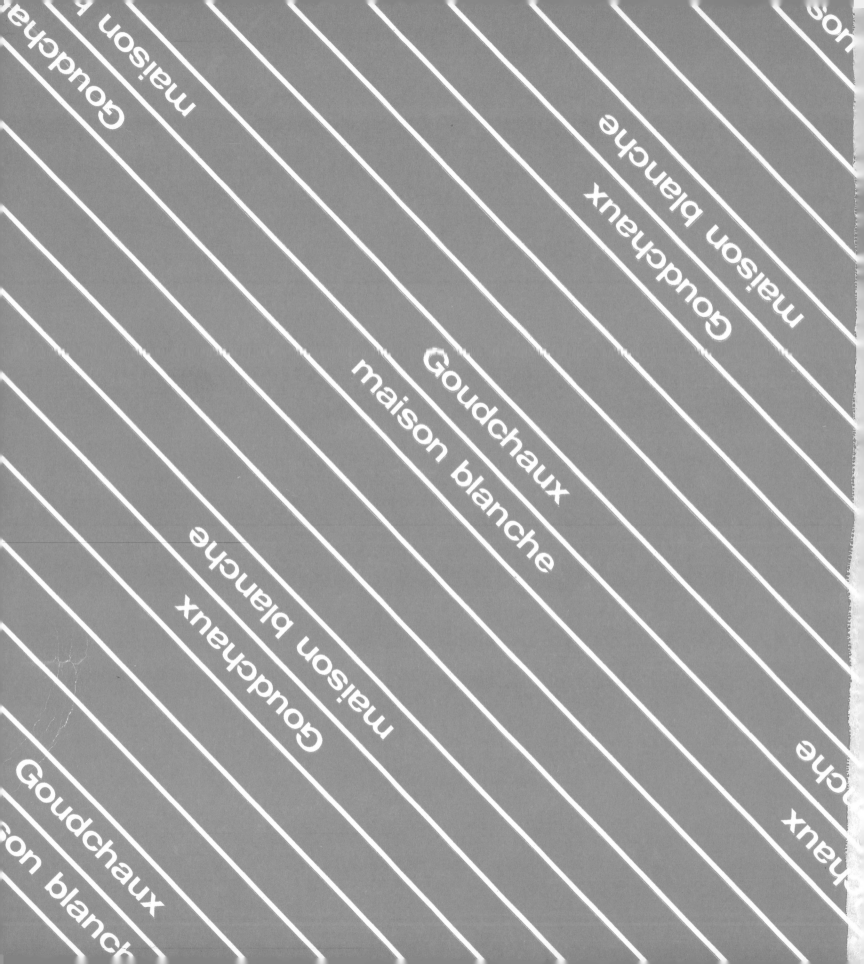

WE WERE MERCHANTS

WE WERE MERCHANTS

THE **STERNBERG FAMILY** AND THE STORY OF **GOUDCHAUX'S**
AND **MAISON BLANCHE** DEPARTMENT STORES

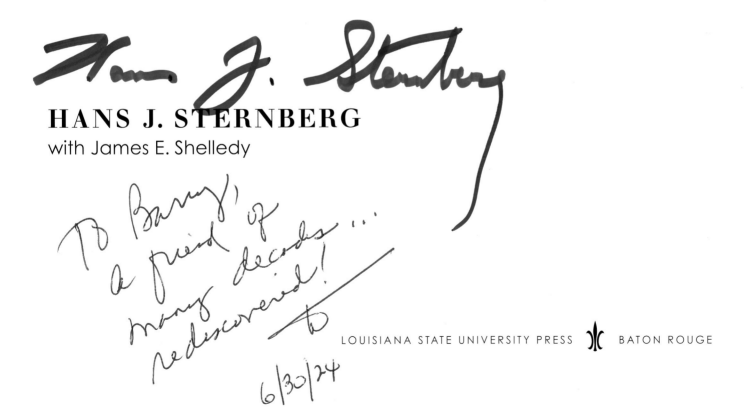

HANS J. STERNBERG

with James E. Shelledy

To Barry,
a friend of
many decades ...
rediscovered!

6/30/24

LOUISIANA STATE UNIVERSITY PRESS ❧ BATON ROUGE

PUBLISHED BY LOUISIANA STATE UNIVERSITY PRESS

Copyright © 2009 by Louisiana State University Press
All rights reserved
Manufactured in Canada
Second printing

DESIGNER: Michelle A. Neustrom
TYPEFACES: Walbaum BE, Century Gothic
PRINTER AND BINDER: Friesens Corporation

Frontispiece: Hans and Josef Sternberg walking through Goudchaux's, 1983. All photos are from the author's collection.

LIBRARY OF CONGRESS CATALOGING-IN-PUBLICATION DATA
Sternberg, Hans J., 1935–
    We were merchants : the Sternberg family and the story of Goud-chaux's and Maison Blanche department stores / Hans J. Sternberg, with James E. Shelledy ; foreword by Bobby Jindal.
        p. cm.
    Includes index.
    ISBN 978-0-8071-3449-8 (cloth : alk. paper) 1. Sternberg, Hans J., 1935– 2. Goudchaux/Maison Blanche (Firm)—History. 3. Department stores—Louisiana—History. 4. Merchants—Louisiana—Biography. I. Shelledy, James E., 1943– II. Title.
    HF5465.U64G637 2009
    381'.1410922763—dc22
    [B]
                                                            2009005543

To my life partner of forty-two years, Donna Weintraub Sternberg, who contributed seemingly endless hours to this emotional endeavor by tolerating my working late into the night, by sharing many memories, by repetitive proofreading, and by providing vital assistance and constant comfort

CONTENTS

ILLUSTRATIONS

FOREWORD

LOUISIANA IS A STATE whose history is filled with unique stories that captivate the rest of the nation, and the story of Goudchaux's/Maison Blanche department stores is no exception. It begins more than two hundred years ago in a small German town and leads the reader through two world wars, the Great Depression, and the history of a family that left an indelible mark on Louisiana.

I can still remember going to Goudchaux's as a child with my mother. The loyalty the store bred in its customers speaks to the dedication of the Sternberg family. Indeed, I remember buying my first winter coat as a student and, many years later, selecting my wedding china at the famous downtown Baton Rouge store.

Hans Sternberg tells us his family's story of inspiration, ambition, and dreams that followed his father Erich's purchase of Goudchaux's from the founding family. Erich left Germany during a time of great uncertainty as the Nazi regime consolidated its power, and he made a life for his family in Baton Rouge.

Erich Sternberg revived Goudchaux's during the Great Depression, a feat within itself, and through daring tactics and true innovation, he and his sons grew their family business into a Louisiana institution. Goudchaux's expanded throughout the state with the acquisition of Maison Blanche in the 1980s, and then into Florida. In so doing, the Sternbergs cemented their family-business place in Louisiana history.

The American Dream truly applies to the path the Sternberg family followed in America. Erich taught his sons, Hans and Josef, to work hard, respect others, and never take anything for granted. It is no secret that these attributes are what helped make Goudchaux's/Maison Blanche into the model for department stores across the nation.

Although Hans has since sold the business, a piece of it lives on with his new venture, Starmount Life Insurance Company, which began as part of Goudchaux's. And though the name is no longer around, Goudchaux's has provided generations of Louisianians with a lifetime of memories. The Sternberg family has shown us all just how far hard work and a commitment to serve can take you.

Bobby Jindal
Governor of Louisiana

ACKNOWLEDGMENTS

ABOVE ALL, I WANT to thank my children, Erich, Julie, Deborah, and Marc, adults with their own families, for their support and encouragement of my efforts in writing this book. They offered suggestions and scrutinized the manuscript; that was especially true of Julie, who herself is an author. In reality, it is for my children, their spouses—Katie Riker Sternberg, Paul Schoeman, Michael Roth, and Katie Goldstein—and my nine grandchildren that I write this book. A family's story, with so many important lessons to tell, must be committed to paper if it is not to be forgotten.

There are many others whom I wish to thank for their assistance in bringing this project to completion.

Insa Sternberg Abraham—my sister, who watched me at eighteen months toddle down the gangplank into my father's arms as we arrived in New York from Germany—shared memories, collections of articles, and photographs. She has been constant in her love of the family and the stores. Dr. Mel Sternberg, now of Mobile, Alabama, whose uncle in New Orleans helped my father connect with Goudchaux's, provided memories and research. Helpful, too, was Mary Ann Sternberg, spouse of my late brother, Josef, who volunteered her research notes, observations, and remembrances, particularly her interviews with early Goudchaux's employees.

Irmgard (Frances) Sternberg Hodes of Orlando, Florida, my cousin, whose memories of Germany and our migration to Baton Rouge remain crystal clear in her fertile mind, shed much light on portions of this story. Paul Sternberg, grandson of my uncle Max, shared memories and memorabilia. Carol Knurr Cain of Chicago and Werner Knurr of Colorado provided details of the Knurr family tree. Florent (Pon) Hardy Jr., of the Office of Secretary of State for Louisiana, helped with historical information from the state archives, of which he is director.

The state's newly elected governor, Bobby Jindal, with whose family we have been acquainted for decades, generously provided a foreword to this book, donating time he did not have during his hectic transition into the Louisiana governor's office and the initial days of his administration. Appreciation also goes to his then-director of communications, Trey Williams.

Phyllis Cutrer, my devoted assistant for more than thirty-three years, provided input about the stores, not to mention much proofreading and typing, the latter at breathtaking speed. She has learned not to let me read anything with a pen in my hand. Colleen Landry, a talented Starmount employee, put her skilled touch to photographic enhancements and cover proposals.

Richard Lipsey added details to our accounts of struggles with political bad guys over the years. We won a lot more than we lost, and it was always great sport. Lance Hill of the Southern Institute for Education and Research, along with the Anti-Defamation League of New Orleans, responded to our requests with valuable notes on the prejudices and politics of the times, especially those surrounding David Duke and former congressman John Rarick.

Former Maison Blanche executives Steve Tisdell, Don Bell, Pam Petite, Charles Unfried, and Tom Cagley poured out a wealth of information—particularly Tom, who shared pertinent pages from a diary he kept while at the store. Many invaluable memories of Baton Rouge's early days, and of Erich and Lea Sternberg and banker Leroy Ward, came from Laura Clark.

Jack Farber, former CEO of City Stores, graciously provided, from his unpublished memoirs, details of our negotiations to purchase Maison Blanche. (Jack, you said such nice things about me—did I pay too much for MB?) Richard Steinberg of Mall Properties spent considerable time researching the establishment of Goudchaux's first branch, at Cortana Mall. William Freedman of Troutman Sanders in New York City supplied information on the financial details of the Maison Blanche purchase. And Milton Rubin, a retired New York investment banker and Princeton classmate of mine, helped in reconstructing details surrounding MB's recession-prompted meltdown.

Advocate columnist Smiley Anders invited his legions of readers to send in recollections of Goudchaux's, which he forwarded to us for inclusion in the book. Those "Goudchaux's Moments" greatly enhanced the finished product. Smiley gets a gold star. Rabbi Martha Bergadine helped with the spelling of Hebrew words that I far too often mess up. Ian Arnof, former CEO of the First National Bank of Commerce, First Commerce Corporation, offered his insights into the banking community in the early 1990s, when one in three Louisiana financial institutions failed. And my attorney, Lee Kantrow, fielded legal questions, although I am responsible for any errors. (You can relax now, Lee.)

Ashton Phelps Jr., publisher of *The Times-Picayune* of New Orleans and friend and confidant, doesn't agree with a few of the harsher judgments we included in this book, but I have always regarded his advice highly. Kevin Roche of *The New York Times* regularly sent observations and editing suggestions during the writing of the manuscript. Daniel McBride, while a student at Louisiana State University, aided us in uncovering details of the early Sternberg family story through his translations of German documents. (In the process, he learned that his father, Perry McBride, now of Shreveport, worked for Goudchaux's while attending LSU in the early 1970s.)

And, of course, my sincere thanks to LSU Press director MaryKatherine Callaway and acquisitions editor Margaret Hart for their unwavering faith in the book (and tussle over the title). Their suggestions, patience, and professional approach were much appreciated. Catherine Kadair, senior editor, combed the copy for style errors and low-visibility editing misses. Her work made for a better read. Designer Michelle Neustrom's talents shine throughout. All of them shared with me a desire to ensure a Goudchaux's touch of class to the book.

Roger M. Williams, former *Time* magazine bureau chief in Atlanta, did an excellent job on the first copy editing of this book.

Finally, my gratitude goes to the many others—most of them quoted in the book—who helped by sharing their memories. I ask forgiveness from those inadvertently missed in these formal acknowledgments.

Hans J. Sternberg

WE WERE MERCHANTS

INTRODUCTION

PEOPLE SELDOM WRITE BOOKS for the fun of it, although it can be an enjoyable endeavor. There must be some sort of prompt. Mine is threefold:

First, Goudchaux's and, later, its adopted, slightly older sibling, Maison Blanche, were not simply stores. They were department stores, near-magical wonderlands in the retailing landscape.

Second, Goudchaux's and Maison Blanche weren't *ordinary* department stores. They were Louisiana legends, emporiums of courtly graciousness, personalized service, cradle-to-grave merchandise of high quality, the place where dreams came true.

Third, they reflected the handiwork and passion of five generations of merchants, which, of course, becomes the final rationale for such a detailed account as this book offers. My antecedents may not have operated their department store in the grand, modern-day fashion, but their enterprise formed the embryo of what was to come.

While the title "world's first department store"—at least as we have come to visualize that institution—has no shortage of claimants, operations of that type were popping up in the major cities of Europe during the mid-nineteenth century. By the 1890s, they were well established in the cities of the United States. (Smaller communities had their equivalent: the general stores.) After World War II, this country boasted hundreds of local, regional, and national department stores worthy of the title.

Today, there may be as few as twenty, and even then only if you count the likes of J. C. Penney, Sears, and Kohl's (which I don't).

In twentieth-century America, few things exceeded the cultural force of the true department store. The concept on which department stores built their strength was straightforward and two pronged. One-stop shopping was a powerful convenience to the customers. Just as supermarkets revolutionized grocery shopping by putting the butcher, the baker, and the candymaker under one roof, department stores joined the men's department with the women's, children's, home furnishings, and other departments. Previously prevalent mom-and-pop, freestanding specialty stores were sorely tried, and many lost that competitive battle and closed.

Department stores had another advantage over specialty stores: They were based—and still are—on the synergies of multidepartment sales. A cluster of departments, each attracting its own clientele, became a larger force. If, for example, the men's department attracted one thousand shoppers and the women's department another one thousand, cross-shopping between the two added customers to each. In a department store operation, the whole adds up to more than the sum of the parts. If one department temporarily falls out of fashion, others carry the company until the weakness is cured. Department stores, in other words, have built-in business parachutes.

The department store concept worked effectively for decades. Then low-cost discounters arrived, the Wal-Marts and Targets, followed by category-killers, such as Home Depot, Best Buy, and Bed, Bath & Beyond. Department stores lost some of their competitive appeal. But before those malls and discounters, before big-box stores and outlet malls, before Internet shopping, the local department store was a dominant economic and social magnet, a wondrous place to see and in which to be seen.

At their inception, all genuine department stores were single venues situated in or near the merchandising center of a city—which was always "downtown" until the second half of the twentieth century. Those stores started out independent and family owned. They defined a city's taste and style, and often the national fashion trends of the day. Their internal presentations, as well as their display windows, were choreographed with imagination and verve that attracted and delighted customers of every age.

Department stores would have faded into a fifties sunset had it not been for two of those dynamics: the popularity of women's ready-to-wear clothing and the formalizing of store buying groups, the latter a concept that began in the 1930s to increase individual purchasing power.

Department stores also gave themselves increased longevity, beginning in the mid-1960s, by sprouting branches in newly developed suburban shopping malls. That move formed the core of a retailing strategy to bring merchandise closer to customers who had been migrating since the 1950s from old city neighborhoods to the suburbs.

Retailers depend on crowds of shoppers to produce the high volume required to support their massive operations. Such special events as anniversary celebrations, holiday seasons, and sales geared to the calendar produce just such crowds. Stores turned to full-page and multi-page newspaper advertisements, as graphically gorgeous as they were enticing, to announce and generate interest in those events as one of two main ways, along with displays, to promote. Department stores put much care and many resources into those advertisements.

No ad, however, could pack the visual punch of in-store presentations, which became elaborate after window displays diminished in importance in the latter half of the twentieth century as most department stores of that time were built without windows. As style became key, magnificent displays were built within the store, each with the ambiance and appeal of the individual vendors, such as Liz Claiborne, Ralph Lauren, and Tommy Hilfiger. These presentations became stores within a store and they remain central to today's retailing.

During the time when retail windows were in vogue, nothing topped the effort—and expense—of Christmas displays. They seldom were worth the cost, but nobody blinked. Going downtown to look at the department-store holiday windows was an annual event for many families. (Maison Blanche's Mr. Bingle, a wooden, puppetlike Christmas figure, was among a half dozen holiday-window icons that gained national status.)

Around the turn of the twentieth century, department stores, traditionally anchored in the heart or the vicinity of the central business district, began building bigger and more ornate retailing palaces, each store attempting to architecturally outdo its rivals as owners strove for singular identity and prominence. The buildings on Canal Street in New Orleans represent such structural elegance. Many of the store façades remain today, including that of Maison Blanche (now the Ritz Carlton Hotel) at Canal and Dauphine.

Department store operations usually were profitable but always a bit risky. Ownership changed hands often. By the 1920s, chains began to appear. By the 1950s, some four thousand department stores were operating in America, but in 1965 the annual sales for discount stores, where mass-produced clothing and low-priced imports became the norm, exceeded those of department stores. It was the start of a thirty-year slide.

The first to go were the cash-strapped family-owned stores. They either went public, closed their doors voluntarily or by force of creditors, or a national chain bought them. Soon, however, chains were devouring their own. By the 1980s, a department store bankruptcy or merger was as common as a January white sale. Goudchaux's/Maison Blanche, at the time this country's largest family-owned department store, was among the last holdouts.

Today, *corporate* department store chains remain in

operation; except for the nation's largest downtowns, nearly all are located in malls, which they "anchor." With few exceptions (Nordstrom's, Neiman Marcus, and Saks Fifth Avenue come to mind), the personalities of department stores are as interchangeable as those of banks. Merchandise is plentiful, but customers are faceless charge cards. Management is tucked away in some far-off city, unrecognizable even when it conducts an occasional inspection of a local store.

This book therefore is dedicated to an era when the department store was part of the family, when youthful faces pressed against display windows signaled the Christmas season had arrived, when someone actually measured your foot and helped you select the perfect new shoes, when someone getting a makeover in cosmetics could transfix onlookers, when a visit to the toy department was mandatory if children were tagging along. It was a period when browsers and buyers alike were greeted and remembered, when they were treated like visiting royalty.

In writing this book, I recognize with enormous gratitude and respect the vision, courage, and wisdom of my parents, Erich and Lea Sternberg. They have been an unending source of inspiration. Their decision in 1933 to leave Nazi Germany not only saved our lives but also set us on the road to fulfilling a retail dream in America, the country my parents adopted and adored throughout their lives.

So that the memory does not fade for the middle-aged and the elders, so that a younger generation may comprehend the nostalgia of that era's shopping, so that the tale of one immigrant family's role in all this doesn't evaporate with the passage of time, I have written the inside, largely untold story of Goudchaux's and Maison Blanche. To paraphrase Irving Berlin, the song may have ended, but let the melody linger on.

1 ‖ GENESIS

FOR FOURTEEN MONTHS, I had been the lone steward of a two-hundred-year-old family legacy: a small German store that evolved into America's largest family-owned department store. On February 10, 1992, the Goudchaux's and Maison Blanche stores slipped from my hands. It was the second-worst day of my life.

The worst had occurred several weeks earlier when I informed my eighty-eight-year-old mother we were selling "The Store" to a national chain and that we no longer would be able to refer to ourselves as merchants. The end came two centuries after my great-great-grandfather opened a clothing store in Aurich, Germany. Some said it was inevitable; others said it was the culmination of an unfortunate set of circumstances. Count me among the latter group.

As I walked away from the beleaguered chain's headquarters at 1500 Main Street in Baton Rouge, I found myself second-guessing my decision to sell. What would my forebears, merchants all, have said? What would the founder of this line of storekeepers, Samuel Sternberg, have thought? What counsel would great-grandfather Meyer Sternberg or grandfather Jacob Sternberg have offered? Would my father, Erich Sternberg, who entered that very building for the first time in 1936 after fleeing Nazi Germany, have done the same thing? Would even my late brother, Josef, with whom I was joined at the mercantile hip for more than three decades, have agreed?

Not only was I turning my back on nearly ninety years of immediate family and Louisiana history, I was fifty-six years old and out of work, at least the type of work I had long considered a vocation and an avocation. Granted, I was hardly broke. On top of my share of the sale proceeds, the new owners would pay me a million dollars to stay away from retailing for five years.

I got into my car on that cool February evening and gazed at the sixty-five-year-old structure that six years earlier had been featured in *Ripley's Believe It or Not* and had been corporate headquarters for twenty-four stores, a chain that had a national reputation for fashion, innovation, and service, in its time a Nordstrom-like legend. Selling was the only viable option, I kept reassuring myself as I started the car, slowly made my last exit from the parking lot, and headed home. But I was nagged by the notion that the next time any member of our family entered a Goudchaux's or Maison Blanche store, it would be as a customer.

Unthinkable.

My emotions notwithstanding, the family business had accumulated nearly a quarter billion dollars of debt, prompted primarily by its rapid expansion during a national recession. Things were bleak, and we faced a sea of red ink. The truly unfortunate part was that I had constructed a plan that might have saved us, but international events had intervened to eradicate that possibility.

And we weren't the only ones in big trouble. Department stores everywhere were falling in droves in the late 1980s and early 1990s.

Perhaps it was nothing more than a sign of the times, inevitable recognition that family-owned department stores had had their day and must merge, go public, or fade away. The rational, business side of me knew that selling was the correct course of action. The emotional tug-of-war, however, turned the ride home into a remarkable parallel journey traversing two centuries and five generations.

Sometime in the 1790s, Samuel Sternberg opened a store in Aurich, a town tucked into the northwest corner of Germany near the North Sea and the Dutch border. Samuel started a merchant legacy that ended two centuries later, perhaps to the year. Some might consider family lineage and future business acquisitions distinct stories, but I believe them to be fused. These are inseparable tales.

We can't identify our Sternberg line much before the mid-eighteenth century. Nor can we be certain of the genesis of the Sternberg name. With an absence of surnames, family trees disintegrate into a genealogical bramble.

Samuel, a Jew, was said to have been a hat peddler from nearby Grossefehn prior to his arrival in Aurich. There is a reference to Samuel originally hailing from the Rheinland-Pfalz area of southwestern Germany, on the border with France. Samuel had a surname; perhaps his father, who was called Solomon or Saloman, did also. An obscure footnote in *Die Juden in Ostfriesland*, by Max Markreich, says Solomon came from the ethnically German area of Sternberg, Mähren (present-day Moravia, a region in the Czech Republic).

When in 1787 the Austro-Hungarian empire decreed that Jews must register a permanent surname, it makes sense that Solomon would have adopted "Sternberg" from the city, which may well have been his birthplace, or from the imposing and nearby Castle Sternberg. There are more than a dozen Sternberg sites (towns, castles, geographical points) in central Europe, so who knows? There also are references to Sternbergs as Frenchmen (which would make some sense, given Solomon's and

Samuel's time in Rheinland-Pfalz) and as Spaniards. To add to the confusion, the first Jews in the Aurich region were Italians, invited there by the reigning prince in the 1400s, according to *Die Juden in Ostfriesland*.

Whatever the case, the German noun *Sternberg* means "star mountain" or "star mount"—a mountain so tall it, allegorically, touches the stars. And that is where the story of Goudchaux's/Maison Blanche begins.

Samuel Sternberg had three children: Wolf, who went to England; an unnamed middle son who died at birth; and Meyer, who was born August 18, 1821, and who took over the Sternberg store in the mid-1800s, renaming it Meyer Sternberg's.

That the Sternbergs were Jewish is coincidental to the first 150 years of this story; it is central, however, to the final half century. The totality of this Sternberg legacy—our family, our business, our religion, our merchant genes, passed on and embraced for five generations—comprised the cornerstone for what would become Goudchaux's/Maison Blanche.

The Nazis provided the catalyst.

The town of Aurich, set in the center of Ostfriesland on the moorlands of the North Sea, began as a farming community. Its cattle and horses were known as far away as the Mediterranean region. Periodic bickering among feudal leaders played havoc on Aurich, but an imposing castle, completed in 1464, nurtured a half century of relative peace and prosperity. Castle and town were burned to the ground in 1514 during Saxon conflicts, only to be rebuilt in the mid-1600s. Aurich became a center of government for the surrounding area, as well as for business, craft, trade, and an imposing aristocracy.

Aurich had roughly six thousand residents as the twentieth century dawned. Jews, nearly all Orthodox, made up about 7 percent of the population, considerably more than in Germany as a whole. (The country encompassed more than a half million Jews at this time, about three quarters of a percent of the general population, with an estimated 70 percent residing in urban areas.)

According to research done by the Diaspora Museum in Jerusalem, Jews first arrived in Aurich in the late thir-

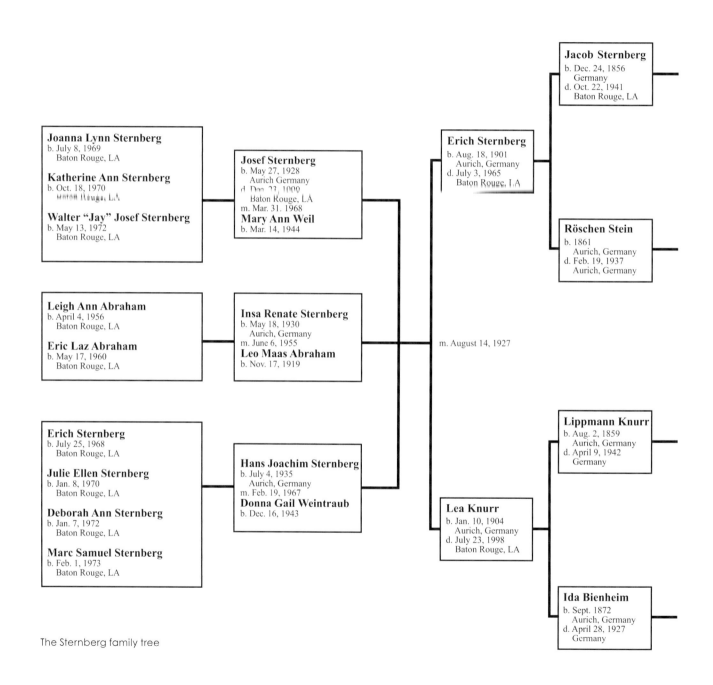

Joanna Lynn Sternberg
b. July 8, 1969
  Baton Rouge, LA

Katherine Ann Sternberg
b. Oct. 18, 1970
  Baton Rouge, LA

Walter "Jay" Josef Sternberg
b. May 13, 1972
  Baton Rouge, LA

Josef Sternberg
b. May 27, 1928
  Aurich Germany
d. Dec. 23, 1999
  Baton Rouge, LA
m. Mar. 31, 1968
Mary Ann Weil
b. Mar. 14, 1944

Erich Sternberg
b. Aug. 18, 1901
  Aurich, Germany
d. July 3, 1965
  Baton Rouge, LA

Jacob Sternberg
b. Dec. 24, 1856
  Germany
d. Oct. 22, 1941
  Baton Rouge, LA

Röschen Stein
b. 1861
  Aurich, Germany
d. Feb. 19, 1937
  Aurich, Germany

Leigh Ann Abraham
b. April 4, 1956
  Baton Rouge, LA

Eric Laz Abraham
b. May 17, 1960
  Baton Rouge, LA

Insa Renate Sternberg
b. May 18, 1930
  Aurich, Germany
m. June 6, 1955
Leo Maas Abraham
b. Nov. 17, 1919

m. August 14, 1927

Erich Sternberg
b. July 25, 1968
  Baton Rouge, LA

Julie Ellen Sternberg
b. Jan. 8, 1970
  Baton Rouge, LA

Deborah Ann Sternberg
b. Jan. 7, 1972
  Baton Rouge, LA

Marc Samuel Sternberg
b. Feb. 1, 1973
  Baton Rouge, LA

Hans Joachim Sternberg
b. July 4, 1935
  Aurich, Germany
m. Feb. 19, 1967
Donna Gail Weintraub
b. Dec. 16, 1943

Lea Knurr
b. Jan. 10, 1904
  Aurich, Germany
d. July 23, 1998
  Baton Rouge, LA

Lippmann Knurr
b. Aug. 2, 1859
  Aurich, Germany
d. April 9, 1942
  Germany

Ida Bienheim
b. Sept. 1872
  Aurich, Germany
d. April 28, 1927
  Germany

The Sternberg family tree

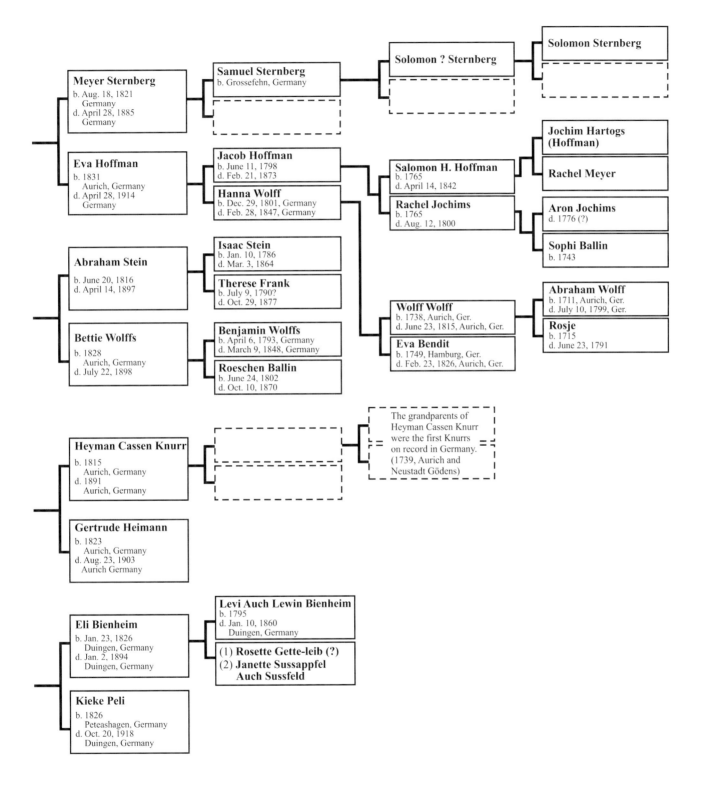

Meyer Sternberg
b. Aug. 18, 1821
Germany
d. April 28, 1885
Germany

Eva Hoffman
b. 1831
Aurich, Germany
d. April 28, 1914
Germany

Samuel Sternberg
b. Grossefehn, Germany

Solomon ? Sternberg

Solomon Sternberg

Jacob Hoffman
b. June 11, 1798
d. Feb. 21, 1873

Hanna Wolff
b. Dec. 29, 1801, Germany
d. Feb. 28, 1847, Germany

Salomon H. Hoffman
b. 1765
d. April 14, 1842

Rachel Jochims
b. 1765
d. Aug. 12, 1800

**Jochim Hartogs
(Hoffman)**

Rachel Meyer

Aron Jochims
d. 1776 (?)

Sophi Ballin
b. 1743

Abraham Stein
b. June 20, 1816
d. April 14, 1897

Bettie Wolffs
b. 1828
Aurich, Germany
d. July 22, 1898

Isaac Stein
b. Jan. 10, 1786
d. Mar. 3, 1864

Therese Frank
b. July 9, 1790?
d. Oct. 29, 1877

Benjamin Wolffs
b. April 6, 1793, Germany
d. March 9, 1848, Germany

Roeschen Ballin
b. June 24, 1802
d. Oct. 10, 1870

Wolff Wolff
b. 1738, Aurich, Ger.
d. June 23, 1815, Aurich, Ger.

Eva Bendit
b. 1749, Hamburg, Ger.
d. Feb. 23, 1826, Aurich, Ger.

Abraham Wolff
b. 1711, Aurich, Ger.
d. July 10, 1799, Ger.

Rosje
b. 1715
d. June 23, 1791

Heyman Cassen Knurr
b. 1815
Aurich, Germany
d. 1891
Aurich, Germany

Gertrude Heimann
b. 1823
Aurich, Germany
d. Aug. 23, 1903
Aurich Germany

The grandparents of
Heyman Cassen Knurr
were the first Knurrs
on record in Germany.
(1739, Aurich and
Neustadt Gödens)

Eli Bienheim
b. Jan. 23, 1826
Duingen, Germany
d. Jan. 2, 1894
Duingen, Germany

Kieke Peli
b. 1826
Peteashagen, Germany
d. Oct. 20, 1918
Duingen, Germany

Levi Auch Lewin Bienheim
b. 1795
d. Jan. 10, 1860
Duingen, Germany

(1) **Rosette Gette-leib (?)**
(2) **Janette Sussappfel
Auch Sussfeld**

My great-grandparents, Meyer Sternberg (*left*) and Eva Hoffman Sternberg (*right*), ca. 1870

teenth century by invitation of the ruler of the East Friesland region. They remained about one hundred years, then left for reasons unrecorded. A new Jewish community formed four centuries later. Jews lived there until, to the last person, they were driven out in 1940.

By 1900, though, the Jewish community claimed about 150 families. There has been a Jewish cemetery in Aurich since 1764, and the synagogue was consecrated in 1811, having been designed by the regionally renowned Conrad Bernard Mayer. Aurich's Christian community donated to its construction, according to reports from that period.

Jews and gentiles lived side by side in relative peace. When Aurich's Lutheran church was damaged by a fire in the nineteenth century, for example, the Jewish community offered its synagogue for that congregation's Sunday services during the renovation, and the gesture was gratefully accepted.

Part of Aurich's commercial bustle was Meyer Sternberg's apparel store for men, women, and children. It boasted a loyal and religiously diverse clientele.

Meanwhile, the clan expanded. My great-grandmother, Eva Hoffman, was born in 1851. There is evidence indicating that ancestors on her mother's side left Spain in the 1400s and two centuries later migrated to northwest

Germany. Eva married Meyer, who was ten years her elder, in 1854. The union produced four sons and five daughters. First-born Jacob, my grandfather, arrived on the day before Christmas in 1856. Other offspring, in birth order, were Joseph, Wilhelm, Esther, Siegfried, Cecilia, Rosa, Johanna, and Emelia. Meyer died in 1885. Eva, with traceable family roots to the late 1600s, lived for another twenty-nine years.

Two of my grandfather Jacob's brothers, Joseph and Siegfried, left for the United States as young men. Joseph went to New Orleans and Siegfried to Asheville, North Carolina. Both found American brides in their adopted nation. (Nearly a half century later, Joseph's son, Mel, would be instrumental in introducing his first cousin, Erich, my father, to Bernard Goudchaux in Baton Rouge.)

Jacob married Röschen Stein in 1887, and they had six sons: Max, Alfred, Bruno, Leo, Joseph, and Erich, who was born August 18, 1901. Including my father, four of Jacob and Röschen's children emigrated to America; one laid down his life fighting for the Kaiser and one, Bruno, died from an unrecorded malady at the age of nine.

On my mother Lea's side of the family, my grandparents were Lippmann and Ida Bienheim Knurr. Their third child, Lea, entered the world on January 10, 1904. She had three brothers—Harry, Erich, and Herman—and a sister named Gerta. The Knurr family also was in the retail trade business, with its store offering, like Meyer Sternberg's, clothing, furs, rugs, draperies, feathers, notions (sewing items), and piece goods (fabrics).

The first Knurrs lived in Aurich in 1739 (yes, long before the American Revolution), and started the Knurr store, the predecessor of H. C. Knurr's. This was more than a half century before Samuel Sternberg opened his doors. Knurr's eventually stood at the corner of Marketstrasse and Nordenstrasse, a block north of the Sternberg store, both in the city's bustling business district. The Knurr building stands to this day, protected by historic designation. The Sternberg store is gone, although elderly residents still recall it with fond memories. The Sternberg family home remains.

The Sternbergs and Knurrs were direct competitors. Think of them as Aurich's version of Macy's and Gimbel's.

Jacob and Röschen Sternberg with their children, ca. 1904. *From left,* Röschen, Max, Erich, Leo (in chair), Alfred, Jacob, and Joseph. Bruno, another son, had died at the age of nine.

A business rivalry notwithstanding, the Knurr and Sternberg families respected each other. Lippmann Knurr was known for taking in orphans. Four or five would be employed at his store at any given time, and more often than not, they ate and slept at the Knurr home. Educated and cultured, the Knurrs were pillars of Aurich's Jewish community, which, in the first third of the twentieth century, numbered around four hundred men, women, and children.

Erich Sternberg went to school through the eighth grade, normal in those days for individuals being steered into business. His schooling was followed by an apprenticeship. That seems rudimentary by today's standards, but in early-twentieth-century Germany, it amounted to considerably more education than was received by the population as a whole. At age eighteen, after four years of apprenticing with a retail business in Alsberg, Erich joined a healthy family business.

The Sternberg and Knurr families were upper middle class. My parents' childhoods were relatively happy, comfortable times, with frequent outings to the North Sea

Joseph Sternberg, age seventeen, who was killed fighting on the Russian front as a volunteer for Kaiser Wilhelm during World War I

beaches about thirty miles distant. My mother always remembered with fondness Aurich's red brick homes, tiled roofs, tree-lined streets, and gardens of loganberries and gooseberries, as well as her pleasant childhood.

But three events brought sadness to the Jacob Sternberg family in those otherwise relatively idyllic times. The first was Bruno's death, which has already been mentioned. The others centered on another son being "given away" and a third son dying in defense of the Fatherland.

Jacob's brother Siegfried emigrated to North Carolina in the late nineteenth century and married Anna Lichtenfeld, whose father had left Aurich for America a few years before Siegfried. Siegfried and Anna returned to Aurich in 1907 to visit. The couple, without children at the time, was prosperous and continually extolled the opportunities in America. They persuaded Jacob and Röschen—

with surprising ease, it was said—to allow them to take Alfred, my father's older brother, to the United States to become part of their family.

The attraction of America and the advantages it offered were too much for Alfred's parents to ignore. And Alfred, who had little to say in the decision, was sent to accompany his aunt and uncle. Alfred never forgave his parents for sending him away, even though they acted with good intentions, and he rejected attempts by Siegfried and Anna to adopt him. As soon as he turned eighteen, he moved to Jackson, Mississippi. In the midst of the Depression, Siegfried's scrap-metal business failed, and he and Anna moved to Philadelphia to begin anew.

The family's military fatality occurred during World War I, when Max, Leo, and Joseph served in the German army. Leo received the prestigious Iron Cross Second Class (Jews were not permitted to receive a first-class Iron Cross) and the German version of the Purple Heart, having been wounded twice while serving with the Seventy-third Fusilier Regiment. Leo spent considerable time recuperating in a field hospital in France. Max suffered a head wound, the result of an artillery shell explosion that killed the brother of his future wife.

Joseph, only sixteen when the war broke out in 1914, rushed to enlist, joining his two older brothers as part of an estimated 40,000 German Jews who volunteered to serve in Kaiser Wilhelm's Imperial Army. (Another 60,000 Jews were conscripted.) Parental attempts to dissuade Joseph from this impetuous act proved futile.

On December 5, 1914, having just turned seventeen and fighting the Russians, Joseph reported that he was ill. His superiors thought he was faking and forced him to march into battle. Several hours later, a czarist sniper ended his life. Jacob and Röschen never forgave themselves for permitting him to enlist at such a young age.

Other than Alfred, my father was the only one of the brothers who did not serve in the military—because he had a kidney problem that temporarily placed him in a wheelchair. It was successfully treated, but he had just turned seventeen when a ceasefire was arranged to this exhausting and senseless war. The military probably would have turned Erich away for medical reasons; but in any case, my grandparents were not about to make with him the mistake they had made with Joseph.

As Jacob's surviving sons grew older, the matter of succession in the business began to play out; the baton would pass to the eldest and youngest sons, Max and Erich. As it happened, Leo had other plans for his future. The Meyer Sternberg store had twenty-eight employees by the time Erich and Max bought the enterprise from their father in September 1919. Max (who was twelve years older) would get two-thirds of the business and Erich a third; Jacob, who had owned the store with his younger brother Wilhelm until the latter's death around the turn of the century, would retain the wholesale hide-and-fur operation. Because he was only eighteen when the papers were signed, Erich had to wait until his twenty-first birthday to gain official ownership of his one-third interest.

Business was highly competitive in Aurich. Jacob would rise at 4 a.m., before his rivals were awake, hitch his horse to the wagon, and head into the countryside to have first choice of the honey gathered by farmers in the rural areas. To keep from telegraphing his head start as the horse clopped along Aurich's cobblestone streets, he would wrap the animal's hooves in cloth.

Jacob could be a practical joker. Once he had a fake newspaper printed with the picture of a friendly competitor on the altered front page. The story said a reward was offered for his capture. He handed it to the basically illiterate farmers with whom he did business. As good citizens, they proceeded to capture the "wanted man," and the police had to rescue him.

Jacob enjoyed the first morning milk delivery in Aurich. It seems a farmer moved to town with his ten children in the early 1900s. He needed clothing for his children but did not have the cash to buy it. Since he had no place to pasture his cow in Aurich, he offered Jacob the animal in exchange for new clothes.

My grandfather told the farmer to keep his cow and gave him permission to feed the animal from a Sternberg field near town where Jacob pastured his own cow. In return for clothes, the farmer would have one of his children milk both cows in the morning and deliver fresh

The Meyer Sternberg store in Aurich, 1923

milk to the Sternberg household daily. They shook hands on it. Among the most senior citizens of Aurich, as discovered by several of our family members who visited there in recent years, this story remains a favorite.

By the early 1920s, Erich Sternberg was considered one of Aurich's most eligible bachelors. Although small in stature (5-foot-5), he was good-looking, hardworking, fun loving, well read, and especially sharp with numbers.

Young Lea had several potential suitors, and she came home from finishing school at eighteen with a couple of proposals of marriage, each spurned. By all accounts, she

Lippmann Knurr, Lea's father

"I'll show you I can catch him," she replied, and she did. Their first date occurred when Erich escorted her to sing at her cousin's wedding. And he proposed after their first kiss—a quaint action by today's standards.

It was an easy courtship. For one thing, they had many interests in common (with one noted exception: Lea loved to dance and Erich did not). Lea had played in her father's store until, at eight, she was given responsibilities. She had learned the retail trade watching her father and uncle, and was fascinated. Erich and Lea would talk shop on their dates.

The town was abuzz with the news of the betrothal, many feeling the marriage would propel my father a notch or two up Aurich's social ladder. Lea had more education and cultural knowledge than my father, but there also was the unspoken issue of a religious pecking order. In that respect, the Knurrs definitely were above the Sternbergs.

The Sternberg commercial operation was larger than that of the Knurrs, but the latter family had more status within the Jewish community for at least two reasons. Lippmann Knurr was a spokesman for the community. When a dispute involving business or the Jewish community landed in court, Lippmann's testimony often would be accepted as expert opinion.

The clincher, however, was the fact that the rabbi would take dinner at the Knurr home, but not at the Sternberg's. The Sternberg household wasn't considered as kosher as the Knurr's. Being part of an Orthodox community, all stores in the Jewish quarter closed on the Sabbath (Saturday), including Sternberg's. The rabbi, however, had heard—quite correctly—that Jacob occasionally opened the store's back door on the Sabbath for especially good gentile clients who found themselves in urgent need of the latest finery.

So it was that Erich and Lea announced their engagement. The wedding, however, would not take place for another five years. Lea made it clear she would not marry Erich while she was caring for her critically ill mother. Ida Knurr died in April 1927. And on August 14, Erich and

was as cultured as she was beautiful. Lea had the equivalent of two years of college, was an accomplished singer and pianist (she gave recitals at family events), and could speak French and English.

Lea and Erich had known each other since elementary school, and they lived only two blocks apart. Initially, however, neither appeared interested in the other. She, for example, didn't think Erich that good-looking and was not romantically inclined toward him. But her father liked what he saw.

One day, the crafty Lippmann teased his daughter: "There is one man, Erich Sternberg, who doesn't seem interested

Lea were married in the Aurich synagogue—the groom four days shy of twenty-six, and she, twenty-three.

Whether my father "married up" ultimately didn't matter to either him or his bride. They were in love. Because Lea would give up all claims to the Knurr business when she left home, Lippmann provided the Sternbergs with household goods and a substantial $15,000 dowry (which had the same buying power as approximately $170,000 in 2007). Family legend has it that there was even a bit of friendly bartering about it.

Their first child, Josef, my older brother and future business partner, arrived on May 27, 1928, barely nine months after my parents exchanged vows. My mother said the town gossips were counting the days. (Note the German spelling of "Josef" versus the more biblical "Joseph" of his namesake. The influence of anti-Semitic attitudes could present itself even in the subtlest of things.) Sister Insa was born two years later, almost to the week, on May 18, 1930. I didn't arrive for some time—and was quite a surprise when I did show up. By that time, though, a third child was the least of my parents' worries.

As most people know, anti-Semitism did not originate in twentieth-century Germany. From the Spanish Inquisition to Russian pogroms, it had long lurked in Europe's shadows, making life difficult and at times dangerous for Jews. Hitler took what had been a dark undercurrent in the continent's legacy and elevated it to horrific levels.

In Germany, it had always been difficult for a Jew to enter medicine or law, and Jewish military officers were rare. Discrimination, subtle and otherwise, permeated German society: My mother and her Jewish friends, for example, were not allowed to play tennis on Aurich's public courts. It is interesting to note, however, that the teachers at the public high school attended by Lea's brother, Erich, came to the Knurr home in an unsuccessful attempt to convince his parents that he ought to study law. And prior to the 1930s, violence was the exception.

European Jews had learned to function on uneven playing fields. Discrimination created in them an inner strength. Germany, ironically, was felt by many Jews to

Lea Knurr during her courtship with Erich Sternberg in Aurich in the 1920s

be more civilized than the rest of Europe. Jews tended to be loyal, industrious, civic minded, family oriented, and law abiding. Those characteristics and that demeanor appealed to the German sense of order, work, and nationalism, so many German Jews thought there would be no lasting trouble.

Nothing could have been further from the truth.

2 CODED MESSAGE

THE EARLY 1930S GAVE rise to Nazi power. Economically, Germany suffered grievously in the post–World War I years—hyperinflation in the 1920s followed by an economic depression that was experienced worldwide. My mother remembered that during the inflationary period a barrel of Deutsche marks rolled to the grocery store would buy little more than one loaf of bread. High unemployment followed inflation—raw ingredients for a dictator with simplistic solutions and a doorstep upon which to place blame.

By 1933, the Nazi party had embraced a crude and hateful antithesis of scientific and historic fact as a theological tenet: the notion that "Aryans"—a mystical (and mythical) "race" of German-speaking, Nordic people—were a super-race that had been, and would continue to be, responsible for all advances in civilization and morality. Jews, the Roma (gypsies), Africans, liberals, the mentally and physically handicapped, communists, homosexuals, intellectuals, and Slavs were considered *gemeinschafremde*—aliens. The Nazi thought process evolved into a national policy of ethnic cleansing. Until 1933, these perverted ideologies were just delusional theories. Adolf Hitler, who had been named chancellor of Germany, had yet to consolidate his power and did not wish to frighten moderate Germans by putting into practice all of what he preached to his followers. Yet he was not above using Jews as scapegoats when seeking votes.

He blamed Jews and communists for the poverty, unemployment, and nationalist baggage inflicted on Germany. The persistent opposition of dissidents, intellectuals, and moral critics—traditional banes of totalitarian regimes—gained them a prominent position on the Nazis' list of undesirables. And the economic privation, brought on largely by the shackling peace treaty imposed by the vengeful victors, had produced massive resentment among the German citizenry. The bitter attitude played into Hitler's hands as he became more maniacal.

By early 1933, Nazi policy had progressed to active and open persecution of Jews. On April 1, 1933, Germans were told to boycott Jewish stores, doctors, lawyers, and teachers. My family has a 1933 photograph of my grandfather Knurr's store being picketed with a billboard on the side of a nearby truck reading "Kauft Nicht in Judischen Warenhausern," which translates, "Do not shop at Jewish stores." A policeman and his attack dog complete the chilling photo.

A week later, the Law for the Restoration of the Professional Civil Service was passed, prohibiting Jews from holding government jobs. Those positions henceforth would be reserved for "Aryan" Germans.

August 1934 brought the death of German president Paul von Hindenburg, hero of earlier wars, and the Weimer Republic all but dissolved into a toxic pool of hatred and megalomania. Hitler, who earlier had coerced and cajoled his way to von Hindenburg's side, immediately combined the powers of president and chancellor. He took control of the Reichstag, the law-making branch of the German government, but he need not have bothered. With the army swearing allegiance to its "fuehrer," Hitler's word became law. The Nazis seized control of German society, and few raised a voice in protest.

My father, on the other hand, had had enough. "Germany is no longer my country," he publicly declared in 1933 after Jews were prohibited from attending most public schools, even though his school-age child went to a private school. It wasn't the only negative comment he uttered in front of others. The condemnations did not go unnoticed.

Matters became more complicated when, in late 1934, a somewhat shocked Lea discovered she was pregnant with her third child. She had undergone what she thought was a hysterectomy after Insa was born. As explained by the doctor, there was a one in a million chance of her conceiving again. Delivered by a midwife, I arrived—all 13 pounds of me!—on July 4, 1935, a million-to-one baby ready for life to shine just as Germany was sliding into darkness.

Our family had left our neighborhood home earlier that year, moving into living quarters above the Meyer Sternberg store to save money and gain increased security. There has to be more than a little retailing in my blood: I was born above the store.

Lea soon reached the same conclusion as her husband about severing ties with Germany. Any lingering doubt evaporated the day she went to check on Josef at a private Aurich kindergarten, one of the few that still accepted Jews. She found him in the schoolyard, standing alone. The other children were pelting him with stones and calling him a Jew. The teacher stood by watching, making no attempt to interfere. Lea grabbed the hand of her five-year-old and hurried home.

During this period, many Jews held out the hope that the present difficult situation would pass, that civic-minded Germans would see the Nazis for what they were, the dregs of German society, brutish thugs, and would re-

place them with saner governance. Unfortunately, it was too late for democratic reform or even sanity. My parents reluctantly recognized that.

The extended Sternberg family discussed sending Erich to America to test the waters for a business there. He and his oldest brother, Max, had been running the Meyer Sternberg store. (Their brother Leo had joined his wife's family store in nearby Emden.) If Erich could secure a base, emigration for all would be considered. Mother and children temporarily would remain behind. If and when Erich succeeded in his quest, they, too, would leave for America.

My father was hesitant about the idea, primarily because he had a business in Aurich and was worried about leaving his immediate family and other relatives in a deteriorating, potentially dangerous situation. But his hesitation did not last long.

The Nuremberg Laws were enacted in September 1935: Jews were no longer considered citizens and, as a result, had no rights. It was decided Erich should leave for America at the end of the year. The venture would require a considerable sum of money. This was a problem. Although Germany in 1935 still was allowing visits to other countries and, at that point, officially preferred that Jews emigrate, the Nazis would not permit anyone to leave the country with significant sums of cash.

My father had Lea's $15,000 dowry plus several thousand dollars of his own money. These funds would be used to get to America and establish a business there, and Erich's parents would help my mother and the children while he was gone. Legally, he could not take that much money out of the country, so he had to devise a way to smuggle it out of Germany. He would need the cash at the ready when he reached the United States. It was a highly perilous game.

Initially, Erich hid money under the radiators of passenger coaches on trains he took for business trips to Holland. He would take the added precaution of riding in an adjacent car. If he were searched at a border crossing, he would be carrying only an amount of cash normal for a business trip. If the cash were discovered in the railcar, he would be sitting nowhere near it.

On one occasion, however, some non-Jewish acquaintances sat with him after he hid the money. He could not retrieve his cash when he arrived at the Dutch rail station. Erich knew the train would remain in the city's rail yard overnight before making the return trip to Germany the following day. So my father and one of his relatives sneaked into the yard later under cover of darkness, boarded the deserted train, and collected the undetected cache from under the radiator.

After that hair-raising experience, Erich looked for another method. He decided to place money in false soles in his shoes, but he could not transport large sums that way. The solution: Lea sewed money in the lining of furs or hides he transported to Holland by train to sell to garment makers there. Then a safer plan unfolded. As a matter of normal enterprise, he shipped furs and hides to relatives in the clothing business in Amsterdam. Erich would invoice the relatives for less than the goods were worth. They, in turn, would deposit the difference in a bank account under his name.

By the end of 1936, he had more than $24,000—roughly $340,000 in today's dollars—in a Dutch bank account. Erich and Lea knew the Gestapo routinely opened and read letters leaving and entering Germany, so they agreed on a plan of communication: He would write to her at the Sternberg store address, but she would post her letters across the nearby border in Holland. They devised a coded message that would alert her and the family to his having found a business. This would be the signal for them to leave Germany for America.

After obtaining a visa from the U.S. consulate in Bremen and the necessary exit papers from the German government, Erich Sternberg set sail from Hamburg on January 27, 1936. Lea bravely watched the USS *Majestic* slip from sight, then let the tears flow. She feared she might never see her husband again.

Following an uneventful voyage, Erich's ship docked in New York City on February 5. Armed with a temporary visitor's visa and permanent resolve, he set off to search for his version of the American Dream—a term that, ironically, had just been coined as the nation struggled to shake itself free of the Great Depression.

Able to say little more than yes and no in English, he immediately boarded a train to Philadelphia to stay with his uncle, Siegfried, who had moved there from North Carolina two years earlier. Erich arrived the same day and arranged for the Dutch bankers to wire his $24,026.52 to the Philadelphia National Bank. Within twenty-four hours, the deposit was made. Erich was given work in his uncle's hide-and-fur business, and by the time he left, a few months later, his account showed a $26,426.56 balance.

Although Erich was off to a promising start, the situation in Aurich was turning increasingly ugly. In fact, our mother later told us, "Had I known how bad it was going to get in your father's absence, I would have taken you and left with him." A new German Law banned Jews from holding professional positions, effectively removing their influence in the sciences, industry, law, education, and politics. One of those already forced out was Albert Einstein, who left for America in 1933. Nazi party members were becoming increasingly brazen—and violent. Hatred had seeped like a North Sea fog into Aurich and many other German cities and towns.

On one harrowing occasion, my mother was wheeling me in a stroller down an Aurich street, with Josef and Insa walking beside her. Coming toward them was a gang of Nazi thugs, singing songs that spoke of killing Jews. She quickly turned into a driveway, as if it were her own, and hid in the house of a gentile friend.

Erich's brother Max, his wife, Ida, and their son, Manfred, soon would join Lea and her three children in the apartment over the Aurich store. In 1930, signs had appeared in Aurich preaching that Germans ought to shop at Christian stores only. By 1933, those signs had been replaced by billboards *demanding* that they not buy from Jewish merchants. Making that practice illegal was but a small step away.

Business at Meyer Sternberg's was meager. Many Jewish stores had closed for lack of sales. To make matters worse, Jews could not shop at non–Jewish-owned stores. Only one Jewish store in Aurich had food for sale, and precious little at that. Jews were even being turned away from pharmacies and hospitals.

Not every gentile, however, turned his or her back on

Jewish neighbors. Mother recalled that friends would throw food into the window of a home near hers. It would in turn be tossed into the window of the adjacent home, finally making its way through the Sternbergs' open window.

In Philadelphia, Erich salted hides during the day and took English lessons at night. He seldom was without his small German-to-English dictionary. The Philadelphia experience lasted only a couple of months. Disliking the work, he struck out for Jackson, Mississippi, to see his brother Alfred. Still smarting from his involuntary move to the home of his aunt and uncle, Alfred was the owner of the Sternberg Pecan Company. The pecan growing and shelling business was not the career my father had in mind, either. He wanted his own retail clothing business, a field in which he felt comfortable and was quite good.

While in Jackson, he wrote to my mother that he was becoming discouraged, bored with his work there, and homesick for her and the children. He discussed returning to Germany. Several weeks later, a letter from my mother arrived. Resolute that a return to Aurich was not an option, Lea insisted her husband stay put, find a way to earn a living, and bring his family to America. She had good reason to be adamant. The Nazis, she told her husband, were obscenely intensifying their punishment of Jews financially and politically, the next-to-last segment of their segregation plans. Government contracts would not be awarded to Jewish businesses. And Aryan doctors henceforth could only treat Aryan patients.

Erich had another problem, though: His visitor's visa would expire in several weeks. A foreign visitor at that time could not renew his U.S. visa or apply for a new one while in this country. The applicant had to leave and reapply from outside the U.S. borders. If the applicant had proof of a guaranteed job or an American sponsor, however, he could obtain a permanent work visa rather easily. So in mid-May, Erich boarded a train for New Orleans, where he made contact with his first cousins, Mel, Jay, and Sam Sternberg.

These New Orleans Sternbergs were sons of Joseph Sternberg, Erich's uncle, who had come to America in 1878 at the age of seventeen. Sam was a physician, while Mel and Jay owned a well-regarded manufacturing busi-

Lea with her three children when we lived in the apartment over the store in Aurich, 1936

ness called Famous Sternberg Clothing, an enterprise begun by Joseph. Originally, the company was called Joseph Sternberg Clothing; when Joseph bought another manufacturer, Famous Clothing, he combined the names. Joseph died eight years before Erich arrived in America. Famous Sternberg used the brand name Deansgate; its primary competitor was Haspel Brothers.

It was decided that Erich would travel to Cuba, a two-day trip by ship from New Orleans, and apply for a work visa there. The New Orleans family agreed to write a letter of sponsorship for Erich that he could take with him. With the guarantee of a job and a U.S. sponsor, such visas were routinely issued. Erich set sail for Havana on May 26. Upon arrival, he went straight to the U.S. embassy, and seventy-two hours later, he was on the steamer *Santa*

17

Maria, arriving back in New Orleans only a week after he had left.

In celebration, the New Orleans branch of the Sternberg family took Erich to dinner at the renowned French Quarter restaurant Arnaud's. Dad's English was rudimentary at best. They ordered him a steak, which, of course, he thoroughly enjoyed. When one of his hosts asked how he liked his steak, my father wanted to say "good," but the word in English temporarily escaped his memory. He knew everyone at the table understood the Hebrew term *mazel tov* means "good luck," so he focused on the word *tov*, meaning "good," which in English sounds like "tough." He pointed to the steak and said "tough, tough." The ever-attentive waiter scurried over and attempted to remove what he thought was overcooked meat. Explanations calmed the waters.

While in New Orleans, my father lived with Mel and worked for Famous Sternberg Clothing, folding pants for twelve dollars a week. Mel traveled in much of Latin America and South Africa selling Famous Sternberg products. He went to such remote places that at times he was forced to arm himself to keep from being robbed. Legends abound in the family that Mel was a soldier of fortune and, at times, a mercenary. The rumors weren't true, but he was a hero.

On one occasion, in Bluefields, Nicaragua, Mel was standing on the dock when a ferry began sinking as it was about to unload. He and a friend saved many lives when Mel cut the ropes holding the gangplank, thus lowering it from the level of a ship's deck to water level. The two men worked their way down the gangplank to the water and boosted numerous passengers onto what had become a lifeline to the dock.

At this point in his life, Mel was chief sales executive for Famous Sternberg. Although my dad fell in love with New Orleans, he did not want to work for the company as a career. He explained to Mel that he wanted his own retail business, and he had accumulated a sizable down payment for just such a venture.

Erich at this time had about $25,000 in a checking account at Whitney National Bank of New Orleans. Desiring to earn interest on at least part of that money, he attempted to transfer $5,000 into a savings account, which

paid 1.5 percent. In early July, Erich sent the Whitney Bank a check to open the savings account. This was still the Great Depression, however. Few had the means to borrow. Banks, which loaned at a prime rate of 2.5 percent, had too much cash in their vaults and too few people who could qualify to borrow it, or even desired to. The interest on savings was damaging their low, Depression-era profits. The Whitney Bank therefore wrote Erich that new savings accounts were being limited to $2,000 and returned his $5,000 check. Macroeconomics didn't work well in the Depression. Because the country was still in its grip, however, prices were low, and there were commercial bargains to be had for those who had the financial means. Mel, who traveled the region, knew of two stores whose proprietors wanted to sell.

One was Marks Isaacs Department Store, named for the founder, a merchant prince of turn-of-the-century New Orleans. The family-owned operation was located on Canal Street from 1909 until the mid-1960s, when it closed. Erich was hesitant about buying Marks Isaacs. He worried that the competition in a large city might strain the limits of his capital.

The other opportunity was Goudchaux's Department Store in Baton Rouge, one of Mel's good customers. Mel had learned of the sale possibility from the sister of Bernard Goudchaux, proprietor of the store. Goudchaux, a leader in the Baton Rouge Jewish community, wanted to sell his store because his brother and cofounder had died a few years earlier and Bernard's son, Harry, was not interested in taking over the business. Besides, father and son didn't get along: The latter had a reputation as a party boy.

On a Sunday in early July, Mel drove Erich to Baton Rouge to meet Mr. Goudchaux, an admired and respected businessman known throughout the city as "Bennie." Waiting with him inside were members of his immediate family. Goudchaux's sounded promising to Erich—until he saw the location of the 10,000-square-foot store.

Bernard and his brother Jake were sons of French Jews who had immigrated to the town of Bunkie in central Louisiana in the latter half of the nineteenth century. They founded their 6,000-square-foot Baton Rouge store in 1907 with three employees. (That same year, coincidentally, Al Neiman, Carrie Marcus Neiman, and Herbert

Marcus opened Dallas's Neiman Marcus, the renowned, high-end emporium.) In 1927, Bennie and Jake had moved their store two blocks down the street to the 1500 block of Main. Jake, somewhat of an oddball bachelor, died in 1933.

The Baton Rouge economic environment my father had to assess was a hotbed of retail activity, and the competition was fierce. In addition to Goudchaux's, popular stores included Rosenfield's Dry Goods, Henry Strauss, and S. I. Reymond (later Dalton's, then bought by D. H. Holmes). (Another Baton Rouge landmark, Farrnbacher Dry Goods, had closed two years earlier.) Competition, however, was of little concern at that moment. What bothered Erich on that hot and sticky summer day in 1936 was Goudchaux's location.

The Main Street store was a dozen blocks east of the more prestigious downtown shopping district and bustling Mississippi River wharf. Even worse, in Erich's eyes, was the fact that dead-end streets bordered the store on three sides. A cemetery completed the uninviting perimeter. (Adjacent railroad tracks didn't help the neighborhood, either.)

Mel drove Erich around the building three times. Then, without leaving the car, Dad asked Mel to head back to New Orleans. He had seen enough. Referring to the neighboring cemetery, he remarked, "I cannot make a living selling clothes to dead people." (Yet, for years afterward, we did exactly that. As a community service, we would open our stores at all hours of the night and on Sundays when the funeral homes called in need of suitable clothing for someone who had passed away.)

Bennie and Harry Goudchaux, along with their wives, were left standing literally at the counter of their store. Bennie naturally was upset, but he was not ready to surrender his retirement plans. He called Mel in New Orleans and, through him, persuaded Erich to take another look the following Sunday. This time he made Erich promise to come inside, look around, and meet the family. Things went better on the second scouting trip. Erich was interested, no doubt, but not convinced. The business had been operating for nearly three decades; the books showed it made around $275,000 in annual sales. My father wanted a more focused look at the operations before investing, so he struck a deal with Bennie: He

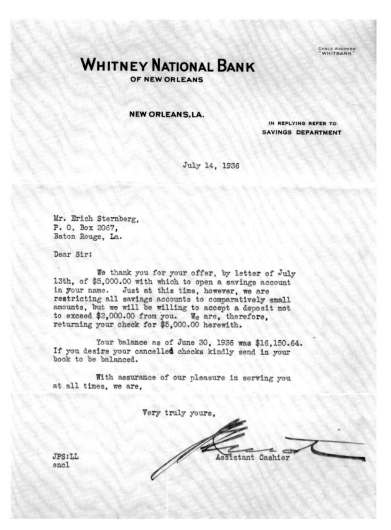

Depression-era letter from a New Orleans bank to Erich informing him it did not want his $5,000 in a savings account. Although not stated, the reason was that the bank would have to pay interest on the money and no one was borrowing. Years later, Whitney Bank offered to buy this letter for its historic collection.

would work in the men's department for a brief time to test the traffic and sales patterns, and, not wanting to feel obligated, he insisted the test period be without pay. Undoubtedly impressed by the offer to work free of charge, and delighted by a nibble, the owner insisted my father be compensated. The two merchants struck a deal: Erich would be paid one dollar a day.

So Erich moved to Baton Rouge, rented the second floor of a small home within walking distance of Goudchaux's,

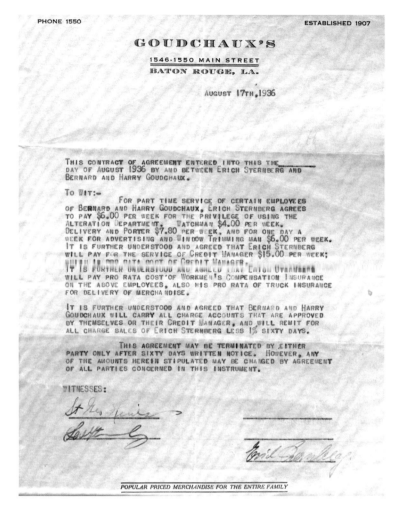

PHONE 1550   ESTABLISHED 1907

GOUDCHAUX'S

1546-1550 MAIN STREET
BATON ROUGE, LA.

AUGUST 17TH, 1936

THIS CONTRACT OF AGREEMENT ENTERED INTO THIS THE_____
DAY OF AUGUST 1936 BY AND BETWEEN ERICH STERNBERG AND
BERNARD AND HARRY GOUDCHAUX.

TO WIT:-
       FOR PART TIME SERVICE OF CERTAIN EMPLOYEES
OF BERNARD AND HARRY GOUDCHAUX, ERICH STERNBERG AGREES
TO PAY $6.00 PER WEEK FOR THE PRIVILEGE OF USING THE
ALTERATION DEPARTMENT. WATCHMAN $4.00 PER WEEK.
DELIVERY AND PORTER $7.80 PER WEEK, AND FOR ONE DAY A
WEEK FOR ADVERTISING AND WINDOW TRIMMING MAN $6.00 PER WEEK.
IT IS FURTHER UNDERSTOOD AND AGREED THAT ERICH STERNBERG
WILL PAY FOR THE SERVICE OF CREDIT MANAGER $15.00 PER WEEK;
WHICH IS PRO RATA COST OF CREDIT MANAGER.
IT IS FURTHER UNDERSTOOD AND AGREED THAT ERICH STERNBERG
WILL PAY PRO RATA COST OF WORKMEN'S COMPENSATION INSURANCE
ON THE ABOVE EMPLOYEES, ALSO HIS PRO RATA OF TRUCK INSURANCE
FOR DELIVERY OF MERCHANDISE.

IT IS FURTHER UNDERSTOOD AND AGREED THAT BERNARD AND HARRY
GOUDCHAUX WILL CARRY ALL CHARGE ACCOUNTS THAT ARE APPROVED
BY THEMSELVES OR THEIR CREDIT MANAGER, AND WILL REMIT FOR
ALL CHARGE SALES OF ERICH STERNBERG LESS 1% SIXTY DAYS.

       THIS AGREEMENT MAY BE TERMINATED BY EITHER
PARTY ONLY AFTER SIXTY DAYS WRITTEN NOTICE. HOWEVER, ANY
OF THE AMOUNTS HEREIN STIPULATED MAY BE CHANGED BY AGREEMENT
OF ALL PARTIES CONCERNED IN THIS INSTRUMENT.

WITNESSES:

POPULAR PRICED MERCHANDISE FOR THE ENTIRE FAMILY

Original agreement between Erich Sternberg and Bennie Goudchaux, 1936

and continued to take English lessons at night from a local language tutor, Angie Williams. By mid-August, he had decided that Goudchaux's might well be the opportunity he was seeking. He believed, and wisely so, that his money would go farther in a smaller city, such as Baton Rouge, than in relatively expensive New Orleans.

Still not quite ready to pull the trigger, he made a transitional arrangement with Bennie in mid-August. Erich would lease the men's department, cover his own inventory and employee costs, and market and operate the department as he saw fit. He would pay his share of the store overhead and keep any profits. It was a good deal: Nation-

ally in department stores, men's wear was more profitable than women's, and Baton Rouge proved no different.

The one-page contract set his portion of the overhead at $6 a week for using the alterations department, $4 a week for his share of the night watchman, $6 a week for advertising and window displays, $7.80 a week for delivery services, $15 a week for the credit manager, and a pro-rated cost for workman's compensation. There was an understanding that, if all went well, he would buy the entire store.

Baton Rouge attorney Victor Sachse Jr., who became a lifelong friend and was the Sternberg personal and business attorney until he died in 1978, drew up the papers for the business arrangement. Victor also prepared immigration papers for our family to leave Germany. The legal community customarily did this without charge, but not every attorney would take the time. Victor, on the other hand, could not do it fast enough and would not let my father leave his office until the documents were complete.

My father now had a business, steady income, a home, and a fast track to proprietorship. The Sternberg line of merchants would survive. He had everything but his family, and in this matter, time was of the essence. The very day the Goudchaux's agreement was signed, Erich sent the long-anticipated message to Lea at the Aurich store.

The trans-Atlantic cable from Baton Rouge undoubtedly was boring reading to an outsider. It certainly did not convey the urgency it actually represented. Neither did the cable arouse more than cursory interest from the Gestapo agent who passed it on for delivery. Mother, on the other hand, savored every exciting word, her eyes returning to a single sentence in the body of the short message. It was the prearranged code that would separate her from home, friends, extended family, and everything she knew. Emotions notwithstanding, Lea mentally had packed her bags the day Erich left. She had been preparing for and eagerly awaiting this green light for months.

And there it was: a single, five-word, seemingly banal sentence that saved our lives and, ironically, was the genesis of an American department-store legend. In traditional cablese, it stated:

"TODAY WAITED ON 1ST CUSTOMER STOP."

Erich Sternberg (*second from left*) and his brother Leo (*far right*) in Goudchaux's men's department in 1936.
Roy Chapman, window trimmer, is second from right, and Erwin Bourgoyne is on the far left. A men's shoe buyer,
Bourgoyne spent his entire working career at Goudchaux's, retiring in the late 1980s.

3 | NEW ROOTS

ROUGH WINTER SAILING IS the rule on the North Sea and North Atlantic, and our voyage was no exception. The weather was foul, particularly the first week. Punishing waves relentlessly buffeted the pitching USS *Washington*, its bow steadfastly pointed westward. Occupants of the Sternberg cabin were seasick, and I—not yet eighteen months old—also was suffering from a dangerous case of double pneumonia. Mother had only a new sulfa drug to give me. (It worked, I am pleased to report.) The doctor had warned her that the trip was a major risk to my life and that I might not make it. Yet Lea instinctively knew that not leaving Germany was an even greater risk.

With the physical and emotional stress of leaving, coupled with three sick children, Mother was at her wits' end during the voyage, a passage made all the worse by the rising and falling of the ship. She playfully began teasing us children as we vomited. Finally, she, too, became sick, and Insa remembers telling her that now she could not laugh at us any longer. (The trip took such a toll on Mother that she vowed, if they made it safely to New York, she would never again board a ship—a promise she kept her whole life, even when family and friends invited her to take cruises with them.)

Confined to the cabin much of the voyage, Lea had time to gather her thoughts. The last four months had been a whirlwind of preparation, exhilaration mixed with anxiety and sadness. The U.S. consulate in Bremen issued special visas for her and the three children to enter America and to reunite with her husband, our father. The immediate family would be safe. And since Erich owned part of an established American business, we would not be a burden to Americans or their governments at various levels.

My mother had purchased tickets on the *Washington*, scheduled to leave Bremen on December 27, 1936, but the Nazi authorities did not give final approval to leave until forty-eight hours prior to departure. Lea had discussed the situation with the Sternberg and Knurr families after receiving Erich's telegram in August. My grandmother, Röschen Sternberg, was too sick to travel, and in any case, neither she nor Jacob was emotionally prepared to leave their home. (Röschen died five weeks after Mother, Josef, Insa, and I landed in America.)

Lea's father, Lippmann Knurr, was seventy-seven (three years younger than Jacob) and told everyone he would be okay because he was "too old, the Nazis won't bother me." Lea's brothers, Harry, Herman, and Erich, who were running the Knurr store, either were not yet convinced they needed to leave or didn't feel they could at that time.

For a brief while that year, the Nazis turned quasi-tolerant as they played host to the Summer Olympics. Hitler was showcasing the country, exploiting the Berlin Games to paint a positive picture of the Third Reich. He especially wanted to show that reports of Jews being persecuted were greatly exaggerated. When world leaders and members of the international press returned home, however, it was business as usual.

Leo Sternberg, one of Erich's older brothers and the proprietor of his in-laws' clothing store in Emden, a seaport town thirty miles to the southwest of Aurich, also knew it was time to go. His business was suffering, as were enterprises owned by Jews throughout Germany, but a pair of related personal incidents convinced him of the urgency.

Riding his bike home one day, Leo saw his thirteen-year-old daughter, Frances, walking ahead. She had beautiful blonde hair and possessed so-called "Aryan" features. He caught up with Frances, stopped his bike, and gave her a hug. An Emden woman who witnessed that bit of paternal affection reproached Leo, a Jew, for daring to touch a "German" girl.

A short time later, two members of the Gestapo entered Leo's store and pistol-whipped him. He thereupon shuttered his store and prepared to find a new home in America as quickly as possible. Leo would go ahead of his family, just as Erich had done in January. His wife, Recha Wolff, known as Resi, and Frances would follow once he was established. In July, about the time Erich was testing the American mercantile waters at Goudchaux's for one dollar a day, Leo sailed from the Hamburg harbor on the USS *Aquitaine*. He landed in New York on July 24 and boarded a train for New Orleans.

My uncle Max had elected to stay in Aurich to run the Sternberg store and help care for his mother. His wife, Frieda Wolff, known as Ida, would remain with him. Max and Ida wanted their only child, fourteen-year-old Manfred, to remain also. But Mel and Ethel (née Rosenthal) Sternberg, who had befriended Erich when he got to New Orleans, convinced them otherwise. They had no children of their own and wanted Manfred to come to New Orleans to stay with them. When the boy's parents resisted, "Uncle Mel" told him that if he "wanted to come to America, I will do everything in my power to bring you here." Mel promised a good education, including college, and, if need be, adoption.

Gerta Knurr, Lea Knurr Sternberg's sister

The situation was resolved by the April departure of Leo's family for America. Resi and Frances booked passage on the *Washington*. Max and Ida prevailed on Resi to take Manfred with her. On April 21, 1937, nine months after Leo stepped foot on American soil and four months after my mother settled in Baton Rouge, Resi, Frances, and Manfred Sternberg landed in New York. They took what was becoming the "Sternberg Trail" to New Orleans, briefly residing with Sam and Jay Sternberg while Leo secured a home in Baton Rouge. Leo had been working with Erich in the men's department at Goudchaux's, but he would leave within a year to start a variety store a half block from Goudchaux's.

Officially, the Nazi regime's policy was to encourage Jews to leave the country, and eventually nearly half of them did. Nevertheless, it was a hardship, given emigration taxes and the prohibition on leaving with sufficient money to get a new start. In practice, that relatively benign official policy lasted until England and France declared war on Germany after the Wehrmacht's September 1939 invasion of Poland. Emigration slowed to a trickle as the clock ticked down to "The Final Solution." Even if Jews got clearance to leave Germany and occupied countries, fewer and fewer other nations would accept refugees, and if they did, it was with numerous restrictions.

From today's vantage point, it is hard to imagine there would be Jews reluctant to leave Germany while there was still time, but in 1936 and 1937 such a move was complex as well as emotionally harrowing. My parents' decision to leave took considerable fortitude. To abandon one's physical, cultural and generational home, to tear oneself from loved ones, to uproot children and say good-bye to family members you may never see again, and to become a refugee are painful and traumatic decisions. Only those with strong commitment and an iron constitution—qualities both my parents possessed—can do so when a clear and present danger is obscured. It would be 1939, or even later, before the most optimistic Jews would come to realize that remaining in Germany had become a death sentence.

In 1936, some Jews still believed they could endure discrimination as others had before them. The sense of urgency had not yet emerged *en masse*. "This will pass," was a common refrain. The Nazis, it was felt, would be turned out by clear-thinking Germans.

Many German Jews, especially those with means, stigmatized emigrating. One left for America to evade creditors, military service, the police, poverty, or political (as opposed to ethnic or religious) persecution, and emigrating for the last reason was not new to mid-1930s Germany. Following political havoc in 1815 and 1848, mass emigrations were especially common.

More than a few Jewish leaders felt they had to stay to provide strong community leadership. Such naïveté was not confined to Germany. Incredibly, the rabbi of the Jewish community in Baton Rouge came to my father's home soon after he arrived and urged him to consider returning to Germany because "Germany needs good Jews," presumably to help guide that nation back to normalcy. (I have heard that such ill-conceived counsel was offered in other U.S. communities, so there may have been a small clique of American rabbis who advocated this suicidal move.)

Finally, as discrimination turned into persecution, persecution morphed into violence and violence into mass roundups for concentration camps, panic set in—but by then the escape routes had closed.

Because Lea refused to sail on a German ship, she had to delay our departure for two and a half months—until space on an American vessel became available. When the Nazi authorities finally approved our departure, they permitted her to take only ten Reich marks in personal funds and five marks for each of the three children. The exchange rate was about 2½ marks to the U.S. dollar. That meant we had a total of about ten dollars for the trip! Additionally, Lea had to pay a 15,000-mark emigration tax.

The shipping of household goods out of the country, amazingly, was not restricted. The Nazis liked to think of Germany as an exporting nation. Lea preshipped her furniture and other family heirlooms to Baton Rouge. She also bought substantial amounts of linens and silverware, liquidating what she could not otherwise take out of Germany. She intended the linens and silver for Insa's future dowry.

The day we left Aurich, a dozen Gestapo agents entered our apartment over the store and searched the house and luggage for contraband. As one agent approached a suitcase that contained hidden papers Mother did not want them to have (we never learned what they were), family legend has it I made a baby sound that distracted him. An agent followed the sound to my crib and played with me for a few moments. The search ended and we were allowed to leave.

It was a sorrowful, memorable farewell as Lea kissed her father good-bye, knowing she might never see him again. As our car pulled away, Lippmann Knurr ran along the side of the vehicle and handed his daughter the Knurr family's Friday night silver *Kiddush* cup. (It has been in our family ever since.) Lea's departure was doubly painful for them both. Her younger sister, Gerta, had contracted pneumonia and, denied medicines and proper medical care, died just four weeks earlier at age twenty-four.

The Nazis inflicted one last insult before the *Washington* slipped its moorings. Gestapo agents boarded the ship to scrutinize, yet again, the belongings of Jewish travelers. They physically searched my mother, looking for diamonds or cash she might be smuggling out of Germany. They took her into the cabin's bathroom, forced her to place one foot on the toilet and searched her body. Lea never forgot the humiliation of this experience.

The agents once again ransacked our suitcases and trunks, throwing everything on the floor and leaving a mess. They even broke into tiny pieces a cache of homemade cookies that Grandmother Röschen had given us, and they shredded sausage Lea's brother had given us to sustain ourselves between meals. Nothing but crumbs remained.

As the Gestapo agents left the room, the furious Lea, demonstrating her backbone, stood up, pointed to the clothes strewn about, and defiantly ordered: "You took them out, now you put them back." Surprisingly, they complied.

Apparently, the Nazis were more intent on harassing a Jewish family than they were on confiscating items that might compromise Germany's security, for they ignored several maps Mother had packed in her luggage. They were part of a school project, meticulously detailed. The maps included points of interest that would not normally appear on commercial maps, such as factories and military installations. The cookie-crumbling Nazis ignored them, but they were of keen interest to U.S. agents when we landed in New York City on January 9, 1937. Mother eagerly gave the maps as gifts to immigration officials.

Erich had taken the train from Louisiana to New York City to meet us. Insa remembers he waved as we docked and that I scooted down the gangplank into his open

arms as fast as an eighteen-month-old could toddle. Josef, Insa, and Mother followed. It was an emotional reunion, I'm told.

We took the 30-hour train ride to Baton Rouge, the state capital with some 30,000 residents. (In fifteen years, the population would triple. In seventy years, East Baton Rouge Parish, where the city is located, would be nearly 14 times that figure.) Erich had described Baton Rouge in a letter the previous summer. By his description (or lack of it), Lea was at a loss as to what to expect. When a picture of Erich wearing a seersucker suit arrived, she thought it strange, telling friends she thought it looked like a prison uniform.

We were welcomed by Julia Goudchaux, the New Orleans–born-and-bred spouse of store owner Bennie Goudchaux, and Buffington Mayer Sr., who was, like Bennie, a prominent member of the local Jewish community. Father's rented "home" was the upstairs of a Laurel Street residence adjacent to the Jewish synagogue. That Friday, all but one of the Sternbergs were escorted to that temple by the Goudchauxs and four other families to offer thanks for a safe trip. I was deemed too young to attend, and the Goudchauxs' daughter-in-law took care of me.

Julia and Bennie went out of their way to make us feel welcome. The family was well respected, referred to by Baton Rougeans as "front-porch" people. Later, members of other religious faiths came to our home to introduce themselves and welcome us to the community.

We always have been grateful for the warm welcome Baton Rouge gave us as an immigrant family. Many took time to extend a hand of friendship, something we never forgot. Teachers, business people, and neighbors were forthcoming and giving. "The people of Baton Rouge were just marvelous to us," Lea said in an interview many years later. Considering from whence our family came, it was a heart-warming experience, one that still gives rise to many emotions.

Baton Rouge was not at all like Mother imagined. By the description in her husband's letters, Lea assumed the family would be coming to hot desert country or a jungle. The Louisiana temperature and humidity, until we adjusted, were certainly uncomfortable, but trees were

Erich and Lea Sternberg with their children upon arrival in Baton Rouge, 1937. We lived in a rented home on Main Street, five blocks west of the store.

eighteenth century, and named for a red totemlike pole or stick the Indians had thrust into the bank of the Mississippi River, Baton Rouge was claimed by five nations in its first one hundred years under white man's rule—France (1699–1763), Britain (1763–1779), Spain (1779–1810), the Republic of West Florida (1810), and the United States (1810–1812). Technically, since Baton Rouge lay on the east side of the Mississippi and north of Bayou Manchac (which marked the beginning of the Isle of Orleans), it was not part of the Louisiana Purchase. The city belonged to Spanish West Florida, a loosely administered territory claimed off and on by Spain, Britain, and the Republic of West Florida (established by American settlers who revolted). West Florida became a U.S. territory in 1810 and Louisiana gained statehood in 1812. Baton Rouge became the permanent state capital in 1879.

The southern portion of Louisiana was a gumbo of fun-loving, free-flowing Cajuns who were largely Catholic; the culturally rich descendants of enslaved Africans whose immigration was hardly voluntary; and settlers from the northern and eastern United States, many of whom brought with them a Protestant work ethic and rigid moral proscriptions. Immigrants from Canada, the Caribbean, and other European nations soon arrived, followed by pockets of Asians, all hoping to realize their dreams.

With each addition, Louisiana's ethnic stew became more flavorful. I would like to believe we German Jewish immigrants were an integral ingredient as well.

It didn't take Lea long to decide that the second-floor home on Laurel Street was too small. In fact, she described the residence as "miserable." Within two weeks of our arrival, she had Erich on a diet and initiated a move to a larger home at 1001 Main Street, five blocks west of Goudchaux's, to which my parents would walk daily. Our furniture arrived from Germany soon after the move.

The five of us—soon to be six with the arrival of Jacob, my grandfather—lived for more than four years in that house with its screened porch, two bedrooms, one bath, a combination living/dining room, and a kitchen with an old gas stove and icebox. (Yes, the latter was cooled by

abundant, foliage was lush, and the yards had flowering gardens. In many ways, the physical appearance of Baton Rouge reminded my mother of Aurich. Politically, Louisiana was just emerging from what some considered this country's closest brush with a dictatorship, the administration of Governor Huey P. Long. People talked about it, but I am sure my father inwardly chuckled. He had firsthand experience with a genuine dictator.

As with Aurich, the flags of many nations had flown over Baton Rouge. First settled by the French in the early

real ice delivered weekly by the ice man in his horse-drawn wagon.) The landlord promised to fix problems in the kitchen for nearly five years. The home had a radio and an attic fan. Good cross ventilation got us through Louisiana summers.

The three children slept in one bedroom and our parents in the other. Both space and money were tight at the start. Frugality was the order of the day. Mother remembered asking for a broom and a mop within hours of settling into the house, only to be told by her husband she could have a broom *or* a mop, but we couldn't afford both. She probably chose the broom. Everything we had was

I stand with the help of Insa and Josef for this picture, taken within weeks of arriving in America in 1937.

invested in the store. The money situation would improve as the sales volume increased.

Mother enrolled Josef, eight, and Insa, six, in Nicholson Elementary School, about a block away. The school was excellent, its principal and teachers outstanding. I remember most of them by name. Insa was in first grade, and Josef should have gone into the third grade, but school officials were concerned about his inability to speak English. He, too, was enrolled in the first grade. Three months later, he was moved to the third.

The family had only the clothes it brought from Aurich, so Josef started school outfitted in the traditional garb of a German schoolboy in February—wool sweaters, knickers, and long socks. He came in for some good-natured ribbing, of course. There are people in Baton Rouge who still remember those knickers.

Mother soon joined my father at Goudchaux's, six days a week. Raised an Orthodox Jew, Lea worked on Saturdays, the Jewish Sabbath, for the first time in her thirty-three years, but work she did! Once Insa and Josef were off to school in the morning, she walked to the store. She would retain a lifelong German accent, but she already spoke English, having learned it at school. My mother understood and related well to customers, quickly becoming a superior sales manager.

Around noon, Lea would walk home to check on me and to make lunch for Josef and Insa. In those days, most schoolchildren walked home for the noon meal. I was being cared for by a housekeeper and cook, Lovie Talbot Hampton, who worked for our family until she died in 2005 at the age of eighty-five. Lea enjoyed a reputation for being a fabulous cook, and she mentored Lovie in the culinary arts. (It can be noted here, however, that Lea always left out one ingredient when she passed along her recipes. Whether to family members or friends, it did not matter.) Lea daily prepared a hot lunch for Erich during their first fourteen years at the store. A Goudchaux's driver would pick up the food and take it to the store. My father had lunch at the store until my brother Josef joined the business in 1951. After that he ate at home. Lea would return to Goudchaux's for a while in the afternoons before meeting the children when school let out.

Sundays were reserved for outings. Neither of my parents could drive—their families never owned a car—but Erich purchased an automobile anyway. It was a 1936 Willis Knight, a nine-cylinder wonder made for only a few years by the Willis Motor Company of Illinois. Costing several thousand dollars new, it was not an inexpensive automobile, even in used condition. It mostly was employed for Goudchaux's business, but on Sundays the family got to enjoy it. Father hired a driver, Robert Gudney, a Goudchaux's employee, to take us on outings we thought were wonderful.

We piled into our small Willis for a day of adventure. How we all managed to fit, I am unsure to this day. When we unloaded, it must have looked like one of those circus acts where dozens of clowns roll out of a car. Being cramped wasn't the only thing of note. This was wartime. When the National Anthem played over the car radio, all except the driver stood up—at least the best we could in such crowded conditions. That was standard practice for many families until President Roosevelt, during one of his famous fireside chats, declared that perilous act of vehicular patriotism unnecessary.

Our one-day round trips to Jackson, Mississippi, to see Uncle Alfred and his wife, or to visit our cousins in New Orleans, or to the Gulf Coast for fun on the beach, always brought us home in time to open the store early Monday morning. My father would take no actual vacations until well into the 1950s, when Josef was trained sufficiently to manage the store.

Back in Aurich, Max was running Meyer Sternberg's. When Erich announced his departure for America, Max insisted Erich sell him his one-third interest in the store. Max rejected an offer Erich had proposed before he left: a dual partnership in the German and soon-to-be-American businesses. Max did not have faith in the overseas venture and wanted to remain in Germany. (Within a short time, however, business in Aurich became so depressed owing to Nazi edicts and persecution that Max had no choice but to leave.)

Grandfather Jacob didn't want to leave, either. He still considered himself a German, believing the current situ-

ation was a "rural thing" and that if he moved to Berlin, a metropolitan, cultured city in which one-third of Germany's Jewish population resided, things would be better.

Although the Nazis still were permitting Jews to leave the country at this point, it was not easy. In addition to emigration taxes, the government would assess those who stayed behind for any "missing" monies and to "repay" the state for education costs and other "investments" the state had made in those who left, on the grounds that the Fatherland would no longer benefit from their labors. As more and more Jews emigrated, the ones remaining became increasingly poor, if not destitute.

Max and Ida remained uncertain about when they should cut their losses and leave for America. Their indecision vanished when Aurich authorities jailed Max in

The Aurich synagogue, burned to the ground by Nazi hooligans during Kristallnacht in 1938

the spring of 1938. Officials alleged that money was missing and that Max knew where it was. According to vague accounts, still remembered in Aurich to this day, a rumor spread that Max had money hidden under the floorboards of his home. The rumor came to the attention of Nazi authorities, who searched the home and found nothing. Max remained behind bars for several days before someone who knew the judge convinced him that the charge was only a rumor and that Max should be released.

By April 1938, nearly all Jewish companies had closed or been forced to sell at artificially depressed prices. Max sold the business for ten cents on the dollar. He had two choices: Sell at whatever was offered or watch the business go up in smoke. (Later, he and my father learned that it would have been financially advantageous to have chosen the latter route.)

Max encouraged my grandfather, now a widower, to come with them to America. Erich could sponsor them. Jacob, eighty-one years old, was reluctant and still talking about going to Berlin. But realizing that his entire family would be a continent away, he finally agreed to leave. However, Lea's father, Lippmann Knurr, who was seventy-eight, steadfastly resisted for another eight months or so. By then, Nazi Germany had become a prison for Jews.

On June 6, some eighteen months before the borders were sealed, the last three Sternbergs walked down the gangplank of the *Queen Mary* (ocean-liner royalty in that era) in New York City and headed for Baton Rouge. Once there, Jacob chose to live with his youngest son, Erich. He slept in the bedroom with the two older children. Still a toddler, I slept in my parents' room.

Max and Ida were reunited with their son, Manfred. Max joined Leo in helping Erich at Goudchaux's. Neither Max nor Leo would remain long, however, preferring to start their own businesses in their newly adopted country.

Max, Ida, and Jacob Sternberg had left Germany just in time. The situation there was about to get demonstrably worse for Jews. On November 7, 1938, a German diplomat, Ernst von Rath, was murdered in the German embassy in Paris by Herschel Grynszpan, a seventeen-year-old Polish

Nazis picketed the Knurr store in Aurich in 1933. The sign warns citizens against shopping at Jewish-owned businesses.

Jew. Germany's minister of propaganda, Joseph Goebbels, used the assassination as a pretext for retaliation.

Three days later, the Gestapo and its vigilantes struck. In what became known as the "Night of Broken Glass," or Kristallnacht, 267 synagogues and other Jewish houses of worship were torched, including the one in Aurich. Some 7,000 Jewish businesses were vandalized, many destroyed completely. Books were burned, and nearly 100 Jews were killed. Piling atrocity upon atrocity, the Nazis then required Jews to come up with one billion Reich marks to repair the damage.

In addition, some 26,000 Jews were rounded up and sent to temporary prison camps. The Gestapo had a list of "special" people they believed to be agitators and began calling for them to come forward. Lea's brother, Herman Knurr, was at one of the camps. Although Erich had

The same Knurr building, modernized, in today's downtown Aurich

left for America two years earlier, Herman heard Erich's name called, no doubt the result of less-than-discreet remarks made about the Nazi regime before he left. My father had committed another "offense": Before his engagement to Lea, he dated a non-Jewish woman, which undoubtedly did not sit well with the Nazis and their Aryan views. Those present when their names were called were taken away, never to be heard from again.

When Herman was released, he returned to the Knurr store to find it completely stripped of merchandise. Walls and floors were bare. Even the light bulbs had been taken from their fixtures.

After August 17, 1939, Jews had to add "Israel" or "Sarah" to their names, and a large "J" was imprinted on their passports. In September, non-Jewish doctors were forbidden to treat Jewish patients. From *Kristallnacht* forward, the Nazis dramatically accelerated their program of persecution and terror. German Jews had no further doubts about the need to leave. The question became, could they leave? Tragically, emigration doors began slamming shut as the desire to flee intensified. Nations sat by as Hitler swallowed up what was then Czechoslovakia

and the heavily Germanic Sudetenland (the latter near the area from which Solomon Sternberg may have emigrated nearly two centuries before). The world seemed ready to buckle to the Third Reich.

In 1938 and 1939, Erich and Lea Sternberg redoubled their efforts to extract those left behind in Aurich. Lea's brothers —Harry, Herman, and Erich—and their families were fortunate: They came to the United States through Holland and France—among only 27,000 people allowed out of Germany in 1938. My father recruited Herman to run the men's division and to help manage Goudchaux's, which he did until his death from a heart attack at work in 1974. Harry and Erich settled in New York City and Montgomery, Alabama, respectively.

My father also helped nearly one hundred other relatives, friends, friends of acquaintances, et al., escape the Nazi death trap. They got out with letters of sponsorship he signed, often while walking the floors of Goudchaux's. He was able to do this because he had a business and could offer jobs, critical criteria at the time for obtaining visas into the United States and out of Germany. People he didn't know stopped him in the store with sponsorship paperwork that needed signing. Erich would tell them to turn around and place the life-saving documents against their backs, and he would sign the forms.

In 1985, the family, Erich posthumously, received an international award from B'nai B'rith, mainly for those remarkable humanitarian efforts. Dad didn't consider himself particularly virtuous. His actions stemmed more from his firsthand knowledge of what was happening in Germany. He was in America and in a position to help, and he did so.

Fortunately, few of those immigrants would travel to "isolated" Baton Rouge seeking work at Goudchaux's. My father's sponsorships notwithstanding, his small business could not have put many of them to work. In all, a third of a million Jews fled Germany and Austria in the years leading up to World War II. By 1941, when emigration was officially and totally forbidden, the German Jewish population of more than a half million had declined to approximately 163,000, according to the Holocaust Memorial Museum in Washington, D.C. A vast majority of those subsequently lost their lives in Nazi death camps.

It wasn't just to America that Jews were fleeing. From New Zealand to China to South Africa to the Dominican Republic to Argentina, the world experienced a tsunami of Jewish immigration. In an attempt to open more doors, President Roosevelt convened a conference on the refugee question in Evian, France, in 1938, but only the Dominican Republic agreed to lift its immigration quota.

Those left behind in Germany included Lea's father, the seventy-seven-year-old Lippmann Knurr, who delayed his exit decision too long. Aurich's Jewish community had honored him in 1939 as "one of the best known, most highly regarded and leading personalities" in the town, further noting that his children, including my mother, "were brought up in order to carry with them a genuinely Jewish way of life." Ironically, only lay people would attend the ceremony; the rabbi had long since left Aurich.

Erich concentrated on obtaining emergency visas for Lippmann and his sister-in-law, Henrietta Bienheim Knurr. But the U.S. immigration quotas were oversubscribed. One still could, however, pry loose a visa for a married couple. Lippmann had been a widower for more than fifteen years, and Henny, who was two years younger than he, was a widow. That gave my father an idea.

He wrote Lippmann and Henny, instructing them to "marry" each other in a civil ceremony. That way he could get them into this country on a husband-and-wife visa. Once here, they could go their separate ways. Henny, a strict Orthodox Jew, refused on religious grounds. In their case, two brothers had married two sisters. Religious rules prohibit marriage between a widowed brother-in-law and a widowed sister-in-law. With no rabbi in Aurich to issue a ruling that life-and-death situations trump tradition and rubrics, Henny's rigidity sentenced Lippmann and herself to death—Henny in the Treblinka extermination camp in Poland and Lea's father under a different, but scarcely less tragic, set of circumstances.

Accepting his fate, Lippmann left for Bremen with Henny on February 29, 1940, and moved in with relatives. Shortly after they left Aurich, the Nazis forced every Jew

Hennie Bienheim and her husband prior to his death. Hennie was Lippmann Knurr's sister-in-law and refused to marry Lippmann (both were widowed) in order to get a visa to the United States. She died at Treblinka concentration camp in 1942.

from the town. Lippmann wrote my mother a postcard in early 1941—one of two that got out before Germany declared war on the United States and all mail service ceased—that two anti-Semitic hooligans had attacked him on a streetcar, causing him to fall from the trolley. The rear wheels severed his foot.

The Nazis inevitably found Henny and put her in a boxcar to Treblinka. We learned she was killed on September 23, 1942, shortly after her arrival at the camp. Lea eventually received word from the Red Cross that her father had died in Bremen from unknown causes in April 1942, at the age of eighty-three. Given the fate of so many others, at least it could be said he died a free man.

Along with Henrietta Bienheim Knurr, fifty-nine of my father's and mother's relatives—men, women and children—were executed by Nazis, according to a list Leo compiled. Two cousins survived the death camps. About half the Jewish population of Aurich perished in the Holocaust. While Aurich escaped Allied bombing, nearly 80 percent of Emden, which was a seaport and, therefore, more strategic, was leveled. Three in four Aurich Jews had left by 1939. When the remaining 148 were ordered from the city in late 1940 and early 1941, the town council proudly proclaimed, "As of today, Aurich is free of Jews." Of the estimated 11 million human beings of all faiths, races, and ethnic backgrounds the Nazis murdered in their concentration camps and in mass field executions, six million were Jews, including almost 1.5 million Jewish children. This was two thirds of Europe's Jewish population; one third of world Jewry.

I often wonder how Germans handle the guilt today. The conscience-numbing burden has to be—and eternally will be—excruciatingly heavy. Even today, when I meet a German of the appropriate age, I feel compelled to learn what year he or she left Germany. If it was after World War II, my feelings remain complex—but raw.

Although Lea visited Aurich to see how the city had changed and to view family graves, I have not traveled back to my native Germany, even though the city of Aurich offered me free airline tickets. I cannot even watch *Schindler's List* and other Holocaust-focused films.

In the decades since the Holocaust, Aurich has been radically different—ironically, "Jew free," as Hitler wished. Only one Jew currently resides there.

4 NEW MERCHANT IN TOWN

BENNIE GOUDCHAUX URGED MY father in 1939 to purchase the store outright. It was time—for both men. Erich's prowess as a merchant had impressed Bennie, who soon asked Erich to be the overall store manager. Bennie loved golf and got away most afternoons for a round. He also sang in the Third Street Harmony Club. In addition, his son, Harry, who squabbled with his father over how the store should be operated, also wanted out (he went into the insurance business in Alaska). Although Bennie was ready to leave, Erich was fresh and energized.

Dad still had much of his original capital, plus money from his investment in Goudchaux's. He believed he could borrow another $15,000 from a bank for working capital. Bernard Goudchaux wanted a bit more than $100,000 for the entire operation—a price tag of more than $1.4 million in today's dollars—but he was willing to let Erich purchase it over time. Financing, however, turned out to be far from a sure thing. Two of Baton Rouge's three established banks, one owned by a Jewish family, turned down Erich's loan request. Leroy Ward, head of Fidelity National Bank, did not. (Goudchaux's eventually became one of Fidelity's two largest customers.)

Ever strategizing, Erich had his own plan: He would buy Goudchaux's in two pieces. He bought the business, including the inventory, in 1938 with his cash on hand, but leased the building until he had the financial wherewithal to purchase it. That milestone came on June 15, 1945, when he purchased the bricks, mortar, and land for an additional $87,000.

The building marquees would continue to say "Goudchaux's." Whatever ancestral or sentimental pull Erich might have felt to change the store's name to "Sternberg's," Goudchaux's had been an established and respected name since 1907. It also would have been expensive to develop new branding and to change the building marquees, stationery, signs, and so on, expenses Erich didn't need in those early days. (He did have one box of stationery printed with "Sternberg's" across the top. In my recollection, he never used it.) When Erich took over Goudchaux's, he had 23 employees. During Erich's twenty-five-year oversight, the store increased in size from 10,000 to 87,000 square feet and in employees to 300.

Bennie Goudchaux had not kept up the store. It was in bad need of a cosmetic refreshing; it also suffered from inadequate lighting. Nevertheless, the place was homey—wooden floors, old-fashioned furniture, piles of clothes, friendly atmosphere—and the overhead was low. Energy control wasn't difficult. It was a matter of reaching up, pulling a string, and turning off a light.

The store was laid out with men's clothing on one side and women's on the other, with fabrics and sewing notions in between. Men's shoes were along a side wall, with cash registers in the middle of the merchandise. Display windows flanked the two front doors. In

My parents always shopped at Goudchaux's in the late '30s. My dad loved to tell about the time we went to buy a hat for my brother. Erich Sternberg tried several hats [on him] that were too small and he would explain, "Whoops, too small." The next hat would come down over my brother's ears, and he would exclaim, "Whoops, too big."

—MARJORIE MILTON

When I was a young kid, back before World War II, I really loved for my mother to take me with her when she went shopping at Goudchaux's on Main Street. It was great fun for me to run up and down those old roller-coaster wooden floors.

—JOHN B. KENT JR.

1939, Goudchaux's shared the 1500 block of Main Street with McConnell's Plymouth dealership, Ben's Bar, Mae's Coffee Shop, a jewelry store, and the Freeman family residence.

Downtown businesses generally offered trendier and higher-quality clothing than Bennie Goudchaux's store. By all accounts, it was a second-rate enterprise. In fairness, however, it should be noted that Goudchaux's merchandise may have been inexpensive, practical merchandise because of the times. Baton Rouge, the state of Louisiana, and the nation were just emerging from the worst economic downturn in America's history. In the 1930s the average family made do with what it had. What few purchases people made tended to be no-nonsense, durable, inexpensive clothing for work and everyday use.

My father's timing in acquiring Goudchaux's could not have been better. By 1939, the ferocity of the Great Depression was moderating, although its effects would be felt for another year or two. Industry was thriving as the United States made ready for war. Most Americans had money and a pent-up desire, as well as need, to shop. They were in a buying mood.

(That desire to purchase durable goods continued through World War II. But unlike the Depression scenario—plenty of merchandise but not so many customers—the war years were just the opposite. With goods and resources diverted to the war effort, Erich and other retailers were forced, for example, to sell shoes made in part from enhanced cardboard, leather having been diverted to military use.)

The merchants on Third Street in downtown Baton Rouge never considered Bennie Goudchaux much of a threat. His store was only 100 feet by 125 feet—and nearly a quarter of that space was storage, in addition to a balcony with the owner's desk and the accounting and credit departments. The store was down-home quaint, with a pot-bellied stove and ceiling fans that nearly blew one over when operating during summer months. (Air conditioning did not arrive until after World War II.) The late Jeanne Whitehead, who began in sales at Goudchaux's in 1928, subsequently admitted that it wasn't "a real department store until 'Mr. Erich' took it over."

Initially, the merchants' association did not invite Erich to its meetings, informing him later what they had decided as a group when it came to store hours. He usually ignored them. Those Third Street business owners would learn—the hard way—that there was a new merchant in town whose mission was to grow and to elevate Goudchaux's to first-class status.

The store Bennie Goudchaux ran obtained its merchandise from traveling salesmen (they were all men in those days) who stopped by when they were in the area. He stocked neither furs nor bridalwear, two specialty items that soon would become among our most popular offerings. Erich instituted buying trips that took Goudchaux's buyers to the merchandise—initially to New York City but later to fashion centers around the world. He wanted original fashions, not those that had been offered to each of his competitors by the same sales reps.

Accompanying him on his first buying junket to New York City in 1939 were Herman Whitehead (Jeanne's husband), brother-in-law Herman Knurr, and Opal Ligon, a buyer of women's clothing (called ready-to-wear). Erich still didn't trust his command of English at this point and relied on others to assist him in communicating with market vendors. A store employee, Frank Bouligney, drove them to New Orleans to catch the Southern Crescent to New York City.

This was everyone's first trip to market. "It was the blind leading the blind—scary," Opal later recounted, except for one thing: "Mister Erich knew furs backward and forward. He always got a good price." With Miss Opal turned loose at market, it wasn't long before bridalwear became a Goudchaux's staple.

It was during that initial outing that Lea, who was in charge during her husband's absences, decided to outfit show-window mannequins with sharp-looking women's lingerie. A delegation of offended people soon confronted her, demanding the "risqué" displays be removed so that "neighbors" would not have to look at them. Mother was never sure who in the adjacent cemetery was offended, but she changed the displays.

(Baton Rouge and the South may have been behind the times on these matters, but not by much. Well into the first quarter of the twentieth century, established department stores deemed mannequins, let alone underwear, morally offensive to the upper-crust clientele they were seeking. Indeed, Benjamin Altman, owner of B. Altman's, decreed that no mannequins of any nature would appear in his New York City display windows. It wasn't until 1927, five years after his death, that the ban was lifted. Underwear displayed in windows, on the other hand, remained a controversy into the thirties.)

Erich returned from New York with an impressive array of merchandise and immediately put on a sale the likes of which Baton Rouge had never experienced. Opal Ligon remembered the phenomenon well: "It took a while to get the downtown shoppers to come our way. When the store started to expand and we got better merchandise, people began to notice us. Having a parking lot helped. No other merchant was doing what Mr. Erich did." In all ways, Goudchaux's was becoming a place to be reckoned with—and a place to shop.

In 1961, Opal was featured in a *Time* magazine story on fall fashions. The publication, profiling one buyer's pilgrimages to New York, said Opal was the "better-dress buyer for Goudchaux's, the best department store in Baton Rouge," and described a scene in which she was "cutting through razzmatazz and [making] swift, sharp decisions." An accompanying photo shows my dad sitting nearby in the showroom with a cigar in his mouth.

Never one to waste time in a showroom, Opal was quoted as telling one salesman who was displaying his wares, "I think you're through, honey." To another, who was promoting a dress: "It's heavy as lead, but I love it."

When I started working in 1948, Goudchaux's had wooden floors that felt very homey and welcoming. On rainy days, we would get straight pins out of the cracks in the floor to use for alterations. We never walked over a paper clip or piece of paper on the floor because we knew they were to be "reused."

—MILDRED RAIFORD GARRISON

Opal Ligon (with glasses), an early Goudchaux's buyer, displaying prom fashions in the late 1940s

My memories of dear old Goudchaux's revolve around three great ladies: Lea Sternberg, Opal Ligon, and my mother. Mrs. S helped me pick out my wedding dress. Opal used to commandeer a package cart and conduct us around the store, selecting Christmas gifts for everyone on our list . . . just like Sherman through Georgia.

—MILDRED WORRELL

Bettye Pearson Richard was a Goudchaux's bride. As was [the store's] custom, a bridal consultant went to the home and helped the bride dress, then drove to the church to see that all went well until the bride and her attendants walked down the aisle.

—RICHARD FAMILY

And yet to another: "Yes, I can see how lovely it looks on the rack. You can just leave it there."

Of the twenty-three original Goudchaux's employees, seven remained for decades, until they retired or died. Jeanne Whitehead sold for and then managed the hosiery department for sixty years. She joined Goudchaux's at the age of sixteen. Of Cajun descent (despite her English-sounding name), she spoke only French when she first entered the store. She told Mary Ann Sternberg in the 1980s that Bennie Goudchaux was "a good person to work for, but Mr. Erich was better. Your trouble was his trouble."

My grandfather, Jacob Sternberg, was my first and closest friend in America. I was too young to understand that, or how much my grandfather missed Germany and his beloved Röschen. We played, and he spoke to me in German. Because of him, I spoke better German than English until I was six. He was a math whiz, and my love of numbers came from him and Dad. Grandfather, however, never fully learned English (although his grandchildren tried to teach him), and never truly explored his new world other than occasional Sunday drives in the packed Willis or daily walks to the store to sit, observe, and consult with his son. In October 1941, two months after I started elementary school, Jacob, still longing for his native land, died of stomach cancer at the age of eighty-four.

Seven weeks later, on December 11, 1941, German foreign minister Joachim von Ribbentrop sent a diplomatic cable to the U.S. State Department declaring that in light of America's declaration of war against Japan for the attack on Pearl Harbor, Germany considered itself at war with the United States. Yes, Nazi Germany declared war on the United States—not, as most Americans believe, the other way around.

My father stormed home from work upon hearing the news and announced that, henceforth, German would not be spoken in the Sternberg household. When the Prussian in him made that kind of statement, it was law. A few German phrases would slip out from time to time, but to this day, none of the Sternberg children speak, read, or understand more than a few words in German. It ought to be noted, however, that Erich's fury at the Nazis did not carry over to Germany itself or to those Germans who remained decent in the face of tyranny.

By 1940, business at Goudchaux's was going so well that my father decided we needed to own a home, and a larger one at that. He purchased a lot in Baton Rouge's Garden District for $2,000 (two years later, he added the adjacent lot) and built a 2,300-square-foot stucco house for $10,800. We moved into the new home in 1941. It had duct work but no air conditioning and a double garage but no cars—my parents still did not know how to drive. (Fifty-eight years later, following my mother's death, we sold what had become a brick-veneer house for $300,000. Its original pitched roof was tile-covered concrete and in excellent condition.)

Erich and Lea stand proudly on the lot just purchased for their first and only owned home, on Kleinert Avenue in Baton Rouge, in 1940.

Josef, Insa, and me in the early 1940s

The lack of transportation did not matter when we lived close to the store, but now Goudchaux's was 2.2 miles away. Erich hired Robert Gudney, our family driver on weekend outings, to give him driving instructions. This was, alas, the era of the manual shift, and Erich had no clue how to use the clutch. On the agreed-to Sunday morning, Robert was late. The appointed time elapsed by a few minutes, and Erich had waited long enough. Since patience was not his long suit, he took off behind the wheel of the Willis Knight on his own, jerking and stopping every foot of the way. We found the car parked diagonally across the sidewalk next to Goudchaux's front door.

A year later, on April 16, 1942, Erich, Lea, Josef, Insa, and I became U.S. citizens at a ceremony in the U.S. District Court in Baton Rouge. It was a grand feeling. My father and mother came to America not just because of Nazi injustices occurring in the mid-1930s—they couldn't even have imagined what was to come in the early 1940s—

but also because of respect for a principle. They were strongly motivated by what they felt was right and wrong, by their belief as to how people should live, by how one human being should treat another.

The Sternberg family embraced this country with an intensity not easily understood by those whose past is different. One of my father's most memorable moments was when he walked out of that federal courthouse a U.S. citizen—the possessor once again of the right to vote. He gladly paid his taxes and, during World War II, publicly and proudly purchased war bonds. For us, American citizenship was and remains something quite special.

Service is the key to success, according to my father. Courtly, old-world manners, personal attention to customers, an instinct for what sells, and a keen eye for what was occurring on the floor of his store—all represented the Sternberg way, and they would become Goudchaux's hallmark. Erich would greet most customers by name as they came in the door, even if their last visit was a half year before.

The story goes that during an interview, when one prospective employee asked where his office would be, Erich looked him over and said, "My friend, your office is on the bottom of your shoes." Even buyers did not have offices. Everyone would be on the floor taking care of customers. It remained that way until we bought the New Orleans department stores in the early 1980s and began competing in seven locations in three cities.

Erich loved children and believed they all were beautiful. He would look at a child, smile broadly, and rhetorically ask, "Where do all the ugly adults come from?" Not a bad question. Think about it.

While walking the floor of the store, Erich habitually carried nickels in his pocket for the occasions when children arrived with their parents. He would hold out a nickel, tell the child what a beautiful youngster he or she was, and ask the parent if he could "buy" that child for a nickel—a story remembered by many Goudchaux customers. Erich would then laugh and offer the child the nickel for a Coke, dispensed in the classic, small glass bottles from a machine in the store.

Mildred Garrison, a forty-four-year employee, recalled inquiring of "Mr. Erich" on one occasion in the early 1950s what he would do if the parent suddenly took the nickel, placed the child in the proprietor's arms, and ran off. "He looked at me," remembered Mildred, "and said in a quiet voice: 'Then I will quit asking.'"

We sold Cokes for a nickel even after our cost went to six cents. Later, Josef and I instituted a policy of rewarding each report card "A" with a nickel, which young scholars could use to buy a Coke. Later still, we provided the area's public and private schools with Goudchaux's report-card holders, advertising the nickels-for-A's program. Coca-Cola's Web site carries this unsigned "Coke story":

When I was in elementary school in Baton Rouge, there was a department store called Goudchaux's . . . we went there every six weeks to "cash in" our report cards . . . Once we got our nickels, we went right to the center of the store in the main aisle and dropped one in the small, red, shiny vending machine with a crank handle . . . Out came the iciest, coldest Coke you ever tasted. My momma would walk around and shop until we were done . . . That was truly a celebration I looked forward to with every report card.

Goudchaux's had two primary rivals in post–World War II Baton Rouge: Rosenfield's and Dalton's. In the beginning, they were larger. In the end, they were gone. While modernizing the Main Street store, my father grew his business with an eye to quality, detail, and value. He

Who can forget the talk of the town for years: The 5-cent Coke machine. [Goudchaux's] kept that price even when Cokes everywhere else had risen to 25 cents. I believe they kept the price of Cokes at five cents well into the mid-1960s.

—JOEL THIBODEAUX

39

bought better merchandise and promoted it. It wasn't long before shoppers who previously had made Third Street stores their shopping domain were driving east on Main to Goudchaux's. With innovative practices, high-quality merchandise, and the intangible personal touch, Erich proved to be a master merchant.

Opal Ligon recalls a man coming in the store during the 1940s to buy a fur coat for his wife. He had hit every sale, but he simply could not swing the price. When Erich went up to talk with him, the man said, "Mr. Sternberg, I can't afford this fur." With that trademark cigar in his mouth, Erich patted the man on his shoulder and said: "You like the fur, so buy it and see me next year [about payment]." From such customer relationships, retail legends are formed.

Business boomed after the war. Going to Goudchaux's at a time before malls was more than a shopping trip. It was an outing, an excursion, a ritual. Louisiana state treasurer John Kennedy fondly remembers his family's annual trips to the Main Street store. "My mother took us every year to buy our school clothes and to shop for Easter. It was a family ritual." The Rev. Charles Walton wrote that as a youngster in Baton Rouge, he went barefoot. "Going barefoot was a way of life. No one my age ever wore shoes unless they were going to Sunday school or Goudchaux's Department Store."

Dad started his workday at 8:30 a.m. He returned home about 7 p.m., six days a week, bringing work with him in a shirt box. Before the paperwork, however, he would spend time with his children. Chess, checkers, and reading together were the most common evening pursuits. We always ate breakfast and dinner as a family. My parents rarely entertained or went out for an evening.

There was a heavy emphasis in the Sternberg house on homework and scholarship. We three children were pushed to excel in the classroom. There was never a question about doing our homework and completing assignments on time. There would be hell to pay if a teacher complained about us. Grades were scrutinized, although the C's I regularly received in conduct were affectionately forgiven as just a matter of boys being boys. Discipline was tight. I well remember my mother chasing me with a hanger when I misbehaved, but I was never caught.

Erich's focus on the store was uninterrupted by hobbies, pastimes, and memberships. He was a person prone to precise, punctual, and exacting activities. He knew what had to be done and how to execute. At night, before going to bed, he put out his clothes for the next day, down to the handkerchief he would carry. After he learned to drive, he never allowed the car to have less than a half tank of gas lest an emergency arise and he needed to travel some distance. That was part of the refugee mentality he never lost.

Once Josef joined him in 1951, Erich ate lunch at home. He took pride in being able to travel home from Goudchaux's, eat, and return to the store in precisely thirty minutes. Outside of his family, his only diversion was a voracious appetite for books on historical topics. Like his father, Erich could calculate in his head faster than, and as accurately as, any adding machine of the time. (I enjoyed "breaking" and expanding his code of mental math, which I have shared with my children and grandchildren.)

He also had a wonderful sense of humor. A salesperson in the preteen and fur departments, Sarah Todd, who spent forty-two years with Goudchaux's, remembers him remarking that when he died, he wanted to be buried in the adjacent Catholic cemetery. "The devil would never think to look for a Jew there," he laughed.

Erich's mission for the store was simple: increase volume through quality and service. Although he always had time for everyone and sincerely loved people, he was frugal in running the business. Erich worried about paying his bills, but never owed anyone anything other than normal bank business loans.

Unless he was traveling, he always carried the same amount of cash: three nickels and three one-dollar bills. The nickels were for a cigar, a newspaper, and a possible telephone call—each costing five cents back then. The three dollars, he said, were in case he needed "real" money. But he had one spending weakness: He was a sucker for gadgets.

If a vendor had an item that purported to save time or to make the company more efficient, Dad would buy it. National Cash Register was a powerhouse of office machines in those days, always announcing some breakthrough to save money for businesses. When it had a new product to offer, Erich was the first person NCR's local office would pitch. But at least once he woke up to his own vulnerability: When NCR salesman Don Plaisance again entered the store, eager to share with Erich news of yet another labor-saving device, the proprietor called out, "Don, I can't afford to save any more money!"

Erich would not allow a vendor in the store after 9:15 a.m., opening time, or even to appear in Goudchaux's at all between November 15 and Christmas. Such interruptions would interfere with sales. He also minimized the amount of merchandise the company purchased from traveling sales reps. He wanted our stock to be unique.

Most of what we sold was bought at the clothing markets in New York City.

Many in the community thought Erich was somewhat unique because he closed the store for Rosh Hashanah and Yom Kippur, the two sundown-to-sundown sacred holidays of the Jewish New Year. (While maintaining this policy at the Baton Rouge Main Street store, we otherwise discontinued such closures following the acquisitions of the Florida units.) And when some members of B'nai Israel synagogue left in 1948 over the temple's lack of support for Zionism and the State of Israel, they asked Erich to join them. He agreed, then reneged. That caused some hard feelings, but he periodically would attend services at the new, "breakaway" Liberal Synagogue in addition to those at B'nai Israel (established in 1858). Max and Leo Sternberg and Herman Knurr, along with their families, went to Liberal Synagogue. (Our family has belonged to both congregations since the 1960s.)

Erich was proud of being a Jew, but he was not as observant as his spouse. Although Lea worked on the Sabbath because she had to, she lit candles on Friday night, said the Shabbas blessings, and observed Havdalah, the prayer service to end the Sabbath (Saturday), as long as she lived. She had a deep and abiding faith in God; it sustained her during dark times.

In the beginning, Lea maintained an Orthodox observance of our faith in the Baton Rouge household, although she and Dad had to work on Saturdays to survive financially. From sundown Friday to sundown Saturday, we didn't shop, sign a check, mail a letter, ride a bike, or engage in or partake of any form of entertainment. On Saturdays, store staff members knew the store was about to close when the boss lit his first cigar of the day at 6 p.m.

Lea sent to Chicago for kosher meat, which was unavailable in Baton Rouge. When the United States entered World War II, meat of any kind—let alone kosher meat—was difficult to obtain. So my parents abandoned that rule, and household Sabbath observances began to ease. By the time I was old enough to ride a bike or attend a movie, I was allowed to do both on Saturdays.

Lea and Erich check on the construction of a parking lot adjacent to Goudchaux's on Main Street, July 1942. The surface was gravel until after the war. It was the first retailing parking lot in Baton Rouge.

Erich Sternberg was a visionary. Following World War II, cars were no longer a luxury. They had become a necessity in a new, mobile world, and it seemed as though everyone had one. Erich leveled and paved a 200-car parking lot next to the store, enlarging a 1942 gravel lot. It was a Baton Rouge first, and he happily allowed a nearby church to use the parking spaces on Sundays.

A competitor confronted him one day, asking what he was going to do with such a parking lot. Erich just smiled. Later, Josef and I bought adjacent land to provide additional parking spaces. Eventually, the lots could handle 1,200 vehicles. On many days, even that number of parking places was insufficient.

Erich also featured another service rarely found in modern retailing: interest-free charge accounts. That Goudchaux's perk continued until we were one of the few department stores in America still offering interest-free accounts. By 1991, we had 640,000 of them. There are many anecdotes concerning those charge accounts, but Patsy Morales recently related a "Goudchaux's Moment" that underscores Dad's business practices and values:

We had charge accounts with Sears, Goudchaux's, and other stores. In 1959, my husband was killed in an auto accident. We had paid our [Goudchaux's] account on the 15th but the bank account was frozen and our checks returned. Sears called me every week asking for a payment, which I told them I would pay as soon as I got an income; the money I did have was needed to feed my family. I had three children and was expecting a fourth.

Goudchaux's called one time, and I told them the same thing. The lady said not to worry, to pay whenever I could. She never called again. Sears never *quit* calling. When I got an income I paid. I'm sorry the store closed.

The credit manager who called Patsy Morales was M. J. Galloway, one of the first women in Baton Rouge to be hired for a key executive position. That seems hard to believe today, but in the 1950s the few women hired generally were sales associates or clericals.

Within a year of taking over the store, Erich instituted home delivery. The first delivery "truck" was a 1937 Plymouth station wagon. Frank Bouligney, an early driver, would tell anyone who would listen that Goudchaux's would "deliver a spool of thread across the Mississippi River to Port Allen" if a customer requested it.

During the 1940s, the store hired a security staff. It was prompted, according to my mother, by two Baton Rouge police officers cashing their paychecks at the store. Erich was appalled at the amounts. "Is this what a policeman makes?" he asked incredulously. Then he told them he needed two security men, and would they be interested in moonlighting? They indeed were, and that was the beginning of a long and close relationship between area law enforcement officers and Goudchaux's.

Erich was the first one to the store each day, unlocking the doors shortly before 8:30 a.m. He dumped the mail on tables that sat squarely in the center of the selling floor. Set up early each morning, they were removed before the doors opened for business.

As every buyer, department head, or merchandise manager picked up his or her mail and work-related material, Erich had an opportunity to discuss informally what was being scheduled for that day and inquire as to what they had planned for their departments. There was time to discuss even the smallest things. Think of it as an individualized daily management meeting—so wonderfully effective a tool that Josef and I continued it until we sold all twenty-four stores.

In addition to being a management tool, the mail tables also were a place to which Louisiana politicians, elected or campaigning, flocked to shake hands. We would guide them through the store to meet employees. All politicians, of all political stripes, were welcome with two exceptions; they will be discussed in a later chapter.

During the early 1960s, Goudchaux's received two awards from the Kennedy administration for our employment of the handicapped. One of those wonderful employees, Jenny, a mentally challenged woman who was with us for decades, was a popular gift wrapper. People would wait in line for her to gift-wrap their "special" packages. Railroad tracks ran within 150 feet of the west side of Goudchaux's. Contrary to what Dad thought when he first looked at the building in 1936, they proved a boon in those early years. Employees of Standard Oil Refinery (now Exxon) came back from the company's plant on the train daily. So many wanted to be let off at Goudchaux's on Saturdays, which was payday, that the railroad created a special stop there. We continued a practice—started by Bennie Goudchaux—of cashing their weekly paychecks, remaining open later than normal to handle the transactions.

Erich worked tirelessly to market smartly and keep the store fresh and up to date, although it was two decades before he got rid of the cigar-box accounting system he devised in response to a customer complaint. When Bennie and Harry Goudchaux ran the store, Harry would call up to bookkeeper Dippy LaGrange on the store's balcony that so and so wanted to charge such and such. Dippy would check the books to see if the customer was current on payments and shout back an okay or thumbs down.

Shortly after my father took over, a customer asked a salesperson his account balance. The request was orally forwarded to Dippy on the balcony, who called back the balance. The customer obviously didn't like everyone in the store knowing how much he owed and complained to Erich. He agreed it was an invasion of privacy and rigged a cigar box on a cotton string that carried written questions and cash payments silently to and from the sales floor to the accounting department. That worked for the next twenty years.

Erich's abiding philosophy was that the customer was everything. Without him or her, there would be no need for a cash register—or an accounting system, rudimentary or otherwise.

My uncle Max did not remain long at Goudchaux's. He wanted to operate his own store, so he bought his brother Leo's "five-and-dime," the common term in the 1940s and 1950s for a variety store. It was located one block east of Goudchaux's. Erich may have lent him money to get started.

Goudchaux's, ca. 1948, when Main Street was a brick road. Still visible are the former streetcar tracks, from which the steel was removed and used as scrap metal for the war effort during World War II.

According to Max's grandson, Paul Sternberg, Max felt he did not always receive the status traditionally attached to the first-born position. He noted with displeasure, for example, that when the patriarch of the family, Jacob, got to Baton Rouge, he stayed with his youngest son, Erich, not the eldest, as was customary, at least in the old country. Paul said there were indications the two brothers didn't speak for several years.

With the money he received from the sale of his variety store to Max, Leo started a chicken-processing busi-

ness that eventually failed. He then became a traveling representative for a New Orleans meat-packing plant, a job he stayed with until his death from a heart attack in 1983—the last of Jacob Sternberg's children to die. Some forty years prior to his death, soon after the start of World War II, Leo made a remarkable symbolic statement, a patriotic act that rated the front page of the newspaper.

Awaiting his U.S. citizenship, Leo donated to Baton Rouge's United Scrap Metal Drive to aid the American war effort the four medals, including the Iron Cross, he had been awarded for bravery and wounds received while fighting for the Kaiser in World War I. He also donated a bayonet and three ammunition rings. *The Morning Advocate,* in an October 8, 1942, story, quoted Leo as saying he hoped the medals would be made into the bullet that killed Hitler.

The post-war German government attempted to settle with Jews who had lost businesses or property as a result of the Nazis. In a June 14, 1960, letter from a Bremen law firm, the following reparations were offered: Leo Sternberg received 11,417 Deutsche marks, the equivalent of about $3,000 in 1960 dollars, for the destruction of his Emden store. Manfred, Max's son, was given 10,425 marks.

Josef, Insa, and I were each allocated just under $600 and my father $230. The latter refused to accept anything earmarked for our family from the German government and gave our reparations to Leo and Max. Why we were offered any money puzzled us, but it was not for the destruction of the Meyer Sternberg store.

In 1942, Max and Erich had signed an agreement that split equally any family property in Aurich that might be left after the war, or any settlement originating from its destruction. They received nothing, it turns out, because Max had sold the store before he left for America, albeit in a coerced transaction. The post-war German government refused to change or void bills of sale that occurred prior to the war because adjudicating the details of each civil transaction would have been a complex, time-consuming, and near-impossible task.

Each of us children worked at the store from the time we reached school age. Starting at age five, Josef and I picked up Coke bottles and stray paper clips on Saturdays. It was a 3½-hour morning shift for which we each were paid the handsome wage of one dime. We could not wait on customers until we became teenagers, but we did so when the time came.

That dime, though, was sufficient for a nine-cent movie and a one-cent bag of popcorn at the nearby Tivoli Theater on Saturday afternoons. The Tivoli was one of the first "air-conditioned" commercial structures in Baton Rouge. When we later purchased the building and land to expand Goudchaux's, we discovered a large pit underneath it. Joe Barcelona, the theater operator, kept the space filled with water and used fans under the floor to blow across the water and create an air-cooled breeze over the patrons' backs.

From the seventh grade on, I worked every Saturday in the store, all day, for my allowance. We did the same thing on holidays and during summers, with breaks to attend camp. (Josef and I raised our children under a similar regimen.) Other kids earned their allowances by mowing the yard or weeding the garden. To this day, I have never mowed grass or done yardwork. The Sternbergs looked at things differently. We were merchants.

From the beginning, Baton Rouge was an accepting community. I remember only a single incident of overt anti-Semitism. At one time, the KKK had a significant presence in Louisiana, although little influence in the urban areas. By the 1940s and 1950s in Baton Rouge, the KKK, which traditionally had African Americans, Jews, Catholics, and the foreign born in its sights, was spewing most of its hate on the first of those groups. The Klan took the time, however, to spray-paint the letters "KKK" on the Jewish synagogue in the 1960s. To my knowledge, no one was ever arrested.

The Baton Rouge Country Club had been accepting Jews as members long before New Orleans clubs and well before we arrived, but there were other areas of inherent discrimination for Jews. The Junior League, for example, did not accept Jewish women until 1973, when the barrier fell with the selection of Marcia Kantrow. Josef's spouse, Mary Ann, was asked to join the following year and my wife, Donna, a year after that. They were pleased to accept—it was a step forward for all of Baton Rouge.

(Some fraternities and sororities at Louisiana State University began dropping their no-Jews policy in the 1950s. Pi Phi sorority became the first, inviting Jeanne Cohn, my Sunday school classmate, to join in 1952.)

In the late 1930s, a man tried to start a Baton Rouge golf and country club that excluded Jews. He approached American Bank president Clifford Ourso for funding. Ourso, unaware of the restrictive agenda, approved the loan. The bank's advertising agency was owned by Alvin "Pinky" Meyer, who went to the banker and told him what

My high school picture, 1952

was happening. Ourso's reaction was swift. He decided that sort of club did not belong in Baton Rouge and withdrew the financing. The project collapsed.

Baton Rouge High School had a social fraternity called Delta Sigma. Until 1949, it had no Jewish youth. The following year, I was among the first Jews invited to join. Frank Foil was my sponsor. (He later became a well-respected appellate judge.) But I already had decided to change schools, transferring to the Lab School at Louisiana State University.

My cousin Manfred graduated from Catholic High School, and Josef attended Camp Stanislaus, a summer camp run by the Catholic church. For the most part, Baton Rouge practiced religious tolerance.

Josef earned his degree in business from Ohio State University in three years. Upon graduation in 1948, he returned to Baton Rouge to join our father at Goudchaux's following a six-month training stint at Rich's Department Store in Atlanta. But military service loomed.

Friends offered to get Josef into the reserves, which back then would have meant he could remain stateside, but he didn't feel right about it and was drafted in 1952. His orders sent him to South Korea, where the U.N.-authorized conflict required soldiers, but he never saw combat. On his way to battle, he and one or two others were pulled aside after the troops arrived in Japan. His typing skills and college degree landed him a headquarters position as a corporal.

Upon his return in 1954, Josef indicated he might like a split career—retail merchandising and farming. Erich bought Josef a farm north of Baton Rouge that summer at a cost of $125 an acre, and father and son walked the land. The redbugs and mosquitoes attacked so ferociously that both victims required soaking in Epsom salts, a cure-all of Lea's, for hours.

Josef surrendered the farming idea the same day, but we still own most of that land. The original parcel was 400 acres. We sold 100 acres several years later at a price equaling the original cost of the entire 400 acres.

Insa graduated from Baton Rouge High, as salutatorian of her 287-member class, eventually earned an MBA at Tulane, and became the first Sternberg to work at Maison Blanche, a New Orleans–based chain we would later acquire. In 1955, Insa married Leo Abraham, a Baton Rouge physician, and withdrew from daily activity in retailing.

I chose Princeton University for college—rather, it was chosen for me. Dad wanted me to go to the Wharton School of Economics at the University of Pennsylvania. SAT scores were necessary for Wharton, so I took the tests. My scores would be sent without additional cost to three schools. Ohio State, Josef's alma mater, was my second choice. I didn't have a third, but the SAT tests were handled by the Princeton Testing Bureau of Princeton, New Jersey, which had no connection to the university. Nevertheless, the word "Princeton" jumped out, so that became my third selection. I took the tests and then wrote for an application.

I was accepted at Wharton and informed the renowned business school I was coming. Several days later, Miss Teer, my English teacher, asked where I was going after graduation. Wharton, I said, adding I also had been accepted at Princeton. Next thing I knew, she had me in the office of the principal, who was on the phone telling my father it had to be Princeton. And that was that.

In 1951, Abbott and Wimberly Department Store opened on Plank Road in north Baton Rouge with the publicly announced purpose of putting Goudchaux's out of business. The new competition, backed by a number of Baton Rouge businessmen, recruited many of our personnel—including one of our key buyers, Opal Ligon—with promises of high pay. The defections were a blow to Erich, but they helped him focus on what he faced: a retail war in which neither side took prisoners. Dad won. Abbott and Wimberly closed its doors after five years. Erich held no grudges. Opal and most (but not all) of the defectors were rehired at Goudchaux's.

Erich realized as early as the 1940s that he had to expand Goudchaux's if the store was to survive. Abbott and Wimberly's attempt to destroy his business added to his sense of urgency and resolve. In 1952, he added store space to the east of the original building. It was a major undertaking, requiring the buyout over time of a number of adjacent entities: Bryan's Drug Store, a grocery store, the Tivoli Theater, Ryan's Stationery, and Sternberg's Five & Dime (by this time, Max had retired from his business). Years later, we got the city to agree to close the section of North 16th Street between the two blocks, adding to the seamlessness of the structure.

Goudchaux's architect was A. Hays Town, a close friend with a national reputation. He would continue to design our Main Street expansions. After several decades, a Goudchaux building would be his last commercial account.

As the foregoing demonstrates, we Sternbergs formed strong and loyal relationships. For roughly five decades, we used the same bank, law firm, architect, CPA—and, until he retired, the same family physician.

The new east side of Goudchaux's was completed in July 1954, and a corresponding remodeling of the old building—which included the major decision to move the principal, Main Street entrance to the back of the structure, facing the parking lot and Laurel Street—was finished three months later, just in time to inaugurate a women's sportswear department. (By 1991, women's sportswear was turning $100 million in sales.)

A 1957 fire caused $150,000 in damage to the Main Street store. It was repaired, and a new addition to the west side of the building was opened two years later. It was only the beginning.

5 | BOYCOTT

I GRADUATED MAGNA CUM LAUDE from Princeton University with a degree in economics in 1957. Having signed up for the Navy ROTC program, I then served two years as a line officer, ending a lieutenant, j.g. My father was quite proud to have a military officer in the family. It never would have happened in Germany.

I considered teaching economics, but the emotional pull to join Josef and my father at Goudchaux's was strong. I knew the family wanted and needed me there. My inclination toward business may have been partly due to a small lesson learned during my senior year at Princeton. I won the prize for the best thesis in economics and received a $25 check. Another prize went to the best thesis on a business topic. That award was $100. There seemed to be a message.

Josef had been at the store full time for ten years when I arrived in 1960, following six months of training at Foley's Department Store in Houston. In Josef's first year at Goudchaux's, he and my father argued over how to run the store—my father relying on his time-tested formulas and Josef touting new, textbook methods. The Prussian in my father sometimes could be hard to take. Josef quit and walked out three times during his first year. Since he was living at home, Lea would patch things up that night, and he would be back at work the following morning. To ease tensions, Erich "gave" his older son an area to run as

his own. It was the millinery department (women's hats), which at the time accounted for about 10 percent of Goudchaux's total sales. Josef could do anything he wanted with that department; Dad would say nothing—"*gar nicht.*" From then on, Josef and Dad got along famously. Josef had Erich's facility for bonding with customers, not to mention his warmth and genial nature. The genes made for an unbeatable team of merchants.

"Father was used to doing things his own way," said Josef in an interview many years later. "He knew exactly what he wanted, and there was really not much room for variance from his design. And here I was, coming in right out of college, telling him what I thought."

Goudchaux's, twelve blocks from downtown Baton Rouge, received considerably less foot traffic than enjoyed by the downtown stores. The disparity bothered Josef, enough so that in the mid-1950s, he talked Dad into opening a 3,000-square-foot women's specialty store, Carson's, on the east side of Third Street in the prime shopping district. For good measure, Josef also opened a Carson's in Lake Charles, 125 miles west of Baton Rouge. If that venture succeeded, the Sternbergs would consider opening a Goudchaux's there as well.

Carson's was profitable, though no runaway success. Its demise had nothing to do with sales and occurred shortly after I joined the company. My brother was mak-

Erich in the Goudchaux's fur department in the late 1950s >

A *Register* cover from 1960, the year I joined the family business full-time

ugees. When many Cubans fled following Fidel Castro's 1959 takeover of the island, Josef and I, having just joined the company, undertook a strong effort to get the Baton Rouge business community to hire refugees who immigrated to our area. We employed as many of them as we could at Goudchaux's.

In 1961, we put together a major job fair, inviting other Baton Rouge businesses to come to the store and recruit. It was a stunning success, and helped many Cubans find work. Josef even did some recruiting among sugarcane farmers in an attempt to place Cubans with expertise in that kind of work. Many of those we hired at Goudchaux's became some of our best and most loyal associates, and remained with us until we sold or they retired.

Why would the merchant Sternbergs bother with all that? Aside from simply wanting to help people, we understood what it was like being forced to flee a country because of a dictatorial government. That knowledge provided intense motivation for action. Coincidentally, we were becoming civic players in the community.

When my father took over Goudchaux's, the annual sales volume was $270,000, and there was a staff of 23. Sales hit $1 million in 1948. By the time Josef joined two years later, sales had increased to $1.5 million. Ten years after that, when I arrived, they topped $4.5 million. By 1990, Goudchaux's/Maison Blanche's annual sales exceeded $480 million, and employees, including part-time and seasonal help, numbered 8,800.

Time magazine called Goudchaux's the best department store in Baton Rouge in 1961. Three years after that, *Business Week* would say nearly the same thing. On paper, things looked healthy. But potential storm clouds were gathering that had nothing to do with sales volume, innovation, or promotions. It had everything to do with race.

When it came to racial issues prior to the 1960s, there was little doubt where the sentiments of a majority of Louisiana's established political and business powerbrokers lay. African Americans were denied political power, organizational memberships, and full access to public places. They were pushed to the backs of buses and restaurants and

ing one of his routine automobile trips to Lake Charles when he encountered a severe rainstorm, ran off the road, and wrecked the car. Although he wasn't hurt in that otherwise serious accident, Carson's died that night. Erich put the two Carson's stores up for sale within a week of the accident. He always claimed the Carson's sideshow was a distraction to the main event at 1500 Main Street. It also placed Josef unnecessarily on the road and at risk, and that was what really decided it for our father.

About this time, we became involved with Cuban ref-

into segregated schools, swimming pools, waiting areas, and restrooms.

Whites who displayed progressive stands on race relations were notified by the KKK and the White Citizens' Council that that sort of "communist" activity would not be tolerated. Moderates were shouted down, integrationists driven off. Federal desegregation mandates were ignored or circumvented.

The theory of racial superiority was deeply disturbing for a family that fled Germany because one class of people proclaimed itself superior to others and viciously persecuted them. The parallel was too strong for our comfort, and Dad quietly broke racial equity ground for Baton Rouge retailing in the 1950s. In retrospect, I know more could have been done. Nevertheless, our policies drew several warnings from the local chapter of the White Citizens' Council.

The Council was a movement throughout the South devoted to keeping the black and white races apart—in socializing, business, education, politics, transportation, and public events. Eschewing the violence and overt racism of the Ku Klux Klan, the Council attempted to mask its bigotry in professional respectability. It attracted more than one million members, many connected to a community's power structure: bankers, editors, lawyers, law-enforcement types, politicians. Far from everyone joined the White Citizens' Council, but it was a force with which to be reckoned.

The South was circling the wagons in its effort to maintain segregation. States banded together philosophically and legislatively to fight attempts at integration in a movement that became known as "massive resistance."

At the same time, African Americans were preparing their counter-resistance, and Baton Rouge would be a first testing ground in this part of the world.

The local chapter of the NAACP pulled off a major, but mostly overshadowed, victory in the early 1950s. The event: a bus boycott. It was set in the middle of a shameful scene. Blacks could neither eat where whites ate nor use the restrooms where whites relieved themselves. Water fountains were for "Whites Only" or "Coloreds." The Mississippi River ferries had separate decks for whites and blacks. Even laundromats often were separate.

Education at all levels was segregated. White medical patients were treated before blacks. Protestant churches, for the most part, were either black or white. While blacks could attend any Catholic church, once inside they often were relegated to a section of the pews. It became increasingly difficult for blacks to vote. What racist registration hurdles did not stop, pure intimidation did.

Public transportation, namely buses, became the first line drawn in the sand. Demographically, whites inside the Baton Rouge city limits have been in the minority since the late 1950s, although they comprise a majority of the East Baton Rouge Parish population. Whites have never been big users of public transportation in this city. Blacks, on the other hand, customarily have relied heavily on buses. In a stark example of business bias, black-owned bus companies with regularly scheduled routes were declared illegal in 1950. They were deemed too competitive with the city's system. Blacks were 80 percent of the riders, yet they were only allowed to ride in the rear half of the buses, no matter how crowded that section became.

In February 1953, the Reverend T.J. Jemison, a lion to the African American community for his courage in the fight for equality, was at the time a pastor at Mount Zion First Baptist Church, one of the city's largest congregations. The reverend took umbrage with the policy that ensured whites exclusive use of the front ten rows of city buses, which more often than not remained vacant, while the rear ten rows were jammed with African American riders. He brought his grievances to the Baton Rouge city council.

The council surprised many on both sides by unanimously approving Ordinance 222, permitting blacks to fill empty seats from the back forward, so long as they did not sit in front of a white passenger. White riders could fill empty seats, starting from the front and working back. Essentially, it was a first-come-first-served policy. Under this plan, the majority would determine where the line of segregation began. Since four of five riders were black, whites no longer unilaterally controlled the seating arrangements. That's what the ordinance spelled out on paper, anyway. In practice, white riders and bus drivers ignored the ordinance and, at least initially, it was not enforced.

Jemison was a founding member of the Southern Christian Leadership Conference. His father, David Vivian Jemison, led the National Baptist Convention—black counterpart to the Southern Baptist Convention—from 1942 to 1953. (T.J. headed the same organization from 1984 to 1992.) Jemison decided to personally test the new rule and the bus company's directive to its balking drivers by sitting near the front. "I did it to show what leadership was all about," recalled the ninety-year-old Jemison in a 2008 interview for this book. When the driver ordered Jemison to move to the rear, he refused. The driver drove the bus to the police station and asked an officer to remove him. Jemison showed the officer a copy of the ordinance and a court order. The officer sided with Jemison.

The drivers voted to strike after two of them were suspended for not complying with Ordinance 222, and on June 17 the Louisiana attorney general declared the newly enacted ordinance in violation of existing segregation laws—a ruling that angered the African American community. The United Defense League organized a bus boycott the following day.

One of the coordinators, a tailor named Raymond Scott, read the boycott announcement over radio station WLCS, at the time the most-listened-to Baton Rouge station. Scott urged all blacks not to use the buses and, instead, to take advantage of free rides and carpools offered by volunteers. WLCS provided boycott news, up-to-the-minute car-pooling information, and other announcements throughout the protest—the only Baton Rouge radio station to do so. "The white leadership of that station was tolerant and progressive," said Jemison, adding that having a mass medium broadcasting immediate information was "extremely helpful" in making the boycott a success.

One of the five WLCS owners and directors was Erich Sternberg, my father. The station's white managers, Lamar Simmons and Gene Nelson, who were also members of the board, received unanimous backing from the rest of the all-white board—my father, J. B. Chapman of Chapman Furniture, and attorney Charles Wilson of Wilson Blanche Watson & Thibaut.

Crosses were burned at Mount Zion First Baptist Church and at Jemison's home. He received a number of death threats. Armed members of Jemison's congregation stood guard over their church and their pastor's home and car during the night, and personally protected Jemison. Carpools were established, and black-owned gas stations sold fuel at cost for pool vehicles. WLCS announcers would inform boycotters where they could find rides to their destinations. Mass meetings were conducted throughout African American neighborhoods, while black and white leaders negotiated behind the scenes. The boycott was having its effect, and less than a week after it began, Jemison called it off with the announcement that a deal with the city had been cut.

The next day the city council approved Ordinance 251: The first two rows of the bus were reserved for whites and the last two rows exclusively for blacks. Every other seat was up for grabs. Since less than a quarter of the riders were white, most of the seats were available for African American riders. To adhere technically to segregation laws, no black person could sit next to a white person.

In retrospect, Jemison partially credits a "progressive" city council for the stunningly quick success of the South's first desegregation of public transportation, singling out council members Louis Dougherty and Woody Dumas, along with Gordon Kean, the East Baton Rouge Parish attorney. (Dumas would go on to become mayor. When he died in 1993, the Reverend T.J. Jemison delivered his eulogy.)

For the most part, the Baton Rouge boycott was considered a victory for black people, one that served as a template for future bus boycotts throughout the South, including the nation's most famous bus boycott in Montgomery, Alabama. The Reverend Martin Luther King came to Baton Rouge in 1954, a year before his famous Montgomery campaign, to meet with Jemison and other leaders, tilling for details about tactics and lessons learned, particularly the logistics surrounding alternative transportation. King preached in Mount Zion First Baptist Church.

In June 2003, my son Marc organized a two-day, fiftieth-anniversary commemoration of the Baton Rouge bus boycott. National Public Radio was among the news media covering the event. "Before Dr. King had a dream, before Rosa [Parks, the Montgomery heroine] kept her seat, and before Montgomery took a stand, Baton Rouge played its part," Marc told NPR. In fact, it wasn't long before the first-rows/last-rows rule evaporated. With the success of Baton Rouge in 1953, bus boycotts spread to other Louisiana cities, and by 1962, Baton Rouge's first black bus driver, Clovis Henry, was hired.

Then, in 1965, in defiance of a federal court mandate, Baton Rouge High School was scheduled to close in order to avoid integration. Josef and I, along with other business and civic leaders, contributed to the cost of full-page ads that ran several times in the city's morning and afternoon newspapers, owned by the Manship family.

The ads made an economic, social, and political case for keeping open the doors of the high school. The campaign was conceived and coordinated by B. B. Taylor, a Baton Rouge attorney, who, when he came to solicit spon-

KKK flyer distributed after some business leaders published a newspaper ad calling for the acceptance of school desegregation, 1965

sors to help underwrite the ads on an anonymous basis, told me he was "a white, Anglo-Saxon, Protestant attorney. They can't touch me." Taylor accepted no more than one hundred dollars from any contributor. While this sort of activity was dangerous business for him (and donors), he refused to be intimidated and proudly became the public face of this common-sense effort.

Within days of the appearance of the first ad, flyers from the KKK were distributed, notifying supporters that they had been "indexed." A Nazi swastika superimposed over a Star of David was centered above a headline that read, "Dupes Beware!" The text that followed warned,

"You have ignorantly allowed your signatures to be affixed to B. B. Taylor's 20 July 1965 racemixing ad in Manship's Daily Worker, The Baton Rouge Morning Advocate, and its Companion The State Times. Renounce your endorsement publicly!!!"

In addition to publishing the advertisements, *The Morning Advocate* editorially maintained that the federal order must be obeyed and the school doors left open. The newspaper also took a progressive stand on integration, as much for practical and political considerations as for altruistic ones. The KKK responded by burning crosses in the front yards of *Advocate* publisher Charles Manship and editor Douglas Manship Sr. The former's residence was one block from our home. Two crosses were also burned at B. B. Taylor's house.

Eight years after the bus boycott, things were progressing slowly. LSU had admitted its first black, a graduate student, and a federal judge had ordered the New Orleans school district to integrate its first school—immediately. Racist reaction was shrill. At a giant rally in New Orleans, the Citizens' Council vowed civil disobedience and a scorched-earth policy.

The 1960s were rough for Baton Rouge as the last holdouts for segregation became increasingly reactionary and were, in turn, challenged by radicalized black militants. Younger African Americans in particular grew impatient. Diehard segregationists, unresponsive bureaucracies, suffocating poverty, and uneven playing fields proved too much for some. Flashes of deep hatred and severe violence ensued.

Southern University president Felton Clark, worried about the financial stranglehold racist lawmakers had on the nation's largest historically black college, told students they would be expelled if they engaged in sit-ins. The following day, in March 1960, seven students were arrested for a sit-in at a Kress lunch counter. They were jailed on a misdemeanor charge of disturbing the peace. T.J. Jemison arranged for the bail to be paid.

The next day, nine more were arrested at a sit-in at the Greyhound Bus depot. The following day, some 3,500 charged-up SU students peacefully marched to the capitol. The leader of that protest march and the sixteen arrested students were suspended indefinitely. In protest, mass withdrawals from the university ensued. (Clark was a member of Mount Zion First Baptist, and his action caused "some contention" in the congregation, remembered Jemison.)

A Southern University student was killed by sheriff's deputies during a campus demonstration, and a half dozen black Muslims were shot by police in a downtown melee. A TV reporter was beaten severely during the latter confrontation and is confined to a nursing-home bed to this day.

It was during this unrest that Josef and I, as well as others in Baton Rouge, received several kidnap threats, such things being part of a national wave. Whether from white racists or black militants, we never could discover. We got permission from the city to park our cars on the sidewalk in front of Goudchaux's so that store security could keep an eye on us as we walked to them in the evenings. We were advised to remove our telephone numbers from the phone book. We only deleted our home addresses. For three years, as a result of the threats, we each bought a million dollars in kidnap insurance, and my mild-mannered brother started carrying a loaded derringer, stating bluntly, "No one is going to grab me without a fight."

Perhaps emboldened by its earlier bus victory and the strong voice of Martin Luther King Jr., who was in the thick of civil rights demonstrations throughout the country, Baton Rouge's African American community decided in 1961 it was tired of being second-class customers in the city's retail stores. Cash registers, they argued, made the same sound ringing up purchases of black customers as of white ones. In addition, blacks wanted more job opportunities, particularly in sales. But Baton Rouge's business sector remained in a segregationist headlock. By Louisiana law, punishable by fines and potential jail terms, stores were required to provide separate bathrooms and drinking fountains for whites and blacks. Lunch counters were segregated. By individual policy, stores generally did not extend credit to black customers nor allow them to try on clothes before they were purchased. Those that did had separate changing rooms for blacks and whites.

Stores displayed little tolerance in accepting returned merchandise from black customers.

Those policies were not followed at Goudchaux's. We extended charge privileges to every credit-worthy customer and allowed all customers to try on clothing articles before purchasing them. The lenient return policy applied to blacks and whites alike. Dressing rooms were integrated from the start.

Stores also did not allow African Americans to be salespeople. While African Americans had been employed at Goudchaux's as stockers and display workers from the beginning, there was but one black salesperson,

To: THE NEGRO CITIZENS OF BATON ROUGE AND OTHER RESIDENTS OF EAST BATON ROUGE PARISH

Do You Want Freedom?

Freedom is not a gift, but freedom is a merit that is acquired only through determination and sacrifice. We must be determined not to accept RACIAL DISCRIMINATION and SOUTHERN JUSTICE any longer.

To promote our stride for equality, we have been negotiating with the following downtown merchants as to (1) BETTER JOB OPPORTUNITIES, and (2) DESEGREGATION OF FACILITIES:

(1) KRESS   (7) HOLMES
(2) GOUDCHAUX'S   (8) THREE SISTERS
(3) F. W. WOOLWORTH   (9) J. C. PENNEY
(4) WELSH & LEVY'S   (10) ROSENFIELD'S
(5) McCRORY'S   (11) SHOPPER'S FAIR
(6) SEARS   (12) MONTGOMERY WARD

The evil of segregation can be conquered through "SELECTIVE BUYING."

Since we are aware of the fact that the merchants of the forestated stores are dependent upon the Negroes' dollar for a prosperous business, we are appealing to you not to buy at these stores if we cannot achieve our goal of equality in employment and facilities within the next few days.

Again we appeal to you: Don't Let Your Dollars Buy Discrimination!!!!!

THE BATON ROUGE CHAPTER OF THE CONGRESS OF RACIAL EQUALITY

To join or financially support CORE contact:

MISS PATRICIA A. TATE, Secretary
1955 Fairchild Street
Baton Rouge, Louisiana
ELgin 7-8048

Flyer announcing CORE's local selective-buying campaign, 1961

Goldie Kelly, by the late 1950s. Kelly, however, was permitted only to sell to black customers. Few other stores even went this far. Erich got periodic letters from the Citizens' Council decrying our practices. My father did bow to Louisiana law when it came to segregated bathrooms and drinking fountains.

Dad's criteria for opening an individual charge account had nothing to do with the color of one's skin. The store also extended credit to African American organizations, such as the Good Samaritans, a charity that bought toys at our store throughout the latter half of the year to give to needy families in the African American community at Christmas. Since a majority of Good Samaritans' donations came between Thanksgiving and New Year's, their purchases required credit until then, and we gladly extended it—interest free, of course. One year, an officer in the charity absconded with more than one thousand dollars in donations, but Dr. B. V. Baranco, an African American dentist and a Good Samaritan leader, personally covered the loss.

In 1961, the Baton Rouge chapter of the Congress of Racial Equality (CORE) organized a "selective buying" campaign against Baton Rouge's largest merchants, including Kress, Goudchaux's, Woolworth, Welsh & Levy's, McCrory's, Sears, D. H. Holmes, Three Sisters, J. C. Penney, Rosenfield's, Shopper's Fair, and Montgomery Ward. The Baton Rouge boycott followed a similar protest in New Orleans.

"The evil of segregation can be conquered through 'selective buying,'" read the flyer distributed by CORE. "Since we are aware of the fact that the merchants of the forestated stores are dependent upon the Negroes' dollar for a prosperous business, we are appealing to you not to buy at these stores if we cannot achieve our goal of equality in employment and facilities within the next few days. . . . Don't let your dollars buy discrimination!"

The boycott lasted about two weeks, and as the largest retailer in the city, Goudchaux's got its share of the spotlight. There were some extremists on each side. A bomb was thrown through one of our show windows. Chances are it came from a radical boycotter. But since we also were getting threats from segregationists, we could never be certain of the perpetrator. In any case, the crude device proved to be a dud.

When the press interviewed him, however, Fire Chief Bob Bogan described the bomb as a "sophisticated" device and said it was just luck it didn't go off. Bogan didn't want whoever was responsible for building it to improve his handiwork.

(After that incident, we installed bullet-proof glass in our outside doors and show windows. We proudly informed our insurance company that we had the protective glass. Big mistake. The company apparently assumed this meant Goudchaux's was targeted, therefore too risky, and promptly canceled our coverage. We had to scramble for a replacement.)

Overall, the boycott didn't have a significant financial effect on us. We experienced an 8 percent drop in sales. I had always believed Goudchaux's was spared severe economic impact because our estimated sales to African Americans historically had been about 10 percent. But civil rights leaders interviewed for this book offered a slightly different take.

The Reverend Charles Smith, a leader among Baton Rouge's clergy and civil rights ranks and pastor of Baton Rouge's Shiloh Missionary Baptist Church, reasoned that the effectiveness of the economic pressure at Goudchaux's was eroded by two facts: First, many of the boycott leaders had sizable credit balances at the store and didn't want to jeopardize those. (I would have told them at the time that we didn't play that sort of game.) Second, Goudchaux's management was considered racially "progressive" compared to the other store owners.

This 1961 buying boycott primarily was focused on Baton Rouge's Third Street downtown businesses, noted Smith, who as a teenager in 1946–47 had worked as a stocker for Goudchaux's. "Erich Sternberg was considered by black leaders to be a very progressive man at race relations for the time," he says today. "And he continued to move forward." Jemison, who also was in the forefront of the boycott, saw Goudchaux's policies in the same light, adding we realized that black customers meant revenue. "The Sternbergs knew that to grow business one had to serve all communities."

Sears and Kress were among the worst stores when it came to respect for African Americans, recalled Johnnie Jones Sr., a feisty civil rights lawyer who, back then, was CORE's attorney. Jones, too, gave Goudchaux's relatively good marks. "They were always more considerate of black customers than the others. It was the most cooperative place in town. We never had a serious problem with them."

At the end of the picketing, protesters got some of what they sought. In a groundbreaking agreement, the city's major retailers promised to hire a certain number of black employees in sales, cashier, and office positions. Josef and I met with CORE leaders and agreed to employ twelve African American salespeople. (Eventually, a significant number of our sales and buying staffs were African American.) Goldie Kelly and the new African American sales associates were able to sell to anyone who came through the door. Jemison noted in his 2008 interview that, unlike some others, Goudchaux's kept its hiring commitment.

Not every customer appreciated an integrated sales staff. In one ugly incident a short time after we integrated the sales force, a white woman was holding a crystal bowl, admiring it, when Goldie came up and asked if she needed any help. The woman curtly asked for "a salesperson" to wait on her. When Goldie said she was a salesperson, the woman looked at her, held out the piece of expensive crystal in front of her, and slowly parted her hands. The bowl fell to the floor, smashing to pieces, and she strutted out of the building.

There were a few sales associates who also felt threatened by the winds of change. One employee in the men's suit department came to me after we hired an African American salesperson for the area to ask if I wanted him to slip a piece of merchandise into the new man's suit pocket, presumably so we could "catch" him shoplifting. My response was immediate and blunt. Even the suggestion shocked me. Feelings ran strong during that transition period.

A lot of negotiations were under way in Baton Rouge at this time between the Citizens' Council and the NAACP. Separate drinking fountains were a source of considerable irritation among African Americans. The two groups met and agreed that this traditional slice of segregation could end as long as paper cups were available for those who wanted them. Customers reacted positively to this compromise.

Years later, I was complaining about the expense of cups at our water fountains. I called a good friend, Buddy Lipsey, who operated Wellan's Department Store in Alexandria, Louisiana, to find out what he was paying for them. "Why do you have cups?" he asked. I had totally forgotten about this little concession to the White Citizens' Council's racism. The dispensers came down that very day.

Over the years, we actively sought black college graduates for management positions. Given the historical paucity of educational opportunities for that group, it took time to build a qualified applicant pool, but that situation, too, eventually resolved itself. Our standards were high, but we found candidates who met them, frequently competing with national companies and the federal government to recruit the best.

Looking back, I can see that the economic boycott created an opportunity for change, and it was a relief to respond positively. Nonetheless, success often seemed akin to walking a tightrope. Erich, Lea, Josef, and I valued all customers, and in return for their loyalty, we gave them high-quality merchandise, good service, and respect.

6 | PASSING THE TORCH

MY FATHER SUFFERED THE first of his two heart attacks while he was in his early fifties. He traveled to the famed Mayo Clinic in Rochester, Minnesota, for diagnosis and a prognosis. It wasn't good. Until that time, Dad ate what tasted good and smoked a dozen cigars a day. The heart attack, though relatively mild, got his attention. The doctor ordered a reduction of fat, calories, and cigars. From that point, Lea presented two menus for dinner—Erich's and everyone else's.

Erich was fastidious about that diet. If it called for six ounces of meat, he would take a three-ounce portion. His beloved cigars, however, were another story. He slowly reduced his smoking from twelve cigars a day to six and later to three. The formula worked for another dozen years, but his heart—figuratively large, vibrant, and warm—was physically diseased and failing. Still, he refused to slow down.

A Mayo Clinic cardiologist recommended bypass surgery in early 1965. Back then, bypass surgery was new and considerably more dangerous than it is today. Dad declined. (Eighteen years later, his brother Leo died on the operating table undergoing that same heart procedure.) Finally, Dad's heart condition forced him into Baton Rouge General Hospital for several weeks—in itself capital punishment for a person who loved being with people and selling them merchandise.

His patience had its limits, and in late June he simply got out of the hospital bed, phoned a Goudchaux's driver to pick him up at the hospital entrance, dressed, and headed out the door for home. First, though, he wanted to drive past Goudchaux's to view "The Store." The car slowly circled the bustling building before continuing to the Sternberg residence. It would be Erich Sternberg's last look at his beloved store.

Dad continued to convalesce at home for several days. On July 3, 1965, the day before my thirtieth birthday and seven weeks before his sixty-fourth, he was sitting in his favorite chair, the living room lounger. Suddenly, he called out, "Lea!" My mother rushed from the kitchen to find him peacefully at rest. My father was gone.

In coping with the loss of her husband of thirty-nine years, Lea Knurr Sternberg remained characteristically strong, just as she had with past adversities, but inwardly she and we children were devastated. We were an exceptionally close family. Dad loomed larger than life, a lion to us. We could not imagine family life or Goudchaux's without him. He was the patriarch; he *was* the store.

Dad was admired and respected in Baton Rouge. His name was synonymous with hard work, honesty, warmth, humor, and civic pride. At a B'nai B'rith dinner in New Orleans honoring the Sternberg family twenty years later, Albert Fraenkel captured Erich well when he described him as one who "sincerely loved people. He personally greeted everyone who came into his store, had time for everyone, and inherently trusted everyone."

Erich Sternberg was part of Baton Rouge's fabric. His business had grown and prospered with the city. Goudchaux's employees and customers, political and civic leaders, friends and family, townspeople of all faiths came by the scores to the funeral and burial to pay respects and say good-bye. The crowd was enormous. Erich Sternberg, merchant and friend, was buried in B'nai Israel Cemetery on North Street, three blocks from The Store.

A key player in the family's mercantile legacy was gone. Now, under Lea's watchful eye, Goudchaux's would be in the hands of the next generation of Sternberg merchants. The generational torch had passed only four times in 170-plus years. If Josef's and my turn at the helm was successful, it would be because we had remarkable mentors and genes.

The day after the funeral, Josef and I were confronted by employees who literally were numb. For as long as they could remember, Goudchaux's *was* Erich Sternberg. Josef and I immediately decided this was not the time to stand around in a mournful daze. We kicked in with a major sale, which produced inescapable storewide excitement. It was our first important decision without Dad. He would have been proud.

We featured $299 mink stoles (stacked on tables, no less) and three-for-$100 men's suits. Our competitors denigrated the suits—claiming they couldn't be "real" at that price—and asked the head of the local Better Business Bureau to investigate. He did. He found nothing out of line and left—after buying three suits. Our banker, Leroy Ward, offered his congratulations on the strategy.

We also lucked out. The sale beat Hurricane Betsy by a couple of weeks. The third-worst hurricane ever to hit Louisiana roared ashore at Grand Isle on September 9 and tore into New Orleans and Baton Rouge. The storm caused a billion dollars in damages—the first time hurricane damage had hit that milestone—and was nicknamed "Billion-Dollar Betsy." New Orleans was flooded for about ten days. (Betsy's destruction, however, paled next to that of Hurricanes Katrina and Rita in 2005.)

Josef and I were helping cover the store's display windows with plywood around 2 a.m. the night the winds mounted. Suddenly, the wind picked up a sheet of plywood and propelled it straight at Josef's head. He ducked in the nick of time. It was the last October 1 anniversary sale we held. Betsy convinced me that August and September—the height of the hurricane season—must be avoided when it came to large, storewide promotions and costly advertising splashes. From then on, no major fall event would begin before October 15.

On the weekend of my dad's death, I was to have my

first date with Donna Gail Weintraub, who was attending the University of Texas at Austin, earning a Phi Beta Kappa key in the process. (Upon graduation, she would be awarded a graduate fellowship to attend Columbia University.) She thought at the time, "Wow, our first date and his father dies. That must be an omen. He'll never call me again."

I did, of course, and two years later we were married.

Following Dad's death, we had to reorganize the family stock ownership, which, in addition to Goudchaux's, included property holdings that were part of the Fifteen Fifty Realty Company and Erich Sternberg Realty Company. There also were a couple of companies called Starmount (the English translation of "Sternberg"). Josef would become president and CEO of Goudchaux's, Lea and Insa would be vice presidents, and I would be secretary-treasurer. (Soon thereafter, Josef chose to continue as president, and I took the title of chairman. We would be co-CEOs.)

Of the 8,197 total shares in Goudchaux's, the store's retirement trust had 827 shares and the estate of Erich Sternberg 1,661. Mother received 1,459 shares, Josef and I each had 922.5, and Insa held 890; Insa Sternberg & Brothers, a partnership, got 395, and Erich Sternberg Realty held 1,120. We divided the real estate company's stock evenly among the four immediate family members and the estate.

In the mid-1970s, Josef and I agreed that our children's share of the business should be controlled by a stockholder agreement as a fundamental ingredient in the success of a family-owned business. That document was legally binding and set forth future control of the company. It described how the children could join the business and what would happen at age thirty-five if they did not. At thirty-five and beyond, working members received an option to buy the stock of nonworkers. Nonworkers received the right to force the company to buy their stock at an appraised value. We strongly believed that in a family business those who participate in the business should control it.

Goudchaux's was in excellent shape when our father

died. Our regular customers came from within a 50-mile radius, and we had some 40,000 active charge accounts. Except in the case of the retirement trust, which was for the benefit of all the store's employees, no dividends were paid. That policy built capital and enabled us to expand.

Full-time employees, whether the CEO or a stocker, received the same 20 percent discount on store purchases for personal use and a 10 percent discount for gift buying. There was one exception: Women of the family could buy designer and other apparel at cost. (And, yes, we insisted they buy a lot of clothes. We considered it a form of advertising.) Along with health and life insurance coverage, each employee received a two-week vacation after one year of work, three weeks after five years. There were never any preferred parking spaces.

Some employees stayed with us long after the traditional retirement age. Take Sam Biller, a native-born Rumanian Jew who survived the Nazis by hiding in caves. He made it to this country after World War II and went to work for D. H. Holmes in Baton Rouge, running its warehouse. Under pressure, he retired at age sixty-one in 1957, and we hired him to run Goudchaux's warehouse and dock operation. When he retired a second time, we ran an advertisement in *The Morning Advocate* with his picture and a headline that said, "After 33 years with our company, Sam Biller is retiring—at the age of 94."

Goudchaux's/Maison Blanche had a great sales crew. We did our best to recruit natural-born sellers. If I heard of a good salesperson at another store, I poached—shamelessly—but paying more than they were making could get expensive. Normally, staff received either a base salary plus a small commission or a straight commission at a higher rate. Commission pay is good for the sales person —the more sold, the more earned—and for the store. Rewards are proportional and immediate, and the right atmosphere is created because the sales staff becomes more solicitous of the customer. Selling isn't for everyone, but those commissions fostered high service levels— a Goudchaux's trademark—and customer satisfaction.

To a certain degree, especially in the high-ticket departments, each sales associate was in business for herself or himself. Paychecks directly reflected individual effort. Real talent developed in that atmosphere, as well as some exceptional compensation packages—along with equally exceptional salespeople.

Contrary to what many believe, retailing can be exciting. There was nothing dull about our sales associates, either, who were as talented as they were different. One of our wilder types, Lenny Levine, bears discussing as an example of employee eccentricity. Our men's department was high volume, and Levine, who wore an eye patch, was one of our best. Customers came from all corners of East Baton Rouge Parish and beyond, some traveling from other states, just to have him outfit them. He was also the most flamboyant personality I can recall. At one time in his checkered career, Lenny, who wore the flashiest Hollywood brand suits imaginable, was a professional gambler. Unbeknown to me, he had not completely surrendered his old ways when he joined us.

At one point, I discovered Lenny taking bets on horse races over the Goudchaux telephone system. He was operating a small-time bookie operation when business was slow! I immediately confronted him and ordered him to stop taking bets. It was clearly illegal, I intoned. Lenny, standing 6-foot-2, stared down at me with his one good eye and growled, "But you know, Mr. Sternberg, your brother is one of my clients." Josef confessed it was true, that he enjoyed placing a two-dollar wager every week or so with Lenny. Nevertheless, such betting was illegal, and my mind conjured the headline: "Goudchaux's Raided; Bookie Operation Closed." I got red in the face, shook my head, stomped my feet, and ordered, in colorful language, that the betting be stopped. And it was . . . at least, I think so.

Million-dollar salespersons were championed and nurtured. Some were so aggressive they drove everyone crazy and basically hogged every customer who walked into their areas. It became survival of the fittest. Those with talent did well; the others simply left. Sometimes we lost salespeople we wanted to keep because they couldn't compete with such champions as Lecarol Chatelain (also a buyer of designer and bridal departments), Carlyn Rhea, Sarah Todd, Bernard Blanchard, the infamous Lenny Levine, Mimi Siegel, Monie Sabagh, Joy Stahl, and Noha Abou Shala. The stars simply stole the show. They worked in high-ticket departments, where the wolves ate the cubs. Some of these people did outrageous things—for example, throwing temper tantrums on the sales floor, disrupting business. No question, Josef and I wasted a lot of time herding the prima donnas, but none of them ever lost his or her job. They were fireproof, and we loved the talent.

Upon joining the company, I initiated a report measuring each sales associate's productivity (i.e., the pay an associate received as a percent of that person's sales). Calculated by hand every two weeks, the numbers were revealing. A good talker could no longer fake his or her results. Individual sales figures were there for all to view, and we were able with confidence to reward those who truly performed.

Even when we had more than eight thousand associates working, there never was a serious staff complaint about discrimination against a staff member. To protect employees from arbitrary actions by a manager, we established and strictly enforced this rule: No associate could be released without at least two, and preferably three, written warnings, signed by the associate. Exceptions were in place for such things as drinking on the job, physical fights, and theft—but those were rarities. Problem associates had no illusions about their performance. Either they improved or they found another job. Each person was reviewed annually, and we maintained high standards.

Our mid-management was dominated by women, an exception to the rule in Louisiana in the store's early years. We built a meritocracy in which those who were productive thrived. Yes, nepotism was in place. Josef, Donna, Lea, Mary Ann, and I hardly went through rigorous screening to get hired, nor did our children. (You know the old line: Nepotism is okay as long as you keep it in the family.) Frankly, a family-owned department store is just that—family. If your store doesn't possess a family atmosphere, you might as well be Sears.

For the long term, there have to be in place methods for dealing with family members who don't measure up. Those methods can take the form of not hiring them (the best way), of asking them to leave, or of providing a role in which they can be productive but do little harm. There is an old but still practical rule: First you take care of the business, then you take care of the individual. The rationale is easy: Without a healthy business, nothing else works.

That said, outside of Herman Knurr, my uncle, we had only one other full-time hire within our immediate family —Leigh Ann Abraham, Insa's daughter, who worked at our Canal Street store in New Orleans and then at our Tampa stores in the late 1980s. All the children reported for temporary employment during summer months.

Our primary competitors in Baton Rouge during the 1960s were, in descending order, Sears Roebuck, J. C. Penney, D. H. Holmes, and Rosenfield's. Goudchaux's volume in 1967 was nearly $12 million, putting us in solid second place behind Sears, which produced $17 million—not bad, considering Sears sold big-ticket items we did not carry, such as major appliances and furniture. We had notable exclusives, such as the Baton Rouge franchise for

Estee Lauder cosmetics, a major hit with our customers. (In later years, our annual volume for Lauder products reached $30 million.)

Josef and I shared a spartan, 10-foot by 12-foot office. The furnishings included two Formica-top desks, three chairs, a 12-foot-long shelf, a two-drawer file cabinet, and a single, shared computer. Throughout our careers, the office was never remodeled or refurbished. As Dad had pointed out many times, our true office was on the sales floor. Following his example, we normally took work home at night in cardboard boxes; we reserved our briefcases for out-of-town trips.

Connecting to our room was my father's old 8 x 10 office. After his death, we had one of our decorators spruce up that space to provide a decent place to meet with special visitors. (The brass "Erich Sternberg" name plaque that once was on the door to his office now hangs by the office door of my son, his grandfather's namesake.) Walls were lined with family photographs and business memorabilia. Not even our buyers had offices in those early days. They remained on the sales floor. Market research was hands on: We mingled with our customers and learned what they wanted.

People wondered how Josef and I got along so well. A key reason was that most days of the week we would meet at our mother's house after work for tea and cookies, homemade cake, or pie from her German recipes. Ever formal and European, Lea would brew the tea from leaves, never a bag. Around that kitchen table, we would thrash out the day's concerns. Lea and Donna were always there and, regularly, Mary Ann and Insa. These sessions lasted from thirty minutes to an hour. Problems were aired; ideas were shared. Major business planning took place at Lea's kitchen table, which had come with the family from Germany. (My daughter Julie now has it in her Brooklyn apartment.)

As important, though, was the rule—never violated— that Josef and I had veto power over each other. This would be impractical with more than three people working together, but was a powerful tool for us. Whichever one of us came up with a new idea had to convince the other of its merit before it was implemented. The rule

Lea Sternberg, affectionately called "Mama," was the undeniable matriarch of the store. She patrolled the aisles all day. One time a cashier was having an encounter with a customer where the cashier was telling the customer that she was unable to honor her request regarding a return or an exchange. The customer replied, "Okay, who is higher than you?" Miss Lea was walking by and stopped to hear out the customer. When she affirmed that the cashier was correct, the customer said, "Well, okay then, who is higher than you?" Miss Lea pointed to the heavens and said, "God."

—MARIAN LANDRY

forced analysis and concept development, prevented rash decisions, and ensured the company moved in one direction. We would play devil's advocate with each other, constantly changing roles. Debate sometimes became heated but never personal. "I was never sure who was the final authority," recalled the late Bill Hamblin, senior vice president of human resources. That's because, publicly, we rarely contradicted one another. There was never a need to count the stripes on our sleeves.

Anyone thinking Lea had a background role in the store's operation was in for a rude awakening. She had worked at Erich's side for almost forty years. This was her store, too, and she had the same notion about retirement as her late spouse. Lea prowled the floors daily, greeting customers while patrolling for idle chatting, sloppy merchandise fixtures, and unattended customers. "Miss Lea" or "Mama," as she was known, was both feared and loved by employees, depending on the day and circumstances.

Marian Landry, who worked with the family many loyal years in credit, remembers this scene from the men's department: "Miss Lea approached a man standing around in that department and asked what he was doing. 'We don't pay you to stand around looking at the merchandise!' she snapped. 'See if there are customers who need help.'"

"But Mrs. Sternberg," the bewildered man reportedly replied, "I'm just here to buy a suit."

And that was not an isolated incident. Don Bell, a former senior vice president of stores, tells of the time he was working the store's floor when a customer addressed him and said, "Are you going to pay me a commission?"

Don replied, "Excuse me?"

"I was shopping," the woman said, "and Mrs. Sternberg came up to me and ordered me to wait on some customers." She dutifully did and sold them some merchandise.

Lea could spot a shoplifter literally across the floor. She would immediately inform store detectives, who were off-duty police officers. Other times, she would follow the culprit to the parking lot and confront him or her. Greg Phares, who in 1980 was part of Goudchaux's security crew, claimed the best person on the team was Lea. Phares, who later became Baton Rouge chief of police and East Baton Rouge Parish sheriff, knew Mother's formula for spotting a shoplifter, if not her accent, by heart: "Vatch the hands; always vatch the hands."

"The *grand dame* of the family was ferocious when it came to protecting her merchandise," recalled Phares. "If we saw 'Mama' staring in a direction, we knew the hunt was on. Following her gaze often led us to a theft in progress. Usually, the apprehension was accomplished without incident, but there was an occasional foot chase across the parking lot."

Phares also remembers men's department sales staff helping struggling young cops by alerting them to sale merchandise and holding the items for them until the next paycheck. "Most of my Christmas shopping was accomplished while I worked the floor simply by telling a friend in the sales staff, 'I need something for my mother, girlfriend, brother, etc.' and picking up [and paying for] the wrapped package at the end of my shift."

On one occasion, Lea, in her sixties, zeroed in on a woman who appeared pregnant. Lea was not fooled; she knew the customer had clothing stuffed under her dress. How did she know? Easy, responded Mother after the petty thief was arrested. "Her bosoms weren't pregnant."

Lea Sternberg never shrank from correcting staff. Mike Smith, a newly hired director of security, was looking quite upset one day early in his tenure. Credit manager Charles Unfried asked what was wrong.

"Miss Lea just fired me," responded Mike, who probably had not spotted the same shoplifter Lea had.

"Don't worry," said Charles. "She has 'fired' me many times. Just lay low the rest of the day."

Don Bell acknowledges he was "fired" on several occasions. Apparently, Lea "fired" many employees over the years, something I did not know until I began this book.

Josef and I had to smooth feathers a number of times because of Mother's zero-tolerance approach to employee behavior. No one believed she truly wanted the people gone; she simply wanted to get their attention. Fortunately, it seems the rebuke was never taken literally.

The case of the women's sportswear buyer, who shall go unnamed, was a classic. For years, the buyer had not done well in her job. Finally, in 1960, she and Lea had words. The buyer went to Erich and told him he would have to choose: Either Lea or she had to go. The meeting was exceptionally brief. Dad was blunt: "Mrs. ———, I am *married* to my wife."

Her bluff called, the buyer remained with Goud-chaux's. A few months later, I joined the company and, as one of my first tasks, developed profit statements by department. This buyer's numbers were simply awful. I worked with her daily for six months in an attempt to salvage a bad situation. I finally told her to find another job. We disliked turnover—we operated as the antithesis of Donald Trump—but in this case we waited longer than we should have. Lea had been right all along.

She always considered herself a businesswoman, demanding no more of employees than she did of herself. She was an exceptional buyer, teacher, nurturer of talent, and salesperson. Customers loved and bonded with her. She still was making buying trips to New York in her eighties, examining the quality of designer clothing and selecting items for special customers who depended on her exacting taste and candid advice.

She also was a marketing guru, with a passion for better goods, as Baton Rouge attorney Charles McCowan can attest. Just before his twenty-fifth wedding anniversary, he saw an ad in the paper promoting full-length mink coats for $1,299 and headed for Main Street. He ran into Lea, who explained to him the difference in male and female skins, in natural and dyed colors, in split and let-out coats. "I left the store with a nicely wrapped box containing a $7,500 coat," recalled McCowan, who had worked in the men's department when he was in college.

"When I brought it home and gave it to my wife, she smiled, opened it, and reminded me it was our twenty-fourth anniversary. When I told Mrs. Sternberg, she teased me with a quick, 'No returns for being a year off.'" But Charles's wife was happy, and so was he.

Josef, too, had a special bond with customers. He never met a refund request he couldn't grant. This incident comes to mind: A customer bought an Izod shirt for a trip to Asia. He returned after the trip to say the shirt did not fit him. No problem, responded Josef, Goudchaux's would be happy to take it back.

"You don't understand," the customer said, "I gave it away in Taiwan. I wasn't carting that shirt all over Asia."

Josef promptly refunded his money. (It had to be a first: a shirt from the United States exported to Taiwan.) Ultimately, I probably would have done the same thing, but not as quickly. Our father had this philosophy on returns: "A return is an invitation to a sale." We had a liberal return policy—if you didn't like it, we took it back—except for two areas: cocktail dresses and evening gowns. We saw too many of Goudchaux's fashions in society-event photos in *The Morning Advocate*, then brought back for a refund. (Truth be told, customers are *not* always right, but they are always customers. And you want them back.)

"Our customers were very special," recalls associate Pat James, who worked at the store for eighteen years. "They expected service, but they were so loyal." Often, customers had their favorite selling associate and would bring in family photos to show. "We associates were treated like extended family," said Pat.

We did a number of things aimed at young people. During the summer, our Main Street store would hire about 50 high school and college students (eventually the number rose to 150) to replace regular employees taking their vacations. It gave them work experience and won loyalty from their parents. During the 1960s, Josef came up with a gutsy, youth-oriented idea called Budgeteen. It was a program that would give teenagers their own Goudchaux's credit cards—if their parents already had a card. Budgeteen did not require teens to have their parents' permission to charge on the card, which had a fifty-dollar credit

In June 1966, my wife and I were married. We had no extra cash for Christmas gifts, so we wanted to open a charge account in order to buy each other gifts. We applied at Shoppers Fair, Gibson's, and Sears. All said it would take several weeks to get approval, which would have been after Christmas. We then went to Goudchaux's and explained our problem to Josef Sternberg. He wrote something on a piece of paper and signed it, telling us to give it to the clerks when making our purchases. We remained loyal customers.

—CURT BEZET

In July 1963, when Ruby Pearson died at Our Lady of the Lake Hospital on a Sunday afternoon, some family members needed to do some shopping before going to Mississippi for the funeral. Joe Richard located Joe Sternberg through his sister, Insa Abraham, and without hesitation Josef said, "Come to the store and get whatever you need," and he met us there. Such compassion and customer satisfaction are not found today.

—RICHARD FAMILY

65

Goudchaux's was definitely a family store. Children of employees were welcome to become employees. My husband went to work at Goudchaux's in 1957 at the age of sixteen. He [was in] the distributive education program at Istrouma High School. Those in this program would go to school until noon, take a quick lunch, and then go to work. My mother-in-law worked in the infants' department. My mother worked in the toy department.

—A FORMER CUSTOMER

At age eighteen, I got my first job at Goudchaux's—in the handbag department. The main rules were: Don't sit down, and don't lean on the counter. One Saturday, as part of a sales promotion, they dressed me up in a big Mickey Mouse costume and had me greet the young children.

—JOEL THIBODEAUX

limit. Although the program lost a lot of money because minors are not always responsible financially, it got a lot of young people hooked on Goudchaux's.

No solicitor came into the store asking for a donation for a worthy cause, or an ad for a yearbook or school newspaper, and left empty-handed. It might have been only twenty-five dollars, but we participated in every worthwhile local event or charity.

Every Friday morning at 7:30, on the main floor, employees held a brief prayer service for those who wished to attend. One service was Catholic; the other, held in a different area of the store, was Protestant. Invited clergy often came. (There were not enough Jews employed at the store to warrant a rabbi.) We continued this practice at the main building for about twenty years. In addition, we would have a priest, minister, and rabbi bless the store at grand openings each time we expanded.

One of the fringe benefits of hiring off-duty police officers and sheriff's deputies for store security was that Josef and I were immune to traffic tickets. If the officer didn't work at Goudchaux's, his partner or a family member did. When we were stopped, as occasionally happened, the officers would ask for our licenses, check out the name, caution us to be more careful, then order us to "drive on."

Josef lived with our parents after he joined the store in 1950. I, too, stayed with them on my return from college and the navy in 1960, but I moved to an apartment within four years. It was a typical bachelor pad, nowhere more pronounced than in the refrigerator. (On her first visit, Donna found the fridge stocked with nothing but beer and a box of butter cookies.) I took most of my evening meals at my parents' place.

Knowing how few eligible Jewish women lived in Baton Rouge, Josef and I rented an apartment in New Orleans. That way, we would not have to drive 75 miles home after late evenings. Dad would kick us out of the store by 3:30 Saturday afternoon, the busiest day of the week, so we could go to New Orleans. He had his priorities, and one of those was trying to make sure we married in the faith.

In the beginning, I had dated women of all faiths, but at one point stopped after I realized I was not going to marry outside mine. When it came to our children, Donna and I had strong preferences that they, too, take Jewish spouses. For us, 3,500 years of history and tradition are at stake, and that heritage is one of their most priceless possessions. Statistically, children of mixed marriages do not remain Jewish. We finally made this compromise with the kids: For every non-Jewish date there would be a Jewish date—and we paid for the latter. (It worked.)

As it turned out for Josef and me, we indirectly pointed each other to his future bride. I had been on a few dates with Mary Ann Weil, who had graduated from Vassar with a degree in English and who, upon graduation, had been working at the NBC affiliate's radio and television stations in New Orleans. She was the daughter of Walter and Joan Weil. He was a partner in the New Orleans brokerage firm of Howard, Weil, Fredriches & Labouisse. Mary Ann first met Josef when she and I were on a double date with my brother and his date.

Meanwhile, Josef was seeing a woman from Tyler, Texas, whom he had met in New Orleans. Josef's girlfriend introduced him to her cousin, Donna Weintraub, and he introduced Donna to me. Returning the favor, I strongly encouraged him to date Mary Ann. Two romances flowered.

In late 1966, following our fourth date, I proposed to Donna. At the time, she was attending the Graduate School of International Affairs at Columbia University. Her parents, Charles and Sadie, were merchants in Sherman, Texas. Donna left New York, and we were married on February 19, 1967, in Sherman. We parked in front of the courthouse to pick up our marriage license. When we came out, I had a parking ticket, which, in those days, cost a quarter. I thought it was a pretty cheap investment. (Anyone planning to marry take note: It was just a down payment. Future bills got bigger.)

My father advised me against marrying for money. "It's cheaper to borrow at the bank," he would laugh. Health, intelligence, and character were what counted, he said. I informed my parents that I wanted my wife to have brains. Mother responded, "It is not enough for her to have brains. She also must have ambition. Brains are nothing without ambition." I got both. Donna and I have been at each other's side since that day in 1967. We

have been one in our family, our business, our religion, and our social lives.

In late 1967, Mary Ann was the assistant to the news director at WDSU-TV in New Orleans. One of her jobs was to sort through the press releases and decide which ones were worth following up. She spotted one from Goudchaux's that told of a governor's award for hiring the handicapped. She called Josef to congratulate him, and he invited her to dinner that night. The romance took off from there.

On March 31, 1968, at the age of thirty-nine, Josef married Mary Ann, sixteen years his junior. When they applied for a marriage license, they were asked, as a matter of course, for birth certificates. Having been born in Germany, Josef had no designation for "race" on his certificate, presumably because everyone born in Germany in the 1920s was assumed to be Caucasian. Mary Ann, being a native of Louisiana, had a certificate stamped "Caucasian." At the time, Louisiana law prohibited a marriage of a white person to a person of color and the court clerk demanded proof that Josef was white. Apparently, evaluation by eyesight was not deemed reliable. They resolved the matter by going to nearby Algiers, which was more enlightened. Mary Ann did contract PR work for Goudchaux's in the 1970s and returned as a full-time corporate public relations officer from 1988 until we sold.

Six weeks after we married, Donna came to my office in tears, saying she couldn't take another tea, bridge game, or other social event. Donna wanted to work—she, too, was raised in a retailing family—and soon became one of the store's best employees. She moved into senior management within a short time. She proved an extraordinary performer in her own right, merchandising the fur and women's designer departments. Running a profitable fur department with $10 million in annual sales in the Deep South proved her skills and validated her merchant genes.

Josef and Mary Ann, Insa and Leo, Donna and I, and Lea all had homes within a few blocks of each other. We remained close, both geographically and as a family.

Four months after Donna and I were married, Israel was forced to defend itself from a three-pronged attack by Egypt, Syria, and Jordan in what was known as the Six-Day War. I told Donna I wanted to go to Israel and volunteer to fight. She wisely convinced me I could do a lot more good by staying in Baton Rouge and raising money for the Israeli cause. (She also didn't relish becoming a young widow.)

We decided to host a fund-raising event to help Israel. Individual members of the Liberal Synagogue, now called Beth Shalom, and B'nai Israel were behind the effort, but Temple B'nai Israel officially was not in favor of funds going to Israel, and its board denied the use of that temple to hold a gathering. Many members of B'nai Israel strongly disagreed with its board but did not feel comfortable going to Beth Shalom. All sides, however, were more than willing to come to one of the Sternberg homes.

I arranged the meeting for Lea's house as our apartment was too small. She was in New York on a buying trip, but she approved. So Donna and I "broke into" her home and proceeded to raise $85,000 in United Jewish Appeal contributions and Israel bonds that night. That set a record for Jewish fund raising in Baton Rouge and also served as the initial step in the creation of the Jewish Federation of Greater Baton Rouge.

(Years later, Donna joined the American Israel Public Affairs Committee, a powerful Washington, D.C.–based group dedicated to the security of Israel. She became immersed in that cause. Today, she is a board member and has a cabinet post in the organization and travels frequently to Israel. We pray that the Middle East will know peace in our lifetimes.)

In the 1960s, we began a major overhaul of our Main Street store. The $2 million addition, the eighth struc-

tural change since 1939, would give us 86,000 square feet. Our architect, A. Hays Town, designed a main entrance with magnificent columns. As costs mounted, we began to consider scrapping the columns.

The general contractor, Rip Collins, an all-conference fullback for LSU's 1945–48 teams, argued persuasively for us to keep the columns. The cost was only $75,000, he argued, and they would make the building. Rip convinced us, but he died a short time after that conversation and his son was unable to continue the work. The bonding company found us another contractor, who completed the job. (There is a lesson here: Always buy a construction and completion bond when building.) The columns remain to this day on a façade that has stood the test of time.

We unveiled the remodeled Goudchaux's on October 17, 1964. Throughout our renovations, expansions, and remodelings of the Main Street store, we deliberately kept the selling area narrow (the building's width is only 160 feet). Long and narrow has many advantages over a square layout. It is more efficient; exciting merchandise is more easily displayed; customers are less likely to become "lost" when they are away from the main aisle; the sales floor is less of a headache to staff; and it is easier for a manager to see and be seen. (We've done the same things recently in our office buildings.)

By the time we completed our last major remodel of Goudchaux's on Main Street, it would be nearly a fifth of a mile long. That was enough to rate inclusion in *Ripley's Believe It or Not*. In 1986, it named Goudchaux's the longest building in the world—971 linear feet—built as a department store. The expansion that was consuming our thoughts during this time, however, did not center on the size of the Main Street store. It was time to extend our reach.

Nearly a dozen remodels and expansions brought the Main Street Goudchaux's store to over 300,000 square feet.
The building still stands.

Ribbon cutting for the final expansion of Goudchaux's. Lea does the honors while I, Mary Ann, Josef, Insa, Insa's husband Leo, and Donna look on.

7 | BRANCHING OUT

BY 1974, A YEAR before we opened a second location, Goudchaux's sales exceeded those of our Baton Rouge competitors combined. The city loved Goudchaux's, and we loved the city. (When we sold the company, the two stores in Baton Rouge alone were turning $90 million in annual sales.) Our most recent expansion made the Main Street building nearly nine times larger than the operation Erich Sternberg had purchased for approximately $100,000 three and a half decades earlier.

There were solid reasons for this success. For openers, we worked on a lower margin, employing a retail markup clearly less than what was prevalent among our competition and in traditional department stores, then and today. There were government regulations controlling minimum retail prices, and we—and our customers—gloried in mostly ignoring them. We invited legal challenges, but they never came.

Our big sales helped a lot. We had some wild and crazy ones. Goudchaux's annual shoe sale, for instance, was nearly more than we could handle. We had so many people one year at the Cortana Mall branch that we had to call the fire marshals, who only allowed customers in the door of that 240,000-square-foot structure when others left.

These years also were relatively good times for Louisiana. The state was in the middle of an oil boom. Many farmers, accustomed to a tough life on the land, suddenly found themselves rich beyond their comprehension when oil was discovered on their property. Josef loved to tell the story about a farmer who struck it big. He came into the store one day and complained to Josef that he had so much money he didn't know how to spend it. Josef suggested the man remodel his home. "I already put new linoleum on the kitchen floor," he lamented. "What else is there?"

Another store feature was the lay-away plan. With a 10 percent deposit, customers could "buy" an item worth $20 or more, and we would hold it as they continued their payments until it was paid for. Fashion merchandise would be held for sixty days, hard goods for ninety. Customers with limited credit—and even with good credit, but wanting to buy a higher-priced item—often used this method. At one point, lay-away purchases were 10 to 15 percent of our business. In the late 1980s, we weaned ourselves from the lay-away program after deciding the expenses of multiple handling and the aging of the merchandise (some of which was never redeemed) were too high.

Among our services especially appreciated by customers was free gift wrap. Later, we established a $15 minimum-purchase threshold, but below that amount we charged only 15 cents for wrapping. If someone wanted a more elaborate "luxury" gift wrap, the cost was $1 or $1.50. For the store, gift wrap was an expensive cost center, re-

I recall my sisters and me singing merrily along with the radio as we took our mother's charge card to Main Street Goudchaux's:

> You never pay interest or a carrying charge
> At Goudchaux's, Goudchaux's.
> You don't need a money tree to get the finest quality.
> Shop today and you will see and save at Goudchaux's.

—MADELINE HERBERT

quiring considerable materials and labor. Since most of our competitors charged, free wrapping provided a competitive edge.

Alteration charges were held to a minimum. We had a staff of tailors (a rarity in today's department stores), but so did some of our competitors. Where we differed was in offering free alterations for men's, boys', girls', and women's designer clothing, whether regular or sale price. We did charge for the more complicated women's clothing, although it was well below Goudchaux's costs—a "loss leader"—in order to encourage sales. Women simply have more unique "curves," and fitting them can get expensive.

Our tailoring staff was the best. Guido DiSalvo, former head tailor at West Point, managed the staff until the end of his life. His wife, Connie, oversaw women's alterations. Guido was followed by Joe Vasco, a dedicated professional who was recruited for us by the president of Hart, Schaffner & Marx Clothing and who remained with us until we sold the business.

We were among the first to institute "purchase with purchase" promotions. Although common today, they were unique for house-credit programs of the day. A tear-off coupon on monthly statements would allow charge customers to buy an item with a perceived value of $5 to $10 for, say, $1 with another purchase of at least $10. One month we sold 45,000 umbrellas in six stores with this promotion.

Home delivery was free. Since we employed our own staff and trucks, items purchased or ordered before 10 a.m. would be delivered the same day—rare then, unheard of today. The competition never matched this service.

We had a staff of fifty-four in data processing in the late 1970s. One of the department's great accomplishments was automating store procedures. A good example was the stock-replenishment program. If a basic item, such as a dress shirt, was sold, an order—based on the sales trend up or down—automatically was generated for its replacement. IBM South America liked the program enough to buy it.

We paid our employees well by the standards of the day. A staff making decent wages is motivated and customer friendly. Still, employee costs caused us considerable concern. The federal minimum wage of $1 per hour, with overtime after 44 hours, was extended to retailers in 1961. Three years later it went to $1.15 an hour for the first 42 hours; a year after that, to $1.25 for 40 hours. Those raises—25 percent in four years, plus a 4-hour shortening of the work week—had great impact. While we always paid well above minimum wage, the changes forced us to increase our wage scale proportionately. We fretted over how we would afford those levels. Obviously, we managed.

Goudchaux's legendary service and quality of inventory certainly were draws, but everything paled next to our biggest attraction: interest-free credit—unique in the region and rare anywhere else. Normal terms meant no carrying charge for five months as long as the customer made payments on the bill each month. If a customer paid less than 20 percent, the missing amount would be added to the next month's 20 percent. Even then, we added no

Register cover from 1973 featuring Insa, Josef, Lea, and me >

JANUARY 20, 1973 • 50c THE COPY
BATON ROUGE, LOUISIANA

The Register

interest. (When we expanded to Florida in the late 1980s, bank interest and other costs grew, forcing us to amend the policy to impose interest if a person failed to make a minimum 20-percent payment each month.)

As business grew, we installed sophisticated computer software to monitor the accounts. Charles Unfried, the credit manager at the time who later became senior vice president of financial services, purchased a computerized risk-assessment modeling system from Fair Isaac Corporation, a leading provider of statistical solutions to determine individual credit risk by measuring payment activity. As payments on an account slowed, the customer's credit limit would be reduced automatically by the computer. The reverse also was true. Today, this is standard procedure in credit departments; back in the 1970s, we pioneered the process, and some of the largest regional banks came to us for advice on their credit programs.

Customers valued the interest-free credit; collections were well within the limits of financial respectability. One might think Goudchaux's would be the last account paid when a customer got into tight times because it did not add interest. In fact, just the opposite occurred. Goudchaux's usually was the *first* bill paid because it was the last credit line a person wanted to lose. Thus, a zero-interest credit account was a strong part of our business, even when we picked up new stores. At the system's peak in the 1970s, we had converted seven in ten customers to our in-house credit accounts, versus cash and bank credit cards.

In 2007, customer Diane Reynolds related to popular Baton Rouge columnist Smiley Anders that when she was involved in a minor traffic accident many years ago, the investigating deputy kept her driver's license. "I called my husband," she said, "and received these very comfort-ing words: 'Cheer up, honey, it could have been worse. The deputy could have taken your Goudchaux's card!'"

Unfried, who continued successfully in retailing after we sold the stores, expressed it this way: "The Sternbergs always understood the value of credit in promoting business. Surprisingly, not every business understood that [concept]." And the few that did never took it to our level. Goudchaux's was the only store in Baton Rouge offering interest-free credit. Most stores tacked on 1.5 percent interest, compounded, on each customer's unpaid balance. That adds up to an annualized rate of more than 19 percent. That 19 percent was just too tempting a target to ignore as a marketing tool.

We unleashed an advertising blitz that drove the competition nuts. Our advertisements read, "Interest Free at Goudchaux's. If you're paying compound interest of 'only' 1½% per month, it's really over 19% a year."

Those promotions pointed out the obvious: With an annual interest rate of 19 percent, credit purchases anywhere else cost more, much more, than cash or interest-free purchases. (Today, the law forbids compounding of credit card interest, so 1.5 percent per month computes to an annual interest rate of 18 percent. On the other hand, stores now charge interest at 1.75 percent per month, or 21 percent a year. Many charge even more, which seems almost usurious.)

I. H. Rubenstein, owner of Rubenstein's Department Store in downtown Baton Rouge, filed a formal complaint in 1966 with the Federal Trade Commission about our promotions. The FTC sent an order to cease and desist from the practice of mentioning the competitors' annual interest costs in advertising. The subject seems silly today, but official demands from Washington are always chilling.

Mama [Ione Phillips] taught me the meaning of "hush money" as she opened, inspected, and paid the monthly Goudchaux's bill. Goudchaux's credit terms were extremely liberal, and "no interest ever" was a popular slogan all over the area. It certainly was at our house.

—MILDRED WORRELL

Our attorney, Victor Sachse Jr., met with a Federal Trade Commission attorney who traveled to Baton Rouge as part of a follow-up to the letter. They negotiated an agreement. Victor proved the better attorney. The documents we signed simply said that henceforth Goudchaux's would advertise that 1.5 percent a month, compounded, was the *equivalent* of more than 19 percent a year. It was a minor distinction—we were debating fourth-grade math—but I didn't want to give even that much. I had hoped to go to court and slug it out. The free publicity would have been glorious.

During this time, most customers could secure a charge account with a $500 opening limit. Starting in the 1970s, they even received a plastic Goudchaux's charge card rather than one made of heavy stock paper. Erich Sternberg started his business with no cards at all, just a charge account file, since he knew most of his customers by name. In 1983, when we switched to Maison Blanche credit cards, many of our Baton Rouge and Lafayette customers rebelled. They simply refused to give up the plastic cards that carried the name "Goudchaux's." The customer, of course, is always right, so we accepted either card.

On the other end of the scale, there were credit limits as high as $75,000. We had to increase limits for the best customers when I added the fine jewelry department—that and furs were my favorites—because there were items with $40,000 price tags. Selling furs for $10,000 to $15,000 was a regular event, although when you stop to think about it, selling fur stoles and coats in Louisiana is the converse of the cliché about selling refrigerators to Eskimos. (Women's fashions have always been a bit of a puzzle.)

Shortly after my arrival in 1960, we began a program in which Josef and I wrote an annual letter to customers who had track records of paying their bills on or before due dates. We would refer to them as our "Gold Card" customers, thank them for their business, and raise their credit limits.

Goudchaux's had the first "Gold Card" program in the country. It began when I took the store's credit card to a new level in the 1970s. The Gold Card then became separate from our other credit cards and included special benefits such as credit card security registration, travel insurance, free luggage tags, car rental and hotel discounts, free luxury gift wrapping and shipping, free parking in downtown New Orleans (when we opened our Maison Blanche Canal Street store there in 1984), and special, lower charges for women's alterations.

There would be, however, a hitch to these Gold Cards, an unheard-of catch at that time: Gold Cards would cost the holder $30 annually. Josef felt it wouldn't fly and might even erode Goudchaux's credit card fame. I conducted a customer survey, which finally persuaded him to give it a try. As far as I know, it was the nation's first charge for a credit card with special benefits. More important, it was a knock-out success.

In a relatively short time, the Gold Card brought in $1 million in annual fees. Other credit card companies, including American Express, began inquiring about the program. American Express paid us for the right to exclusively market the "Gold Card" name (which we began using in 1960) on one level of its cards. AmExp thought its trademark was threatened by Goudchaux's Gold Card. We decided to play nice . . . and we didn't mind the cash.

Bank cards, such as MasterCard, Visa, and American Express, had appeared on the scene and gained enough traction to concern us by the late 1970s. They were in competition with the Goudchaux's card, so initially we did not accept bank cards. If a customer wanted to charge, it had to be with Goudchaux's plastic. Any purchase with a bank card cost us 2.2 percent plus a transaction fee, and we couldn't capture the customer's name and address, which were important for our mailing lists.

Our reticence notwithstanding, bank cards became too popular with the public to ignore further, and in 1982, when we expanded into New Orleans with its significant tourist trade, we ceased our opposition.

Donna and I made the company's first overseas buying trip in 1971, visiting Japan, Taiwan, and Hong Kong, the markets that at the time offered the best import values. The trip proved quite profitable and added a new dimension to our merchandise selection. We sent buyers back to those markets and, over time, to Paris, London, Rome, Milan, Florence, Tel Aviv, Berlin, Seoul, Montreal, and Bangkok. The breadth of Goudchaux's offerings expanded exponentially.

During this period, we started several in-store ventures that were not so successful: the sale of gourmet food, small electric appliances, and electronics; in-store restaurants; and mail-order catalogs. They were too time consuming, had low returns for the effort, or were a distraction to our core business. We soon abandoned them and moved on with a live-and-learn attitude. We also considered selling furniture, but our in-depth analysis determined that that category's real money was in area rugs, mattresses, and lamps. Those became the only traditional furniture selections we carried.

Another venture begun in the late 1970s was retailing concert tickets. It was a blast! We sold advance admission tickets for Louisiana, Mississippi, and Arkansas events, but we expanded that operation in the 1980s by purchasing the Ticketmaster franchise from D. H. Holmes Department Stores for $1.1 million, a move that added Alabama and Florida to our franchise territory. Concertgoers would be lined up at our stores, waiting for the doors to open on mornings when particularly hot tickets went on sale.

The operation made money and attracted all sorts of potential new customers. You wouldn't believe how many new "friends" the Sternbergs and their children acquired when it became known our stores were offering tickets to sell-out events. Acquaintances would call Josef or me

for tickets. We would transfer them to our administrative assistants, Koota Landry and Phyllis Cutrer, respectively. They, in turn, would do their magic. Nine out of ten times, the tickets would appear. It was great fun.

Although we hated to part with it, we sold the franchise back to the Ticketmaster Corporation for $4 million in 1990 because a recession had hit us hard and we needed the liquidity. Today, Ticketmaster is owned by Barry Diller's publicly traded InterActiveCorp.

Customers were fiercely loyal, and Goudchaux's, hands down, remained the No. 1 department store in Baton Rouge as we moved into the 1970s. The demographic growth of the city, the location of our Main Street building, and the dawn of malls, however, were leaving too many new customers on the table. People throughout the parish knew us, but Main Street was not convenient to a growing number of them.

Our success would have to be transplanted to new population centers if we wanted to protect our retailing franchise. We would attempt to take the winning family-oriented formula with us, but that would not be easy, as we suspected and found out.

Josef and I had planned to put branches in key Baton Rouge locations by the late 1960s. The city was rapidly growing to the east, and Goudchaux's was on the west side. Baton Rouge already had gotten its first mall, Bon Marché. Goudchaux's had been approached to become one of Bon Marché's anchors, but the site was barely three miles from the Main Street store. We needed a location farther away and closer to where new customers lived, not one that would overlap and thus dilute our current shopper base. We passed on the Bon Marché opportunity.

New York developer Mort Olshan announced plans in 1972 for the 1.4 million-square-foot Cortana Mall, huge for the time. It would be located at Airline Highway and Florida Boulevard, farther east than Bon Marché. At five miles from the Main Street store, that worked for us, but we hardly were approached. Olshan initially didn't seem interested in Goudchaux's. The choice anchor spots were offered to Sears, Maison Blanche of New Orleans, J. C. Penney, and Dillard's. When Olshan began handing out

Shopping downtown Goudchaux's was an experience. Nothing like it. Vendors still talk about furs heaped on a table. One was overwhelmed with the commonness of the store and the quality of what was there.

— PAM PETITE, former divisional merchandise manager

invitations for secondary mall locations, he threw a full-fledged pitch for Goudchaux's. We said no thanks.

Not only did we decline, but Josef and I also designed and implemented an alternate strategy. We bought thirty-nine acres of prime property fronting three blocks of Airline Highway, two miles south of Cortana Mall and directly between it and Interstate 12, the primary traffic artery for that area. We announced a competing mall, with Goudchaux's as the lead anchor store. Shoppers exiting I-12 would have to pass the Goudchaux's Center, and we would make sure they stopped and shopped. Before our mall could take off, however, Maison Blanche decided there were too many headliners at Cortana Mall and took a "better deal" at Bon Marché Mall, where it would be a standout.

Olshan came back to us in 1973, offering the mall's choicest spot, now vacant. We closed the deal by conference call—Donna and I were on a buying trip to Paris, and Josef was in Baton Rouge minding the store—and announced the new direction in July. The Airline Highway property was developed as an office park and sold at a healthy profit.

(Mort Olshan and the Sternbergs became friends. During this period, he was closing in on fifty and was still a bachelor. Lea devoted time trying to fix him up with a wife. His partner, Dick Steinberg, finally told Lea her years of matchmaking were wasted: Mort had found his own girlfriend. He and Carole married and had two wonderful children, the first when he was fifty-two.)

Opening a second store at Cortana would be Goudchaux's first move away from home base. It was a quantum but necessary leap, the initial step in a fifteen-year expansion and acquisition campaign. From this point, there would be no turning back.

Even as we developed plans to locate a branch to serve the growing eastern portion of the city, our interest in and attention to the Main Street store never wavered. We completed our tenth expansion of the forty-three-year-old building in late 1970, including parking for 1,200 vehicles. At the opening of the expanded Main Street store, Baton Rouge mayor Woody Dumas lauded Goudchaux's as a symbol of the city. We shared an eighty-pound cake, a replica of the store, with those who attended.

The planning and construction of Cortana Mall and our two-story branch consumed two years. The doors opened in February 1976 to reveal 120,000 square feet of merchandise on one floor. The second floor was an empty shell, an additional 120,000 square feet of space with elevator and escalator wells already constructed. Opening of that area awaited analysis of customer reception and solid sales results. (The second floor went on-line in another five years. It created a shopping space of almost a quarter of a million square feet, nearly triple the space of our Main Street store.)

We did not, however, triple our employee expenses. The sales force doubled and managers were added, but we kept the same credit, advertising, display, buying, and accounting staffs at headquarters. Cortana was a stunning success, and Goudchaux's profitability more than doubled.

We expected Cortana to put a dent in sales at Main Street, however, and that is precisely what happened. Our flagship store generated about $4 million less in 1976 than in 1975. The $29 million sales volume was what had been projected.

We kept promoting our original downtown presence. For example, in November 1972, a small, two-story brick building sitting on a 22-foot-wide piece of land on North Street, one block north of the store and clearly visible, became available. The owner wanted only $8,500. I bought it

Donna and I, with children Erich and Julie, celebrating one of many remodels to the Main Street store with Lea and Josef and had a sign of billboard proportions painted across the side. It blared GOUDCHAUX's with a large arrow pointing to the store a block away. I subsequently sold the building with a stipulation that the sign not be removed for the life of Goudchaux's. While our store is no longer, the building sign continues to this day to prompt the memories of many passersby.

The Cortana move was progressive and made with the company's health in mind, but beneath the hoopla there was a risk: a subtle change in the company's culture at the branches. The big decision for Josef and me in opening a second (and any subsequent) base of operation was management oversight. Would one of us move to Cortana and the other remain at Main Street?

We decided quite early that a one-family-member-per-store policy wouldn't work. It would limit the growth of the company, since we didn't have a third person. The two of us would continue to maintain the corporate base at the Main Street store, recruit highly qualified senior managers for branch stores, give them considerable authority, and spend part of a day each week at the branches. (We continued that policy even when we expanded to twenty-four stores.) We recruited a senior vice president—Don Bell—to become the Cortana manager. He was a superb choice. As usual, we paid more, but the results reflected the talent.

Lea also took her "maintaining standards" patrol to the Cortana sales floor. She was not happy about two features we unveiled there: a restaurant and a beauty shop. "My husband always said, 'Lea, never have a restaurant or a beauty shop in your store.' And here we have both," she informed Don. (Erich had always argued that they took valuable space away from the selling floor.)

"She was totally disgusted," Bell recalled in a 1994 interview in the *Baton Rouge Business Report.* "And, of course, she was right. [Those operations] lost money and gave us more headaches than you can believe." Personnel turnover in those departments was high, and neither ever became other than marginally profitable.

We had plenty of space at Cortana and sometimes, recalls Bell, it was put to uses other than retailing. We donated office space to the newly appointed director of the Pennington YMCA while the physical plant was being built. The still-active Cortana Kiwanis was launched in our coffeeshop, while the first services of Cortana Baptist Church were held Sunday mornings in the employee lounge.

The core challenge for Cortana and subsequent branch openings and acquisitions was translating our store's culture to new sites, managers, and associates. In reality, the hominess and special feel of Goudchaux's Main Street would be hard to transfer to the other stores. While Goudchaux's branches would be first-rate, we knew there would be a difference.

The quality and scope of the merchandise, the sales, helpful staff, the perks, and the interest-free credit would be there, no question; but the first-name greetings, the owner-to-customer relationships, the courtly touches could not be counted on. Although we did our best to impart family attitudes to new managers and staff, the warmth and family feel, hallmarks of the Main Street Goudchaux's, inevitably would erode as the company expanded. Cultural dilution is the great challenge of all business expansion, but we had to expand to survive.

With Cortana, we became the largest family-owned department store chain in Louisiana. Twelve years later, the national title would also be ours.

During this time, we found ourselves involved in political and social unpleasantness in Louisiana. One such incident, heretofore unpublicized, involved the Fidelity National Bank. Among the city's three largest banks at the time, only Fidelity had granted Erich Sternberg's request for financing to buy Goudchaux's in 1939, after others had turned him away. As long as there was a Fidelity, we did business with only one bank. Leroy Ward had retired as president, and Josef had been named to its board of directors.

At the start of the 1980s, Saudi Arabians attempted to buy a controlling interest in Fidelity. This was a period of intense investment interest in American companies by Saudi business types, flush with new oil money. Somehow, Fidelity Bank popped up on their radar.

On paper Sheik Ali Abdullah Alireza was attempting to gain control by purchasing Fidelity shares owned by

United Companies at 1½ times market value, $84 a share, for a total of $7 million. United owned nearly 14 percent of Fidelity. A rumor circulated among the directors that another 10–11 percent of the stock was in play from other sources. Control would be achieved with 33 percent ownership, but apparently 25 percent was acceptable.

It turned out that Sheik Abdullah's Kuwaiti cousin was the money behind the move. The sheiks were represented by Carl Mathews, former president of the Republic National Bank of New York, and a Mr. Warge, a former executive vice president of Manufacturers Hanover, also of New York. The representatives assured the Fidelity board that, while their clients' investment would be major, their role would be passive. (Josef and I knew the United Companies' stake in Fidelity had been on the table for about four months, but the board received only a 24-hour notice of a "mystery" buyer.)

Attending the March 1981 Fidelity meeting were a bank officer, three directors, and the two representatives for the sheiks, who quickly made it clear their clients required 25 percent of the stock, as well as a seat on the board. If there was any controversy or negative publicity surrounding the transaction, the directors were warned in clear terms, the deal was off.

Josef got right to the point. He told the two advisers he was Jewish and asked what position their clients would take in Fidelity and in the community. The two representatives refused to answer questions, not even divulging the name of the director they wanted on the board. Because of Josef's inquiry, they said they would go no further with the acquisition and abruptly left. The United Companies' management was seething and remained upset with Josef for some time. But we never regretted his question, and the hostile reaction he received spoke for itself.

Generally, we avoided public shows of partisan politics. We made it a point to escort Louisiana politicians of every stripe through the stores during election campaigns so that they could shake hands with our associates. There were two exceptions: David Duke and John Rarick.

An Oklahoma native, Duke joined the Ku Klux Klan at seventeen, just before he became a student at Louisiana State University, where he formed a White Youth Alliance and goose-stepped around campus in Nazi regalia. He held parties on the anniversary of Adolf Hitler's birth. Graduating in 1974, Duke reorganized the KKK into the Knights of the Ku Klux Klan (KKKK), a button-down version of the old night-riding, robed thugs, and became its wizard. He traded hoods for business suits, but the message was the same: The enemies were blacks and Jews. Duke's solidly white-supremacist and anti-Semitic KKKK, however, did eschew a pair of traditional prohibitions—women were now encouraged to join as equals, and membership was opened to Catholics. Needless to say, few bit.

Over the next twenty-five years, Duke ran for nearly every elected office in Louisiana (and for U.S. president in 1988). He succeeded in winning a seat in the Louisiana House of Representatives in 1989 as a Republican with 51 percent of the vote. He started out as a Democrat, transitioned to the Independent ticket for his presidential run, and finally switched to the Republican party in 1989.

We actively opposed Duke and contributed substantial sums to his opponents. Some of the first large donations for the anti-Duke effort in the 1991 gubernatorial race were raised at a meeting in Josef and Mary Ann's home in April 1990. It was attended by 35 to 40 people. Those joining Josef, Mary Ann, Donna, and me included the Reverend James L. Stovall and Lance Hill, whose Louisiana Coalition Against Racism and Nazism effectively fought David Duke from the start and received that night's proceeds. Among others attending were Richard and Susan Lipsey, John Noland, and Gordon and Camilla Pugh.

Duke gained national attention in his campaign for governor when he qualified for a runoff with Democrat Edwin Edwards, a two-term governor shadowed by long-standing charges of corruption. The national media had a field day over Louisiana's gubernatorial choices: a Nazi versus a corrupt politician. Bumper stickers read: "Vote for the Crook, It's Important," and "Vote for the Lizard, not the Wizard."

Just before the election, I had a personal run-in with Duke and his supporters. Either Josef or I would visit New

Orleans stores each Saturday. Our opposition to Duke was well known, so I am convinced it was not coincidental that Duke chose a Saturday morning to demonstrate in the parking lot at Clearview Shopping Center, site of one of our stores. It was my turn to be there, so I had to weave my car through the demonstrators. I gave considerable thought to calling the police and having them removed, but decided the headlines would only give Duke additional attention—something he craved. After an hour of posturing, he and his followers left.

A photo of the rally, with the Maison Blanche marquee unfortunately displayed in the background, appeared in the Sunday *Times-Picayune*. The photo was picked up by the Associated Press and published in the now-defunct *Houston Post*. I received a letter from a Houston citizen accusing me of being a supporter of David Duke; otherwise, why would he be using MB as a backdrop? The laughter at our end was pretty strong. I responded, explaining the obvious, and added this postscript: "Relax, we beat the SOB." Edwards won easily with 61 percent of the vote. (He was convicted of corruption in the late 1990s, following his last term as governor, and was sent to a federal prison.)

Duke later received minor notoriety as the author of a sex advice book for women and from being convicted of mail fraud, not to mention his most recent escapade: appearing as a panelist at a December 2006 conference for Holocaust deniers in Tehran, which was opened by another sweetheart, the extremist Iranian president Mahmoud Ahmadinejad.

The other politician unwelcome at Goudchaux's was the racist Democrat John R. Rarick, who represented Louisiana's Sixth Congressional District, including Baton Rouge, between 1967 and 1975. A district court judge, Rarick, according to the *New Republic*, kept a burned KKK cross in his office and openly belittled African American attorneys.

A graduate of LSU and Tulane University Law School, Rarick was a member of the White Citizens' Council (and its successor, the Council of Conservative Citizens) and a cheerleader for the reactionary John Birch Society. As a member of Congress, he spewed anti-Semitic diatribes into the *Congressional Record*. He was defeated in 1974, and Josef and I were more than a little involved in working toward that end.

In 1973, we were approached by Jeff LaCaze, a local broadcast sports announcer, who was embarrassed by Rarick's representation in Congress, as were a great many Louisianians, and sought to oppose him in the Democratic primary. Josef and I had assiduously avoided partisan political activity and told LaCaze that mixing business and politics was not a good idea and that we did not want to get involved.

Jeff came back in a few weeks to report he couldn't raise enough money to run, having been asked by several potential donors of the Sternbergs' position. He persuaded us to donate the grand sum of one hundred dollars to his cause so that he could tell others we were supporting him.

I hoped that might be the end of it, that the tension might go away, but a couple of weeks later I received an interesting call from one "Catfish" Bill Carrigan, who told me he was the "national campaign manager for the Honorable John R. Rarick." He wanted to know if I was bankrolling the congressman's opponent. I said that was not an appropriate question and would not answer. Catfish was persistent. So was I. Finally, I said that if by his question he wanted to know if I was supporting LaCaze, the answer was yes. As for "bankrolling" LaCaze, I said the answer was no. End of conversation.

Following that phone call, the White Citizens' Council publications began claiming that "the Sternbergs and the Steinbergs" were funding the Rarick opposition. Speeches were made employing the same language. Richard Lipsey of Steinberg's Sporting Goods also was supporting LaCaze. The exaggeration and implied anti-Semitism infuriated Josef and me, and we began sending LaCaze real money. Our friends did, too, and the publicity attracted strong supporters, including Shelly Beychok, a local attorney, who recognized the attacks as pure anti-Semitism, and Baton Rouge mayor Woody Dumas.

LaCaze beat Rarick by fewer than 400 votes, four-tenths of a percent, in the primary. In the general election, the liberal LaCaze was "defeated" by Republican Henson Moore by 14 votes out of approximately 120,000 votes cast, a margin so close that it was contested. After it was discovered that a balloting machine had malfunctioned, the state ordered a special election to decide the winner.

Moore fared much better in that contest, beating his opponent (whom we continued to back) by some 11,000 votes. Moore, only the second Republican from Louisiana to serve in the U.S. House of Representatives since Reconstruction, was reelected for five more terms, and we became, and remain, close friends. Rarick never won another election.

Ever since we engaged in the campaign to get rid of John Rarick, Josef and I became more politically engaged. To our father, politics was anathema. There was no partisan activity while Dad was alive. Josef and I tended to be moderate Democrats—social liberals and fiscal conservatives—but never exclusively.

Flush with profits from our foray into Cortana Mall, we began casting a covetous eye at Lafayette, an up-and-coming city about fifty miles west of Baton Rouge and a hub of the state's booming oil industry. Its size, demographics, and per-capita income made it an increasingly attractive location for a third store. In 1977, we entered negotiations with Acadiana Mall developer Bob Aikens. Less than two years later, in August 1979, we opened the doors to a third Goudchaux's.

The Lafayette store was 111,000 square feet on a single floor. It was constructed so that its foundation could support a second floor if that became necessary, but we never implemented it. (Our successor did add another floor.) Competitors at Acadiana were Dillard's, J. C. Penney, and Sears. Jim Nicholson, one of our seasoned merchandise managers, became the store manager and provided excellent leadership.

Lafayette presented a new challenge. Goudchaux's enjoyed nearly 100-percent name recognition in Baton Rouge, but not in Lafayette. My son Erich remembers visiting the construction site and noticing that the construction crew was speaking Cajun French. The world was a bit different in Acadiana, and we had promotional and marketing work ahead of us.

Yet Lafayette accepted Goudchaux's beyond our expectations. With the added revenue from the Acadiana store's first full year of operation, Goudchaux's overall sales volume in 1981 was in excess of $100 million. In 1984, the Society of Louisiana Certified Public Accountants named Goudchaux's the company of the year.

One humorous incident related to the Lafayette store deserves telling. How the story began, however, was not amusing. In early 1980, less than a half year into our operation there, the store's computer crashed. Everything in that branch was frozen. Not a single cash register was working. Dan Smith, head of IT, alerted our Ohio-based vendor, Unitote, which, like any top computer firm, immediately dispatched three troubleshooters by plane late in the afternoon. They arrived in New Orleans around 10 p.m.

The trio rented a car and headed to Lafayette, approximately two hours to the west on Interstate 10. For those unfamiliar with the route, I-10 west of Baton Rouge becomes a raised causeway for about twenty-five miles as it traverses the Atchafalaya River basin, a series of swamps, lakes, and bayous that thousands of years ago comprised the main channel of the Mississippi River. Thick stands of trees line the interstate. In the dark of night, the trees appear to be on ground level with the highway and adjacent to it. They aren't. They sit in water about 12 feet below the expressway and some 40 feet away.

The intrepid "computer doctors," having flown several hours first-class (on our nickel) enjoying the free drinks, were feeling little pain as they winged their way down the road to Lafayette. By the time they reached the Atchafalaya Basin, it was pitch black and raining. The call of nature was too strong for one of them, who insisted the car be stopped on the emergency apron of the then-unlit freeway so he could relieve himself. Not wanting passing headlights to catch him in the act, he made the inebriated decision "to walk over there" to the nearby trees, climbing over the short cement guardrail. The bad news was there was no "there" there. The good news: The drop was into spongy swamp ground.

Architect's rendering of the Goudchaux's store in the Mall of Acadiana in Lafayette, 1977

After several minutes, the two techies remaining in the car wondered what happened to their colleague and one decided to check. Walking to where he thought his friend had gone, he, too, headed for the trees. He stepped over the rail and fell to the "rescue," next to his otherwise-unharmed friend. (The alligators must have already eaten that day.)

The third computer guru wisely stayed in the car, having no clue as to what had happened, and turned on his flashing emergency lights. A Louisiana state trooper came along and summoned the closest fire department. The pair was rescued, but fire trucks are often followed by news photographers, and the next day Goudchaux's made the front page of the *Lafayette Daily Advertiser.* At least "Goudchaux's" was spelled correctly in the headline.

* * *

We hit our first million-dollar day on December 22, 1980, and it came because we opened for business twice that day. Tom Cagley, our general merchandise manager, talked me into a double opening. The Goudchaux's dress buyer had come to us from Rike's Department Store in Dayton, Ohio. She had told Cagley about an event in which Rike's closed its doors at 6:30 p.m. on a normal Christmas-season evening, then reopened them at 7 p.m. with all manner of hoopla and specials.

Just before December 1980, Cagley pitched the idea to me. My reaction was, why close for thirty minutes when we could be open for business? But I agreed to try it. The volume that first day/night was $925,000, beating a 1979 single-day record. We repeated the promotion two Saturdays later and did $984,000 in business. A week later, we hit $1,007,000 for the day.

We also launched a couple of literary careers. In 1982,

FROM Mr. Bingle's Kitchen

A Children's Cookbook
by
Holly Berkowitz Clegg

▼Maison Blanche

Chef and author Holly Clegg used Mr. Bingle as a theme for one of her first cookbooks.

a local caterer, Holly Clegg, teamed with Goudchaux's to publish a cookbook, *From a Louisiana Kitchen*. It hit the book shelves the following year and became a best-seller, with nine printings and almost 40,000 books sold nationally. It was one of three cookbooks Holly did for us before we sold the store. We introduced her to Random House, which became her publisher, and she went on to national fame. We also published *A South Louisiana Bride's Notebook*, edited by Mary Ann Sternberg. It became a popular gift from the store to those enrolled in our bridal registry. She later authored three additional nonfiction books, two published by LSU Press.

Chef John Folse credits our stores for the success of *his* first cookbook, *The Evolution of Cajun and Creole Cuisine*, and for putting his restaurant, Lafitte's Landing in Donaldsonville, on the map. We called John in the fall of 1989 to say his just-published volume had been selected for a Goudchaux's/Maison Blanche upcoming Christmas promotion in our Louisiana and Florida stores. "It was a gigantic break," the internationally famous chef says today. That visibility spawned attendant publicity and a number of subsequent popular cookbooks. Now in its sixteenth printing, *The Evolution of Cajun and Creole Cuisine* remains his best-selling book.

We experimented with many things in those heady days. Some of it shocked the retail world. For example, at one point we sold black-and-white 9-inch TVs for $10 with any purchase of $100 or more. It created a mob scene at Christmas. (The TV sets cost us $12.)

Our success at Cortana Mall and in Lafayette's Acadiana Mall, and the continued popularity of Main Street, made us regional players by the early 1980s. This whetted our appetite for expansion and reinforced our belief that long-term survival in the department store industry was possible only through increased volume and economies of scale.

From the Lafayette venture onward, we began seriously looking at new Louisiana locations. Lake Charles and Alexandria beckoned, but we decided that either the population base wasn't large enough or the demographics and competitive scene weren't right. What did catch our fancy, though, was the Big Easy.

8 | MAISON BLANCHE

IN 1853, THREE YEARS before grandfather Jacob was born, Isidore Newman came to New Orleans as a penniless, sixteen-year-old Jewish immigrant from Kaiserslautern, in the Rheinland-Pfalz region of Germany. Newman never met our immediate family, although he undoubtedly knew my great-uncle Joseph Sternberg, who moved to New Orleans before the turn of the century. Our legacies would be intertwined in another way.

Newman walked down the steerage-class gangplank and registered as an immigrant. Officials listed his occupation as farmer, but that was not to be his career in America. He went to work for his uncle, Charles, helping run his general store in nearby Harrisonburg, Louisiana. He worked hard, saved his money, and soon sent for his two younger brothers, Henry and Charles. The three Newman brothers opened a cotton brokerage in New Orleans.

His timing could not have been worse. The Civil War and its aftermath laid waste to much of southern commerce, including the Newman enterprise. For the only time in his new country, Isidore Newman would be connected with a business failure. He turned his efforts to investment banking, which in the early 1890s gave him the financial wherewithal to acquire the streetcar lines in New Orleans, as well as the Edison Electric Company that powered them.

In 1897, he opened Maison Blanche (French for "white house") Department Store on the corner of Canal and Dauphine streets in downtown New Orleans. He stocked the Victorian-style emporium with fine clothes and home necessities. Maison Blanche became a retail sensation, successful from the start.

By 1909, the year of his death, Newman had torn down the original domed and turreted building on the edge of the French Quarter and replaced it with a 12-story, terra cotta and marble "skyscraper" that remained the city's tallest building until 1921. It still stands, as the Ritz-Carlton Hotel. Being a philanthropist and community leader, Newman created a school for Jewish orphans in 1903. (Open to all parts of the community, Isidore Newman School continues today as a prestigious private school.)

Newman operated his business with the same principles as my father: progress, fashion, value, and customer service. Both merchants believed those to be cornerstones of a successful retail institution, certainly for their times, and history proved them correct.

That tradition was maintained by Newman's family, which operated Maison Blanche until it was sold in 1951 to City Stores, a publicly traded holding company based in New York. City Stores had held a financial interest in Maison Blanche since 1923. (The company's other operations in the South included Lowenstein's in Memphis, Loveman's in Birmingham, and Kaufman-Straus in Louisville.)

By the 1950s, City Stores owned department stores throughout the United States and was considered a poten-

Construction of Maison Blanche Department Store on Canal Street in New Orleans, 1907. At the time, it was the tallest building in the city.

our radar since 1976, when we made discreet but unsuccessful overtures to City Stores. (We opted for opening a Goudchaux's in Lafayette when City Stores displayed no interest in selling.) The five Maison Blanche stores were tempting for many reasons: proximity to our headquarters; a name that was to New Orleans what Goudchaux's was to Baton Rouge; a business culture similar to ours. In addition, the timing for us was right.

As the 1980s commenced, and MB appeared ripe for the picking, Josef and I kept the focus of our covetous eyes confidential. Eventually, that strategy paid off. In the five years since City Stores had dismissed our preliminary overtures concerning Maison Blanche (in reality, a small piece of its overall operation in the 1970s), the situation had changed dramatically. City Stores had filed for bankruptcy protection, its management was overthrown, and the Maison Blanche branch that anchored Bon Marché Mall in Baton Rouge was shuttered.

City Stores had lost money for years, primarily because it was run by bankers rather than merchants. By 1984, City Stores' department store division had closed, and the other entities were dead or divested.

Until the late 1970s, Maison Blanche had been a money maker. It was considered by many the crown jewel of the clothing and department store treasures gracing New Orleans. The city was dominated by local merchants, as reflected in the store names: D. H. Holmes (the oldest, founded in 1842 and sold in the 1980s to Dillard's), Rubenstein's (a posh establishment that opened in 1924 and is still operating), Kreeger's (founded in the 1860s but closed in 1986), Krauss (founded in 1903 and the first New Orleans department store to have air conditioning and escalators but which closed its doors in 1997), Leon Godchaux Clothing (with which we later would experience legal unpleasantries because of the closeness of our two names), and Maison Blanche.

Canal Street was the place to shop, especially in the 1950s and 1960s, before the malls began to siphon off the more mobile consumers. Through the 1970s, Christmas on Canal Street witnessed a sea of human shoppers. Santa would make an annual appearance on the balcony of the Holmes store, while Mr. Bingle, star of Maison Blanche's

tial rival to the industry colossus, Federated Department Stores.

"MB," as it was affectionately known to generations of New Orleanians, was the second store in Louisiana to have air conditioning (1926) and escalators (1933). The Newmans established an MB branch in Gentilly in 1942, and City Stores extended that strategy further, opening three shopping-center branches: Westside in 1958, Clearview in 1969, and Lake Forest in 1974. Maison Blanche also was the first Louisiana retail store to computerize (1960), beating Goudchaux's by fifteen years.

With the success of Goudchaux's expansion to the Cortana and Acadiana malls, we began serious consideration of additional acquisitions. Maison Blanche had been on

Christmas puppet shows, would attract tens of thousands of onlookers to MB's elaborately decorated holiday display windows.

Due to corporate losses at City Stores, MB was forced into bankruptcy protection in 1979. It emerged in 1981 but continued losing money, even though it posted $64 million in annual sales. Nonetheless, we privately were salivating at the possibility of acquiring Maison Blanche. We knew we could run it more efficiently than City Stores. With the financial troubles the parent company was experiencing, the stage was set. When a business needs funding or is forced to sell a division, the potential buyer already has a pair of aces in the pocket.

We wrote Jack Farber, City Stores' new CEO, expressing our interest. The initial response was another "no interest" along with the assertion that Maison Blanche would survive. While on the surface that "no" may have appeared to be a deal-ender, this time it was posturing, part of the game. In fact, City Stores wanted to unload MB. It could no more show an eagerness to sell than we could telegraph ours to buy.

Mergers have a momentum of their own, and this particular deal was carried forward by two factors: The new City Stores management did not consider itself department store oriented, and Maison Blanche continued to bleed red ink. A broker entered the arena and the merger dance began. We were given sketchy financial data (Profit & Loss, balance sheets, etc.) and invited to New York City.

There we met with Jack Farber, a brilliant former senior partner at Price Waterhouse, who had joined City Stores determined to get it out of its financial mess. The company's largest stockholder as well, Farber forced the previous holding company's management to sell its stock, allowing him to take control. He would represent City Stores throughout the negotiations. We formed our ac-

quisition team with a New York law firm today known as Troutman Sanders, which boasted a group specializing in mergers and acquisitions. In addition, we retained experienced acquisition accountants from Touche Ross offices in New York City and Atlanta.

We initially met in June 1981 in the offices of City Stores' legal firm, now called Proskauer Rose, one of New York City's larger law firms. Klaus Eppler, a senior partner in the firm, represented City Stores. In the six months that followed, both sides found themselves surrounded by lawyers, CPAs, and advisers.

City Stores' CEO, Jack Farber

Farber could be moody. In the mornings, he was peppy, lively, and civil. By afternoon, he had worn out, becoming frazzled and irritable, often pounding the table and screaming expletives in my direction. There was always give-and-take from both sides, and not infrequently the negotiations became more than a little tense. Emotions ran high. I wasn't always an angel, either. One afternoon, I made what I considered a particularly "reasonable" suggestion. Jack jumped up, told me I could "go f——" myself, and stormed out of the room, his dozen or so lawyers, accountants, and staff dutifully following. It was like a scene out of Hollywood.

I decided Jack had a low-blood-sugar problem and began stopping at a bakery and buying pastries on my way to the negotiating sessions. Whenever Jack started getting up and pacing, I would shove a plate of Danish his way. He would grab one, eat compulsively, and calm down.

City Stores opened with an asking price that represented the book value for the Maison Blanche business, subject to certain adjustments such as inventory, and a premium of $5 million. Something ridiculous, as I recall, some $20 million. Without flinching or rendering judgment on Farber's price, we sought more in-depth accounting and merchandising information and agreed to a further meeting. We focused on what not to buy, severing those elements we felt were keeping MB in the red.

The financials told a startling story: MB's losses were heavy. By MB's own bookkeeping, the most recent annual loss was $3.5 million. Our estimate exceeded $4 million. The six months of meetings that followed resembled the Vietnam peace talks: Objectives were always known; the only issue was structure. Based on our analysis of the books, we came up with five key, nonnegotiable positions.

For openers, City Stores would have to close Maison Blanche's main store on Canal Street. Ditto for its budget outlet adjacent to the main store. We simply were not going to buy them. While the Canal Street store was MB's biggest sales producer, years of neglect had increased overhead costs to a point that it would take millions of dollars to bring the cost of doing business to a tolerable level. The heating and air conditioning systems dated to the 1940s. Utility bills exceeded 4 percent of sales and were rising rapidly. (Goudchaux's norm was less than 1 percent.)

The building was 522,000 square feet over five floors, exactly the size it had been when opened in 1909—too large to be efficient. Sales had been static for a decade. There was no parking to speak of. Further, the overall retail business in New Orleans' central business district had dropped 3 percent over the last ten years, and it appeared the slide would continue.

Second, Goudchaux's warehouse facility in Baton Rouge was sufficient to handle effectively the combined businesses. The existing MB warehouse, with its annual rent of $450,000, not counting utilities and payroll, would have to be eliminated from the sale, along with its fleet of delivery trucks.

Third, Goudchaux's existing computer system had the capacity to include the New Orleans acquisition. That would eliminate the need for Maison Blanche's accounting department, as well as its buyers and corporate staff. Those, too, would have to come off the table.

Fourth, we wanted nothing to do with Maison Blanche's charge account balances, then in the neighborhood of $18 million plus a $3 million annual handling fee to a New York bank. That did not even include an interest rate of 2.5 percent above prime on money borrowed. We did demand, and would receive, the names and addresses of its customers who held those accounts.

Finally, to fit the Goudchaux's mold, it would be necessary to eliminate any MB inventory not in Goudchaux's regular merchandise mix, for example, furniture and appliances. We estimated that to be more than 10 percent of MB's inventory.

We told City Stores that, based on its own books, Maison Blanche, as a whole, was not salable at any price. We were willing, however, to discuss the purchase of specific assets. Farber rejected that approach, and we canceled further conversations. I prohibited all future meetings between the two sides' legal firms. We had defined our thresholds and walked away, something successful negotiators must always be prepared to do. To underscore our point, we told our CFO, Brian Kendrick, who was in New York working with the accountants, to leave his hotel and return to Baton Rouge. We felt certain City Stores would check to see if he left (and it did).

In reality, however, it was a high-stakes game of chicken—and City Stores blinked. (I can reveal now that we held an edge in that stare-down: An inside player at City Stores in a carpool one morning innocently told an employee of Touche Ross, our accounting firm, that no other buyer was interested in MB.)

Within three days, Mort Olshan, a friend of both sides who was the original go-between with City Stores and us and eventually received $175,000 from City Stores for his participation in the sale, approached us with this inquiry: Was there middle ground? Yes, I said, we would pay more if City Stores kept what we did not want and our attorney would write the contract. While the dollars changed little, there was a dramatic transformation in the structure of the deal. We had moved from paying a premium to compensating the seller for disposing of assets we weren't buying.

By September 1981, we had signed a letter of intent to buy Maison Blanche but were still five weeks away from agreeing on a final price and details. The main hang-up concerned inventory. City Stores gave us a December 18 deadline.

Farber was a tough, highly skilled specialist in selling distressed properties. He knew and practiced every subtlety, including an analysis of our personalities and styles. We were down to the final negotiating session. Although neither side was forced to lie during the months of negotiations, neither side had volunteered damaging information. Our data had been impeccable. Even though Farber swore at us with blistering language and each side teetered on the brink on numerous occasions, there was high-level mutual trust that pulled us through. Farber knew we would deliver what we promised. Apparently, Farber also gained a great deal of respect for us as the negotiations unfolded. In his memoirs, he wrote, "By the time of the detailed negotiations on inventory, it was clear that the Sternbergs knew more about the Maison operations than [Maison Blanche CEO Dan] Lincove or [COO Jerry] Sklar. I learned a lot about real professionals, as opposed to experienced managers that are really amateurs by comparison."

We came to an agreement on a Saturday morning in January 1982. On the previous day, when those final negotiations were to begin, my attorney, Herb Rosedale, whom I greatly admired and respected, advised me to go to my hotel and sleep. It was midday, I reminded him. He knew what was coming: an all-nighter. I did what I was told. (Farber thought Rosedale an unforgettable eccentric, a smart man but an unusual dresser. "He had represented some low-end retailers" in his earlier years, Farber wrote in his unpublished memoirs, "and had tastes consistent with those retailers. He always wore a wash and wear polyester shirt and a reversible polyester tie that he flipped each day so (we would think) he had an extensive wardrobe.")

For various reasons—delayed papers, a sick attorney, and so on—the session at Proskauer Rose, City Stores' law firm, did not begin until 7:30 that evening. Farber remembered the negotiations as "seemingly endless and exhausting." (All big deals seem to end this way.) Two shifts of legal secretaries typed through the night. A Chinese dinner and a midnight snack were brought in. At 7 o'clock the next morning, a chef arrived to fix everyone breakfast. The law offices even had showers.

The final details hammered out, the session ended at 10:30 a.m. We paid $13.8 million for Maison Blanche, including inventory, but we later recovered about $2.2 million on an inventory discount. It was a terrific deal. For $11.6 million, we picked up three suburban stores, inventory, fixtures, personnel, accounts receivable lists (but not the old balances)—a going business that would fit nicely into Goudchaux's existing infrastructure.

Left behind were the building housing the Canal Street store (which City Stores soon sold), the budget outlet store, a warehouse, delivery trucks, severance for MB executives, and inventory that didn't match ours. Further, City Stores would be responsible for collecting its old charge account balances.

In return, though, City Stores received millions in cash and eliminated a source of continuing losses. (Shifting gears in the mid-1980s, City Stores became CSS Industries, a profitable, Philadelphia-based manufacturer of seasonal and everyday decorative products, gift cards and wrappings, with customers throughout the United States and Canada. Jack Farber remained as CEO.)

We had a significant advantage in the Maison Blanche deal: City Stores had to sell or liquidate. The down side for us would have been disappointment and out-of-pocket negotiating expenses, but no serious damage. City Stores knew this. What City Stores didn't know is that we had put a geographical limit on how far Goudchaux's would expand. That two-hundred-mile radius from Baton Rouge covered several good markets—Jackson, Shreveport, Lake Charles, Natchez, Vicksburg, and Mobile—but New Orleans was the plum.

Although available land was hard to find, we could have built Goudchaux's branches in New Orleans instead of buying MB. That said, starting without a charge account base, without an established clientele, without a reputation, without a trained selling staff suggested a staggering overhead potential. The advertising costs alone would have been 50 percent above normal. We were dying to buy MB but disguised our passion well.

By using our own lawyer to write the deal, our legal costs were increased by $50,000, but it was cheap money. Nevertheless, lawyers tend to over-lawyer, so it is your job to control your attorney. My advice: Find lawyers who are business persons. Personally read every word of the contract repeatedly. The maxim still applies: School teaches you how to read the fine print; education is what you get from not reading it. "Your lawyers and accountant are only as good as you are," Erich Sternberg taught us. Don't depend on them to do your work for you.

The most important things to remember in the art of negotiating are to know your walk-away points and have the guts to maintain them. Those who don't mentally set the maximum they will pay or the minimum they will accept before beginning a negotiation risk giving away too much. Often a negotiator's best weapon is the willingness to physically leave. You can't lose money you haven't spent.

(The dozen working strategies used in purchasing Maison Blanche stores and in subsequent negotiations can be found in Appendix 1.)

* * *

An immediate hitch developed in our invasion of New Orleans. Leon Godchaux Clothing Company had been a New Orleans fixture since Godchaux (who spelled his name without the first "u") emigrated from France in 1836 at the age of twelve. He could speak French only, but that worked in New Orleans. He peddled notions on foot to plantations around the city after persuading an established merchant to rent him a backpack filled with sewing paraphernalia. Some three years later, the sixteen-year-old opened a dry goods store forty miles north of the city.

In 1865, the forty-one-year-old Godchaux moved to New Orleans and opened a men's clothing business. While the enterprise continued to be operated by family members, Leon went on to become the wealthiest sugar merchant in the South, a true rags-to-riches story.

In 1926, his grandson moved Leon Godchaux Clothing to the 800 block of Canal Street, a block from Maison Blanche, revamping its focus to cater to middle- and upper-income customers. Women's and children's clothing, jewelry, linens, and so on, were added. Its display windows would highlight high-end novelties, such as black suede shoes adorned with diamonds that sold for $45,000. Still, it always remained smaller than Goudchaux's of Baton Rouge, and it lacked our stores' personality, breadth of merchandise, and promotional zeal.

Leon Godchaux Clothing expanded to the New Orleans suburbs in the 1960s and to Houma and Baton Rouge in the early 1970s, buying the Varsity Shop in the Capital City. In its commercials, it deliberately would call the Varsity Shop "a division of Leon Godchaux Clothing Company" in an attempt to catch a ride on Goudchaux's good name. I came up with a counterlogo: Over Goudchaux's nameplate, it proclaimed, "The difference is U."

Leon Godchaux Clothing feared we would operate Maison Blanche under the combined Goudchaux's/Maison Blanche name and filed a lawsuit to protect its New Orleans turf. The suit did not get past depositions. Because it had done that very thing to us in Baton Rouge, Leon Godchaux Clothing had a difficult time making its case. The company went bankrupt in 1986, so in the end, the point was moot. In Baton Rouge and Lafayette, we operated the stores under the name Goudchaux's/Maison Blanche, while in New Orleans, common sense dictated we use only "Maison Blanche" in advertisements and displays.

The Maison Blanche anchors at the Lake Forest, Clearview, and Westside shopping centers opened for business under new management in February 1982. Josef had pushed aggressively for this acquisition, and he was proven right.

Understandably, there was negative reaction to the closing of the venerable Canal Street store, flagship of the MB group. My mantra to the inquiring news media and civic organizations was that we had saved the eighty-five-year-old institution and would rejuvenate it to what it was in years past. The alternative was to liquidate inventory, sell the buildings, and bury Maison Blanche . . . precisely what City Stores would have done had we not stepped in.

"The very opposite is going to happen," I told *The Times-Picayune,* adding that we were bringing MB ownership back to Louisiana after thirty years. "We're going to expand and build more stores and hire more people." And we did—even more so than we originally planned.

The political situation in New Orleans was not helpful, however. I paid a courtesy call on the mayor, Ernest "Dutch" Morial, after we purchased MB. He was anything but welcoming, deliberately assuming a provincial attitude. Although I had never met the man, he haughtily and deliberately turned his back to me when I entered his office, and his demeanor remained icy and aloof. He did give me permission to hold a parade bringing the puppet icon, Mr. Bingle, back to Canal Street. (More on that in the next chapter.)

It was helpful that we brought to New Orleans a reputation for customer service and the interest-free charge accounts that immediately became available to Maison Blanche customers. We had the most efficiently run department store in the country, according to the July 1981 issue of *Stores* magazine, an industry trade journal. Our sales-per-square-foot (the measure of a store's productivity) from the two Baton Rouge stores and the Lafayette site topped such giants as Bloomingdales, Macy's, and

Josef, Lea, and I on a *Times-Picayune Dixie* magazine cover in 1983, following Goudchaux's purchase of the Maison Blanche stores in New Orleans

Foley's, and were *double* the national average. That sort of consumer acceptance made Maison Blanche sing financially and was a factor in tempting us to change our stance on the Canal Street store.

We hired Maison Blanche's CEO, Dan Lincove, to be president of the New Maison Blanche, as we called our New Orleans division. He was a good manager, but he didn't last ninety days. He voluntarily resigned, a bitter person, resentful that he had to report to our director of stores, Don Bell. On that point, Josef and I would not bend. He joined his brother in a Shreveport business and dropped from sight. We also retained an MB designer buyer, who proved to like the social scene too much. We celebrated when a New Orleans rival lured her away.

Every Canal Street sales associate was offered a transfer to one of the branches. When we acquired it, Maison Blanche was represented by seven unions—including carpenters, truck drivers, electricians, and painters—but we managed to eliminate union representation before we reopened the stores under our management. My problem with unions is simple: They attempt to run the business and in the process push up costs, often making it impossible to compete profitably.

As for inventory, out went the "basement" goods that MB had resorted to in its final years. In came fashion and quality. It proved to be the right move. Our business grew at an annual rate of 20 percent.

With the acquisition of Maison Blanche, we instituted a change in Goudchaux's management structure. Operations now were simply too large for Josef and me to manage as we traditionally had. We instituted an executive committee, made up of ten to fifteen top managers (the number varied over the years) who would call the day-to-day operational shots. In conjunction with this executive committee, we made our second-biggest decision regarding Maison Blanche.

Josef particularly wanted to reopen the Canal Street store. In terms of volume, it had the highest sales of all the MB stores before it was shuttered in early 1982. Josef pointed out that D. H. Holmes's Canal Street store was turning $35 million in annual sales. We estimated it would take $6 million to renovate the property and add a parking garage. (That would be in addition to the $8 million we spent refurbishing the three MB suburban stores.)

I wasn't as sure as Josef about Canal Street's potential for success, and neither was Ashton Phelps, Jr., publisher of *The Times-Picayune*, who advised us against it. Still, we calculated that if we could modernize the store and decrease the overhead, it might just work. And the historic Canal Street structure definitely had that flagship ambiance. The free publicity from its reopening would be worth a million dollars. We decided to do it.

New Orleans businessman Philip Carter, son of the late Mississippi newspaperman/author Hodding Carter, Sr., had purchased the Maison Blanche building from City Stores but was having trouble finding tenants. MB's footprint was more than a half million square feet over the first five floors and the basement. We needed fewer than 200,000 square feet to reasonably replicate the size of our other stores.

We leased the first three floors from Carter and converted 170,000 square feet into retail space—one-third the size of the original store operation. We also purchased the abandoned Kress building that stood adjacent to Maison Blanche on Canal, turning most of it into multilevel, covered parking and leasing the first-floor space to The Gap and Wohl Shoes. The Kress façade, on Canal Street, was returned to its original grandeur.

With considerable fanfare, we reopened the Canal Street store in 1984 in time for the New Orleans World's Fair. Under the promotional slogan "Old Heart, New Beat," we launched a fresh, convenient shopping experience for New Orleans customers. The Canal Street site produced a retailing renaissance for downtown. We got the anticipated publicity and plenty of tourist traffic. The store also catered to the city's so-called carriage trade, the wealthy.

Although underperforming financially, Canal Street proved to be a great success in reestablishing MB's image as a New Orleans institution. And it did make some money. We had taken a retailing *elephant blanc* and converted it into an efficiently run enterprise turning a small profit. Compared with losing $4 million a year, as it had been doing, that represented a significant turnaround.

Remodeling and renovating what were now four stores, as well as the construction of a parking garage on Canal Street, cost us considerably more than our original investment, but was worth it. With the acquisition of Maison Blanche, we moved from being the eighty-fifth largest department store chain in the country to the fifty-fifth.

We weren't the only ones revitalizing Big Easy's downtown. The year before we reopened the doors to Maison Blanche, Saks Fifth Avenue opened a 75,000-square-foot store at Canal Place. Lord & Taylor would open two years later, and Macy's planned to establish two locations in 1987—all this despite Orleans Parish losing population.

We were not intimidated. For one thing, we were nimble. We did not have to wait for corporate approval if we wanted to do something. Josef liked to tell reporters: "There is no greater satisfaction than having my brother at my side, deciding a course of action, and implementing it ten minutes later. I don't have to wait for Chicago to say 'yes.' We don't answer to anybody but our mother."

Developing the New Orleans business was fun. In 1983, for example, we were struggling to expand the Estee Lauder cosmetics franchise to our New Orleans stores. I arranged a meeting with CEO Leonard Lauder during a Young Presidents Organization "university" we both were attending. Leonard was friendly but noncommittal when it came to saying we could market Lauder products in the Crescent City.

Getting up to leave, I said, "Leonard, we can continue the way we are going, but we both understand we are pissing away a million dollars a year." He looked a bit shocked, but four weeks later he and a group of his managers visited New Orleans, toured our stores, and gave us a green light to launch the Lauder line. It was a big deal because D. H. Holmes and Leon Godchaux Clothing had been the only stores with Lauder franchises for the previous twenty years.

"The Sternberg brothers saw the enemy and they aren't impressed," reported *Forbes* magazine in July 1984. We knew how to compete. We bought our clothes for the same wholesale prices as our rivals, paid the same advertising rates, had a strong import program, and had our share of exclusive lines. Actually, I told the *Forbes* reporter, we have the advantage over our out-of-town competitors, because we live in Louisiana and know our customers.

9 | MR. BINGLE AND BEYOND

FROM THE EARLY 1950s, Goudchaux's Santa Claus held seasonal court at the Main Street store in Baton Rouge. A helicopter flew a "live" costumed Santa to the parking lot each year, offering a friendly knee for every child. Pictures with that Santa cost only one dollar originally, and the waiting line could get quite long. But it was the animated, laughing, mechanical Santa that caught the attention of our customers.

First as a fixture in the display windows and then elevated to a sheltered "Santa Room" above the canopy of the middle entrance, the lifelike figure became Baton Rouge's yuletide centerpiece. It was so large and heavy—the seated Santa measured more than five feet tall and weighed hundreds of pounds—that it had to be hoisted to its perch with a crane. Its signature "ho! ho! ho!" was as unforgettable as it was loud.

To this day, customers remember Goudchaux's artificial Santa and how transfixed they once were by its moving hand and knee and belly laugh. When this Santa Claus arrived after Thanksgiving, people came from far away to see him. They loved the animation, and few could resist laughing along. Some of the neighbors were not so jolly when the "ho, ho, ho" boomed through Louisiana's crisp late-autumn air, though expressed complaints were rare.

"Everyone remembers the incessantly laughing Santa at Goudchaux's," says Margo Murphy. "My sister and I would enjoy watching it move every time we waited to pick my mom [an employee] up from the store."

Faye Hoffman Talbot recalls living about eight blocks from the Main Street store as a child in the 1950s. "When the wind was blowing just right, we could hear Goudchaux's Santa 'ho, ho, ho-ing' from our upstairs window." Obviously, the Hoffmans were among those neighbors who actually enjoyed that distinctive laugh.

I well recall the "Goudchaux's Moment" provided by former credit office employee Olive Campbell, who each year vowed, because of the long hours demanded during the holiday season, that that particular year would be her last Christmas at Goudchaux's. A proper and refined woman, she always returned until she retired. "One Christmas Eve," remembers Olive, "Jerry McMahon, Valerie Gonzalez, and I were leaving the store at 9:30 p.m. We had been there since 7:30 a.m. and were dead tired. The old Santa Claus on the roof of the store was 'ho, ho, ho-ing.' I looked up at him and without a thought said, 'Shut up, you old sh———' . . . I still miss that old store down on Main Street."

In the early 1980s, Santa went missing. Incredibly, the heavy figure had been stolen. This was no ordinary theft. The headlines in the local (and numerous national) newspapers screamed, "Santa Kidnapped!" Alas, he never was rescued. My hunch: It was a fraternity prank. The theft was an annoyance, but not devastating. Yes, Virginia, Goudchaux's had a backup Jolly Old St. Nick, a duplicate of the shanghaied Santa. The "ho-ho-ho-ing" didn't miss a beat.

While Goudchaux's was known for its up-on-the-housetop Santa, Maison Blanche in New Orleans had a Christmas symbol that eclipsed our Santa Claus, one so popular we incorporated it in all our stores after we purchased MB. Enter Mr. Bingle, a Christmas puppet dressed as a snowman, wearing an inverted ice-cream cone hat and carrying his signature striped candy cane. The original puppet, created by Emile Aline, a Maison Blanche employee, made its debut in 1947 at the Canal Street store.

It was no coincidence that Mr. B's initials and Maison Blanche's affectionate nickname, MB, were identical. This character was promotional ingenuity at its best. Mothers would bring their children to Maison Blanche, leaving the youngsters to have "Breakfast with Mr. Bingle" while they shopped. The Mr. B's mantra still rings in many ears to this day:

> Jingle, Jangle, Jingle, here comes Mr. Bingle
> With another message from Kris Kringle.
> Time to launch the Christmas Season,
> Maison Blanche makes Christmas pleasin'.
> Gifts galore for you to see,
> Each a gem from . . . MB.

Tens of thousands of Mr. Bingle stuffed-toy replicas were purchased, as were countless Mr. Bingle "Watch Me Grow" wall charts. Mr. Bingle, with his high-pitched voice, got invited to the lighting of the National Christmas Tree at the White House and showed up at the Orange Bowl in 1989. He even had his own radio and television shows.

Mr. Bingle probably would not have survived a second or third Christmas had it not been for Edwin Harmon "Oscar" Isentrout, a carnival worker and troubadour who, according to writer George Gurtner in *New Orleans Magazine,* worked everything from carnivals to puppeteering (with the world-famous Zuzares Marionette Troupe) to playing supper clubs and movie theaters to supplying the bumps and grinds to a striptease puppet at a joint on Bourbon Street. Isentrout's puppet act was billed "Oscar and the Little Woodenheads," and that's how Edwin Isentrout got his nickname.

The Brooklyn-born-and-raised Isentrout, Gurtner wrote, fell in love with the Maison Blanche Christmas

Santa and a not-so-happy customer at Goudchaux's, 1971

windows, with their snowy winter scenes and villages traversed by toy trains. There he was introduced to the cartoonish Mr. Bingle. They bonded immediately. Isentrout sold the Newman family on the idea of letting him put on a Christmas puppet show in MB's windows.

In the early days, MB promotions people would have to comb New Orleans in August to locate Isentrout and direct him to begin preparations for the Christmas show. He needed several months' lead time for his intricate and grand shows, which included several themes, music, elaborate lighting, and stage settings. MB soon decided to make him a full-time employee, who nevertheless would come and go as he pleased except around Christmas.

Off season, Mr. Bingle "lived" on the upper floor of the Westside Mall branch. That was Oscar Isentrout's office and workshop, a place where wires, tools, work benches, and boxes of arms, heads, and hands were scattered about. Employees named that floor "Bingle Land."

Don Bell, director of stores, remembers going to Oscar's studio and, standing outside the door, hearing him having a conversation with the puppet. Not wishing to disturb the colloquy, Bell left. Oscar, in his own world, often talked with Mr. Bingle, doing both voices. The puppet master would eat, drink, and sleep his work, says Bell, but the emphasis, unfortunately, was on drink, and at times he didn't show up for work.

In midsummer 1985, an employee checking on Oscar, who had been truant for days, found him on the floor of his home, dead of a heart attack. He was sixty-two and penniless. Maison Blanche paid his funeral expenses. He was buried in Hebrew Rest No. 3 Cemetery in Gentilly.

Mr. Bingle himself continued on our payroll until we sold the store in 1992. We introduced him in our Baton Rouge, Lafayette, and Florida stores. In Baton Rouge, we regularly sent him, bearing candy canes and holiday cheer, to the children's wards of the two hospitals. Mr. B. carried on his Christmas greetings with but a single change: From the day Oscar died, Mr. Bingle never "spoke" another word. His unique, high-pitched voice died with Oscar Isentrout.

Mr. Bingle still lives. In 2006, he became part of Celebration in the Oaks, a New Orleans holiday tradition in City Park. Dillard's had ended up owning the celebrated character after buying Maison Blanche in 1998. He was gathering dust in a forgotten storage area, and the store was persuaded to loan him to the annual celebration. Mr. Bingle thus became part of the post–Hurricane Katrina healing in that city.

The Louisiana World Exposition, as the World's Fair officially was known, closed in November 1984, a total bust for New Orleans. The fair lost more than $100 million. Most of the previous fairs also had lost money; they

< A life-size Mr. Bingle stands with Santa.

mainly had been catalysts for urban renewal projects, which certainly was true in New Orleans. (There has not been another world's fair held in the United States since.) Officials had estimated they would need 12 million attendees to turn a profit, but only 7 million went through the turnstiles.

Thanks to solid prefair analysis, Maison Blanche did not take the same bath. D. H. Holmes, our major competitor in the Big Easy, purchased $10 million in fair-related goods, most of it with the World's Fair logo. Holmes even leased twenty outlets at the event and dedicated three managers to oversee operations there. Our buyers submitted projections of selling $1.5 million in fair-related goods, a rather reasonable forecast given that Holmes was planning to sell more than six times that amount.

Before approving those modest plans, I sent two junior managers on a scouting trip to Knoxville, Tennessee, site of the previous World's Fair. Their reports were chilling. Knoxville's two leading department stores had achieved only mediocre sales of fair merchandise and overall were helped only marginally by the event. I therefore cut our purchase orders to $300,000 and permitted only one buyer to purchase fair goods. Only he could book the merchandise. We were able to market all of it by fair's end, and realized a small profit.

Even though our operations were doing fairly well, and our debt was down to $9 million, economic storm clouds accompanied the closure of the World's Fair. Goudchaux's/Maison Blanche eliminated 70 middle management positions in anticipation of a downturn. The state's economy went south in 1985, with unemployment running 11 percent. The following year, the figure was more than 13 percent, some 50 percent higher than the national average. The state was operating with a $200 million deficit.

As noted earlier with regard to City Stores, department stores nationally were having problems. The Holmes chain reported a $2.2 million loss for the third quarter of 1985—a period that's normally good for retailers. And several months later, Kreeger's, a New Orleans group of specialty stores featuring mostly women's apparel and furs, sought bankruptcy.

We began to concentrate on cutting costs in anticipation of near-term profit problems. Profits were up, but sales increases were hard to come by with one in eight Louisianians out of work. The store's executive committee was charged with creating a cost structure that permitted a 10 percent pretax profit. That was what we needed for a growth rate that doubled profits every seven to eight years. In addition to 70 managerial jobs, we eliminated the catalog department. We had about 4,000 full- and part-time employees, and I wanted another 100 of their positions eliminated.

I specifically asked for "positions" rather than "people." As with the earlier 70, natural turnover within a workforce as large as ours normally would achieve a 5 percent downsizing of non-sales personnel without our resorting to layoffs. (We wanted no reduction in the *sales* force. The last thing we needed was to lessen service.) With so many people out of work, however, job turnover was lower than in normal years; there wasn't always another opening for those whose positions were ended.

Around this time, Leon Godchaux Clothing of New Orleans filed for bankruptcy. Although that company had made several attempts to complicate our lives over the years, the family was honorable. It was sad—if not a little scary—to see a 140-year-old company crumble. One of the national financial reporting services, the Jewelers Board of Trade, confused our store name with Leon Godchaux Clothing and reported the bankruptcy filing of Goudchaux's. I was furious. Several hundred telephone calls and letters poured in, many of them from vendors. It was a real pain. The conversations between the trade board and me were more than blistering; stuff hit the fan, believe me.

We settled for a strong letter of correction, which I wrote and they signed and distributed to all the reporting service's members. In addition, the board issued a public announcement, and we received a long-overdue upgrade of our credit rating. We had a slam-dunk case for financial damages, but who wants to spend the rest of his life in court?

By the mid-1980s, our overall business was good; life was good. The family had a relatively large, profitable enter-

Donna and I with our children in the early 1980s

prise that required strong, daily direction. It was precisely the time to discuss with our children what they should do if something happened to Josef and me. We weren't being morbid, just prudent. There was an unwritten prompt for this sort of action, one I have not openly discussed before: the refugee mentality and the survival instincts that accompany it. Charles Darwin put it this way: "It is not the strongest of the species that survive, nor the most intelligent, but the one most responsive to change."

If Josef and I died, there would be confusion and angst over the business. The first line of heirs—Lea, Insa, Donna, and Mary Ann—were not interested in running the stores. Neither was Insa's daughter, Leigh Ann, who was working full-time at an MB branch in New Orleans.

Josef's and my children were in high school. Our recommendation in our just-in-case letter was to act firmly and sell, outlining the route to accomplish that objective. (That step-by-step process can be found in Appendix 2.)

Despite Josef's and my prudence, it turned out that I was the one who would pull the trigger on a sale.

Life may have been good, but it certainly wasn't routine. During the early 1980s, the issue of Sunday closures came to a head. The closing law had been enacted by the Baton Rouge city council in 1818 and was thought by historians to be the oldest in the Mississippi Valley. We had taken a rather unusual stance for aggressive retailers in dealing with the 168-year-old "blue law." We supported it.

A blue law is a type of ordinance that enforces moral standards, usually surrounding the observance of a Christian Sabbath. These types of statutes began with Puritan colonists in the 1600s. It is a common misconception that they got their name from blue paper on which Puritans inscribed them. "Blue" was a common, disparaging adjective assigned to rigid moral codes of the eighteenth century and beyond.

These laws were particularly plentiful in southern and midwestern states, often enacted to control Seventh-day Adventists, Jews, non-religious types, and saloon owners. Today, most blue laws have been repealed, declared unconstitutional, or are simply not enforced—but not all. Some remain for convenience. In Louisiana, for example, auto dealers still open are under a prohibition against making a sale on Sunday. A vast majority of them support the law because it allows a day off without fear of competitors ignoring the law. Our support of Sunday closing stemmed from practical considerations plus a desire to have a day of reverence. The anticlosure argument revolved around lost revenue and taxes, but we were not persuaded.

By 1984, Louisiana remained one of the few states in the nation that maintained Sunday statutes against most kinds of retailing. A year later, authorities in New Orleans publicly declared they would no longer enforce Sunday closings. But the law in Baton Rouge continued on a selective basis, with many enterprises legally exempted. Even there, however, support for the law was waning, and significant cracks in enforcement were forming. A federal lawsuit brought an initial response from the judge that the law might well be unconstitutional. In 1984, Josef and I wrote a letter to the editor of *The Morning Advocate* in support of Sunday closings. We based our pro-closure argument on the quality of life of our customers and employees, the preservation of family time, and keeping one day of the week for reflection and prayer.

"It is easy to scoff at those things," we wrote, "but should we? Are we ready to sacrifice yet another bit to commercialism? Are we wise to let the tensions and frustrations of business encroach even more on the way we live? We believe [Sunday openings] will be a mistake . . . [If the judge strikes down the law], the result will be that the majority become the losers."

That said, we were realists, and we clearly stated the obvious: If all department stores remained closed on Sundays, no one would lose business. If one opened, all would have to follow suit (including MB) or suffer financial consequences. We would lose being closed when others were open; but we wouldn't necessarily win if all of us opened on the seventh day. Customers spend roughly the same, whether that spending is spread over six or seven days.

More than a year later, when New Orleans had all but opened on Sunday, we wrote a statement for *The Times-Picayune*, noting that opening was a shopping trend that had gradually spread through the country and reached the New Orleans area. We had been among the leaders in attempting to retain the statute and were among the few major department stores to close on Sundays. We continued: "It has always been Maison Blanche's publicly stated view, however, that competition could force us to alter that position. That time has now come." We would have employees work every third Sunday only. Exceptions would be made for volunteers who *wanted* to work Sundays and for those who could not because of religious restrictions. The Sunday doors at the New Orleans stores were opened at noon and closed at 6 p.m. for the first time on October 27, 1985.

Nine months later, the situation fell apart in Baton Rouge. The legislature had repealed the blue laws, effective December 1, 1986, but some stores began jumping the gun. We prepared to follow suit on June 8, 1986, with the same hours we were keeping in New Orleans. There had been rumors flying that D. H. Holmes would open on Sunday in early June. I phoned Holmes chairman Robert Fiddler to dissuade him. He said he was defending the store against Sears. I promised to keep Goudchaux's closed if he did so with Holmes in Baton Rouge. He would not agree.

The East Baton Rouge Parish sheriff and the Baton Rouge police chief vowed to enforce the law until it was repealed on December 1, so Fiddler changed his mind about opening his store. Unfortunately, he "forgot" to inform us, and we opened our Cortana branch on June 8 in anticipation of matching Holmes, only to have Holmes become missing in action. The police arrived and began issuing a misdemeanor citation to our branch manager. I walked in and insisted my name, as the owner, be put on the citation rather than his. I reasoned the lawyers could worry. I never heard another word about it.

From a public standpoint, the first half of the 1980s saw a number of memorable events for our company. We were accepted as members of Associated Merchandising Corporation (AMC), the world's largest and most exclusive buying office, with members such as Bloomingdale's of New York and Rich's of Atlanta. The accompanying prestige and buying power were enormous. In addition, we built an off-site television production studio for our in-house advertising and began accepting outside work. Our travel agencies exploded in size and services.

The most exciting new venture—one that would have lasting impact—was the creation of an insurance division. The seeds were planted in 1974, when we started a small insurance agency as part of our financial efforts. That was the year my friend Fred Dent persuaded me to speak at an LSU program for insurance executives. Twenty companies were represented in the audience. I suggested that one of them establish an agency at Goudchaux's. As an alternative, I urged them to market products through the store by training personnel I would hire.

Those companies weren't interested, and neither were eight or nine others I contacted around the country through the years. The lack of enthusiasm for the enterprise left me little choice: I vowed to start my own insurance entity. The impetus came when an existing company, Security Industrial Insurance of Donaldsonville, Louisiana, owned by E. J. Ourso (after whom the LSU School of Business is named), refused to allow Goudchaux/Maison Blanche to sell his burial insurance product.

Moderate-income families demonstrably need small policies. We contacted Ourso because his was the largest business in that field and had the best product. He initially agreed that we could sell it. With fanfare, I announced the new program to our staff. Three days before our launch, however, E. J. called and reneged on his commitment. I was angry and publicly embarrassed.

Ourso claimed he had received complaints from his agents that our department store was too large and that if he allowed Goudchaux's to sell his policies, he would jeopardize his relationship with his stable of two hundred agents. I mentally cursed. However, the last-minute cancellation gave me the extra incentive to form my own insurance company, and I did so that very year. Henceforth, we would feature our own products and be dependent on no one. We began in 1983, calling it Goudchaux's Life Insurance Company and, within a short time, changed the name to Maison Blanche Life.

(I kept the insurance business when we sold in 1992, renaming it Starmount Life. "Sternberg" translates from German to English as "starmount," a mountain so tall it touches the stars. That resonates when you are trying to sell life insurance.)

When I opened the insurance entity, Josef automatically owned half, because he and I shared in almost every business transaction. The only exception: a $24,000 investment in rats. A college roommate of Josef's convinced him to help start an experimental rat farm that produced rodents for hospital labs and research facilities. I declined to contribute my share of $12,000, and I turned out to be right. The rat farm venture folded. I, however, am not so sure the family and Josef didn't get $24,000 worth of laughs over the years in recalling it.

Perhaps the most incredible proposal ever to come before us did so in late 1984. It was the deal of deals, the dream of every retailer. We were offered a profitable New York City department store chain at no cost.

And we turned it down!

B. Altman's, headquartered in the Big Apple, was showing a sales volume close to a quarter of a billion dollars annually, but profits were less than 1 percent. It was owned by a tax-free foundation run by the Catholic church, and was being sold under government order. (Recent federal regulation prohibited charitable foundations from owning for-profit businesses.)

The five B. Altman stores along with the Altman business were valuable assets, even though real estate in New York City at the time was severely depressed. Bids arrived from across the nation. The winner, with an offer of $110 million, was a group of investors led by Mort Olshan of New York City, with whom we had forged strong ties while developing our branch stores. The foundation imposed a pair of iron-clad stipulations the winning bidder was required to honor: a guarantee that the operations of the department stores would be continued and that the retail operator be acceptable to the foundation. The foundation's concern was the continued employment of B. Altman employees.

Mort only wanted the real estate, not the business. The retailer with whom he had made the bid, Sandy Zimmerman, was judged by the market as only an average merchant. He had tax problems and little wealth of his own. Mort became concerned. Familiar with our success in New Orleans, he called to offer us a piece of the action. Initially, he proposed we take one-third ownership at no cost, along with a pledge of an additional one-third vote, which would give us two-thirds control. The operating third would belong to Zimmerman, the former president of Abraham & Straus Department Stores.

While our share of B. Altman's was to be gratis, there would be sizable capital needs: $80 million to $90 million to operate the stores and an additional $44 million to remodel the Fifth Avenue store and its branches. The money was readily available, but we turned down the deal because it was not a practical mix: The Sternbergs would be in Baton Rouge. Zimmerman, on the ground at the store, would be calling the shots. We could only lend advice and guidance.

Mort called back a week later, asking if we would take the entire business at no cost. This was an unbelievable, once-in-a-lifetime offer. B. Altman's had a provable net worth of $15 million, which would be ours just for operating it. Mort believed we could turn the business around, just as we had with Maison Blanche. He would get percentage rents on the volume and was gambling we would increase sales, which we probably would have. Again, we declined.

Lea made the point: Our dad often said that one of his strengths was knowing how far his money would take him. Having just remodeled four stores in 1983, opened another store and an eight-story parking garage in 1984, and announced a much-needed expansion of Goudchaux's Main Street for 1985, we already owed more than $42 million. Furthermore, Josef or I would have to move to New York City, breaking up the partnership we considered our greatest strength.

Although we would have free title to the store, remodeling and operating costs would have required more than a $100 million outlay. Experience dictated that was too much debt to assume. To strike out on a new venture involving major borrowings would not continue the conservative mode to which Goudchaux's/Maison Blanche previously had adhered. (Dad liked the traditional concept of a single store because there was little need for branches during his time and malls were unknown. We didn't expand geographically until about ten years after his death.)

Mother liked the homey 1930s/1940s family-owned department store, but she also knew we couldn't stand still. "If you want to progress, you have to go with the times," she would say, adding that she did not think Josef and I would have liked it if the store had remained as small as when we started. She was spot on there.

As the calendar pages flipped to 1987, we had seven stores turning $227 million in annual sales. True, the last two years had seen only 4 percent and 3 percent sales growth, respectively, a far cry from the double-digit annual increases of the early 1980s, but we had just gone through an economic slump characterized by high unemployment and reduced consumer spending. By every measure, Goudchaux's/Maison Blanche was doing better than most of its peers.

The message we heard: Opportunities await. The Altman decision notwithstanding, it was time to go shopping.

10 | HIGH WATER MARK

IN THE LATE 1980s, a letter to the editor appeared in *The Baton Rouge Morning Advocate* from one O. W. Stevens, who challenged Louisiana governor Edwin Edwards' parting excuse that "state government cannot be run like Goudchaux's."

"A person *can* run the state like Goudchaux's," countered Stevens, "and lower taxes and be reelected."

Edwards' successor, Democrat Buddy Roemer, a former congressman who switched to the Republican party during his term as governor, must have read the letter and concurred. Just before taking office in 1988, he asked me to "lend" him my chief financial officer, Brian Kendrick, to help the state emerge from a severe shortfall by "scrubbing" the budget. I did—but I placed a six-month limit on the loan. We would continue to give Kendrick the difference between what the state paid and Brian's store salary.

Roemer's request underscored the quality of our managers. Over the years, we nurtured a good number of Goudchaux's/Maison Blanche employees. In 1990 Kendrick went to Saks Fifth Avenue to become its CFO at a salary of approximately $600,000, about double what we were paying him. (When Saks made the offer, Brian asked me what he should do. I told him to take it.) Sadly, he died a few years later—of a heart attack at the age of fifty-six. He was hardly the only sharp arrow in the store's quiver. His successor, Steve Tisdell, who was with us until we sold, was even better.

One Goudchaux's/Maison Blanche alum became the CEO of Arrow Shirt Company; others spread through the national department store ranks in senior positions. There were many gems, people like Tom Cagley and John Olson. They came to us knowing the opportunities we had to offer them. Cagley wrote that people joined Goudchaux's/Maison Blanche "to work hard and enjoy the fruits of their efforts, and if you put your heart into it, the store became your mother and your father. It was your family and as one went we all went. And it was a merchandising family. Two merchants ran the store, not a controller or the personnel department or advertising or operations. As a whole, what was good for the merchants was good for all."

Indeed, we were merchants. Josef and I took pride in being keen judges of talent and character, as a story from the late 1960s demonstrates. ADT, a large company specializing in security management systems, nearly had a lock (no pun intended) on business from Baton Rouge banks, jewelry stores, and department stores because of its patented burglar-alarm equipment. We were one of ADT's largest local customers.

One day, two regional ADT managers brought the newly hired local manager to our Main Street store to introduce him. Josef and I stood with them on the sales floor and chatted, learning in the process that the new manager had once operated jewelry stores in Gulfport,

Mississippi, and later in Baton Rouge. We all shook hands, and they left.

Josef and I took a couple of steps down the store's aisle, turned to each other, and simultaneously agreed that something was wrong. The guy registered on our dishonest radar. He came across as a potential *ganof* (thief). We called some downtown friends, who confirmed our suspicion: This person, who was about to oversee most of the security in Baton Rouge, had several years earlier been charged with faking robberies at his Gulfport and Baton Rouge jewelry stores in order to collect the insurance. We relayed that information to ADT immediately, and the company got rid of him. The city had dodged a major bullet.

Our ability to judge the potential of acquisitions also showed a solid record. As we grew, success followed. With Goudchaux's expansion from its lone Main Street store, revenues doubled. When we purchased Maison Blanche a few years later, sales volume doubled. So, two years after opening our Canal Street Maison Blanche location, we were on the prowl again.

It is fair to ask, Why tinker with something that ain't broken? We had a good thing going. The answer is that life is not single faceted. Neither are careers, nor the arcs of businesses. We were ambitious, and good things were happening. Josef and I liked to see business and people grow, and we were good at making that happen.

Even when the economy was less than robust, Goudchaux's/Maison Blanche seldom held back on investing in expansion and enhancements. By 1986, for example, we completed the final remodeling of the Main Street store: an $8 million facelift and a 28,000-square-foot addition to the selling space, both of which came in the middle of an economic downturn in Louisiana. The renovation expanded the building's length to 971 feet, earning us that coveted spot in *Ripley's Believe It or Not* as the longest building in the world built as a department store.

By 1986, Goudchaux's Main Street footprint, counting warehouse and corporate offices, was spread over 340,000 square feet—the physically largest retailing operation under a single roof in Baton Rouge, if not the entire state. (The record was the flagship Maison Blanche store on Canal Street prior to our acquiring it. That store boasted nearly a half million square feet devoted to retailing. We reduced its retailing area to about 170,000 square feet when we opened in 1984.)

We also were in the midst of constructing a 740-vehicle parking garage and an 89,000-square-foot addition to the Clearview Maison Blanche store. We also had agreed to open a 112,000-square-foot branch in a new mall at Slidell, a bedroom community northeast of New Orleans. It would be smaller than our normal branches—which averaged 150,000 square feet—and the last store we built.

On the drawing board was a third store in Baton Rouge, near Interstate 10, a deal that fell through when we sold. We also expanded our distribution center in Baton Rouge to 160,000 square feet.

In the spring of 1986, we became interested in the Cain-Sloan stores in Nashville. They seemed ripe since Allied Stores, their owner, was having financial troubles. We also were interested in the much larger Joske's chain in Texas. Joske's, too, was owned by Allied but had just been purchased by corporate raider Robert Campeau of Toronto for $4.3 billion. Campeau, who in a few years would be bankrupt, planned to sell some properties. We expressed our interest in Joske's and Cain-Sloan, and entered a waiting game for Allied's new owner to establish the rules for proceeding.

Five months later, while still talking with Campeau's people, I received a call from First Boston, Campeau's investment banking house, informing me that bidding for Joske's was moot. Dillard's Department Stores of Little Rock had submitted to Allied a preemptive bid of $255 million for Joske's, including $30 million in real estate.

I was surprised and disappointed but had no serious complaint other than the $225,000 I had spent on attorneys, accountants, travel, and so on. Had we been allowed to bid, our offer would have been $227 million. My sense was that Dillard's overpaid by $28 million, but with $2 billion in annual sales, Dillard's could afford to make such a mistake. We couldn't.

After we discovered in the spring of 1987 that Joske's was off the table, Josef and I were in a down mood and began casting about for new opportunities. Goldsmith's

Ripley's Believe It or Not plaque recognizing Goudchaux's as the world's longest building built as a department store, 1986

in Memphis remained tempting, and I explored that possibility. We made a preemptive, $140 million bid to Federated for Goldsmith's after touring the stores. The stores' volume was $165 million, so the price worked in our computer model. We thought we had tendered an offer Federated could not refuse. But two weeks later, it did just that.

Josef had better luck. In July, he made contact with Tom Hays, president of the May Company department store chain, who invited us to his St. Louis headquarters to discuss some Florida properties. CFO Brian Kendrick, Josef, and I were in Hays' office five days later. The properties in play ended up being Robinson's Department Stores, a string of operations in central Florida, based in St. Petersburg. We had been expecting a general discussion of facts and figures in our initial meeting with Hays, but he astounded us by saying his company was prepared

to sell that instant. We forged an agreement-in-principle in about three hours. Negotiations over the details went smoothly and consumed less than two weeks.

We paid $121 million for 10 stores located in Orlando (3 sites), Tampa (2 sites), Clearwater, St. Petersburg, Sarasota, Fort Myers, and Naples, along with a state-of-the-art distribution center. An eleventh store remained part of the deal since Robinson's was under contract to build in Lakeland, Florida. (Completed in 1988, it was a standard 110,000-square-foot operation that cost us an additional $10 million-plus.) May's price tag was high but within reason.

Florida was booming when we negotiated to buy the Robinson's stores. The state's 800-pound department store gorillas were Maas Brothers, based in Tampa, and Burdines of Miami, originally owned by Allied and Feder-

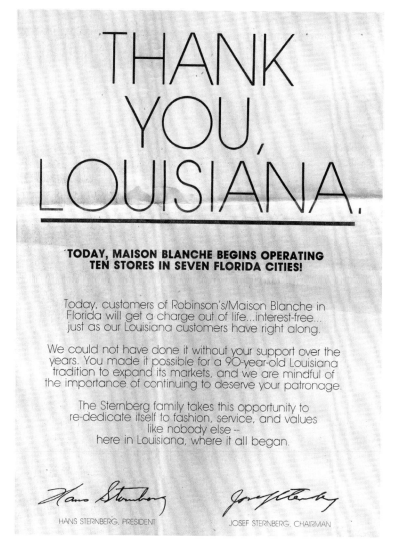

THANK YOU, LOUISIANA.

TODAY, MAISON BLANCHE BEGINS OPERATING TEN STORES IN SEVEN FLORIDA CITIES!

Today, customers of Robinson's/Maison Blanche in Florida will get a charge out of life...interest-free... just as our Louisiana customers have right along.

We could not have done it without your support over the years. You made it possible for a 90-year-old Louisiana tradition to expand its markets, and we are mindful of the importance of continuing to deserve your patronage.

The Sternberg family takes this opportunity to re-dedicate itself to fashion, service, and values like nobody else -- here in Louisiana, where it all began.

HANS STERNBERG, PRESIDENT

JOSEF STERNBERG, CHAIRMAN

Newspaper ad announcing Maison Blanche's incursion into Florida in 1987

ated, respectively, before those two giants merged. Maas and Burdines had both existed more than fifty years by the time Associated Dry Goods Corporation of New York created Robinson's in the early 1960s in the center of Florida's burgeoning population. It targeted a middle-to-upscale clientele. May Company bought Robinson's in 1986 as part of a larger acquisition and, finding itself in need of cash, almost immediately flipped it to us.

We took ownership of Robinson's in the fall of 1987, only two months after Hays shook Josef's and my hands on the deal—an amazingly swift acquisition. We had every reason to be optimistic. Our single concern of substance was the breadth of the operation: Seventeen stores, ten of which were nearly one thousand miles away, would stretch our management. We hired a vice president for our Florida operations, Joe Isola, who had been an executive with Joske's. (He later parted in a huff over a corporate decision to reduce the territory under his authority.) Isola's presence notwithstanding, Josef and I each spent two days per month inspecting the Florida stores; plus, one of us spent at least one day in the New Orleans stores every week.

Our optimism aside, we experienced an unexpectedly bumpy entry into the central Florida market. There normally are surprises in mergers, and they are seldom pleasant ones: Your merchandise doesn't match, your customer files are on another computer, and so on. Mergers are fraught with heartburn.

Wanting a clean break from Robinson's, every item had to be replaced, right down to the price tags. The stores had been run inefficiently. Indeed, Robinson's sales volume of $101 per square foot was the second worst among May's department store divisions. Furthermore, in the last few years, Robinson's had replaced some of its higher-end items with cheaper goods. As a result, many of its more affluent customers drifted to Maas or Burdines.

There also was a morale problem. Personnel had been faced with three owners in less than a year. We eliminated more than 260 positions in Robinson's corporate office, along with four of the ten store managers. Personnel cuts occurred immediately, but were avoided thereafter. Josef and I visited every store, reassuring the remaining employees and managers, and being candid about the future. We made it clear where merchandise, promotion policies, and operating style would change. We spent a lot of time in Florida during that transition. When it came to the name on the building, it took eight months to transition from Robinson's to Robinson's/Maison Blanche to Maison Blanche/Robinson's to Maison Blanche.

Our purchase agreement called for Robinson's to liquidate its older merchandise before the formal handover in September. "This Is It!" sales generated a stampede of bargain hunters. They descended on sales floors like rabbits on a vegetable patch. Home-furnishings departments were stripped bare. We had a major logistical problem getting merchandise replenished fast enough.

Our goal was to improve the quality of the merchandise, but our purchasing staff in Baton Rouge was overwhelmed. Additionally, we were slow to fully understand the buying habits of Floridians, especially during the August-to-October period. Louisiana's back-to-school merchandise consisted of heavier, darker goods. Not so in Florida. It was shorts and sleeveless tops.

New to us, too, was the Florida tourist trade, which comes into significant play between October and March. Many of the tourists stayed longer, especially the sizable part of the population known as "snow birds," residents of northern states who migrate to Florida in winter and return "home" in the summer. Snow birds stay in Florida a minimum of six months and one day so they can claim Florida residency and take advantage of the state's lack of an inheritance tax.

Generally, Maison Blanche customers had household incomes in the late 1980s that ran between $35,000 and $50,000. In areas where we had the Robinson's stores, the household incomes tended to be lower than our Louisiana Maison Blanche demographic. Our customers had been fashion conscious and service sensitive. Now we had to broaden our appeal to a more casual Florida shopper. The latter liked brighter colors and white year-round. They were highly attuned to garment weight. There was a difference between New Orleans glitz and Florida glitz.

Merchandising problems plagued us through November. They might have sunk an ordinary chain, but Goudchaux's/Maison Blanche had a hole card unmatched by its Florida competitors or any other major retailer in the region: interest-free credit. Our credit policy was as popular in Florida as it was in Louisiana. Most of the other stores were charging 19 percent interest per annum on their charge accounts. Free credit got us through those difficult initial months.

By December, higher-quality inventories were on the shelves, our customer service was not only noticed but talked about, and free gift wrapping awaited Christmas customers. We introduced Mr. Bingle, along with a pre-

Christmas early store opening and a Cracker Jack giveaway in which many of the boxes of caramel popcorn and nuts contained discount coupons. One box of Cracker Jacks in each store contained a $500 diamond ring. The customers loved it. (Fortunately, no one accidentally swallowed a ring.) The Maison Blanche motto, "Like Nobody Else," began to resonate in Florida.

It didn't take long for competitors to respond—two of them with what I thought were suicidal tactics. Maas discounted everything in the store by 20 percent for three days. Ivey's took 25 percent off its entire stock for three days. Maison Blanche countered by offering nine popular items at 40 percent off. My rationale is fundamental: Customers do not buy entire stores; they shop for desired items. Steeper discounts on limited selections, if frequently offered, should attract more customers and produce larger volumes with a smaller hit to profits. They populate the store with people who buy other things.

We began converting the Florida employees to commissions rather than salaries. Although hesitant at first, the new associates soon found their paychecks growing. It wasn't long before MB salaries, supplemented by 25 percent discounts on personal purchases (including clearance items), exceeded those offered by competitors. Word got out, and more often than not, we got the pick of the applicant pool.

Morale also improved when we empowered branch managers and buyers to make their own merchandising decisions. "Employees feel like they're included now," one Tampa store divisional manager told *The Jacksonville Times-Union*. We should have started that program earlier and developed it more extensively.

At the same point, we decided to streamline our name to Maison Blanche. It was time for "Goudchaux's" to go. We were already using just "Maison Blanche" in New Orleans, Lafayette, and Florida, but the two Baton Rouge stores retained the hybrid "Goudchaux's/Maison Blanche." We wanted to make the names consistent throughout the chain. There was one significant hitch, however, in our MB-only strategy: Lea Sternberg.

I was sitting with Don Bell and some high-rolling marketing types from New York who were hired to over-

Future First Lady Barbara Bush poses with the Sternberg family during a campaign stop at the Sternberg home in 1988.

see the name switch. Lea walked in and announced we would not be changing the name. "The people of Baton Rouge do not like the name 'Maison Blanche,' so thank you for coming. You can go back home."

I did a "Now, Lea . . ." response, to which she answered, "This is my store, and I am not going to change the name." And she wheeled around and walked out. The group kept on talking until she returned a few minutes later. "Did you not hear me?" she asked. "I said you could go now." We compromised. In Baton Rouge, the "Goudchaux's" sign physically would remain on the buildings below "Maison Blanche."

Mother and I disagreed a lot over the years. We each had strong opinions and were equally stubborn. The arguments, however, were never personal.

* * *

In addition to the business, we were active civically. The store always could be counted on when it came to the arts, especially the Baton Rouge Symphony. We were one of the orchestra's major underwriters. Josef's attachment to the symphony was particularly strong, and there is a great story entwined with that enthusiasm.

In the late 1980s, during a visit to New York City, Baton Rouge mayor Pat Screen noticed that the Birmingham Symphony was playing Carnegie Hall. If an orchestra from Alabama could rate that famous venue, the mayor reasoned, so could one from Baton Rouge. So he called and booked an engagement.

Only after a contract had been signed did Screen learn that the featured Birmingham symphony was from

Birmingham, England—not neighboring Alabama. Nevertheless, the entire Baton Rouge orchestra traveled to the Big Apple and appeared in the famous hall. A large contingent from our city, including Josef and Mary Ann, was in the audience, along with a host of friends and relatives from the New York area. The orchestra delivered a magnificent performance during its moment in the sun.

After Josef died, Mary Ann created the Josef Sternberg Memorial Fund, which helps underwrite many worthy arts, educational, and public radio causes. My mother funded the Erich and Lea Sternberg Honors Professorship, annually awarded by the LSU Honors College.

In 1987, New Orleans received a visit from its biggest world dignitary ever—Pope John Paul II. The crowds would be enormous for the September 11–13 papal visit, and the Catholic archdiocese of New Orleans called a meeting of retailers to plan what the stores along Canal Street would do in terms of welcoming displays on their building exteriors. Although many retailers were at the meeting, I was the only CEO and could therefore announce decisions on the spot. The rest had to go back and get corporate approval.

Maison Blanche would go all out celebrating the occasion, I said, and if the others wanted to keep pace they would have to stretch their budgets, which I urged them to do. For that, I received a certificate from Archbishop Philip Hannan expressing his appreciation, a document that hangs in my office to this day. I also was given the opportunity to be among those at a private welcoming. The pope spoke briefly to us.

Goudchaux's/Maison Blanche's game was retailing and growth, so it is not surprising that Josef and I were back in the hunt following the Robinson's acquisition. We liked what we saw in Florida. Our stores were doing relatively well. Word came in May 1989 that, in order to solve financial problems, D. H. Holmes had sold to Dillard's, and Campeau lost control of Federated in August. Our new Maison Blanche president, John Irvin, tagged Campeau's rise and fall accurately when he said Campeau did not add value to Federated. The attorneys made money, but the customers lost.

Bloomingdale's, Saks Fifth Avenue, and Marshall Field's were on the block, as were Burdines and Maas—undoubtedly along with every other property Campeau owned. There was nothing fundamentally wrong with most of those stores. The department store had been around for a hundred years, withstanding the test of time. It helped shape American culture in the middle third of the twentieth century.

But the financial landscape changed in the 1980s. The investment-banking community found ways, through junk bonds and "free" money mechanisms, to raise unheard-of sums, which they put into the hands of speculators who had no knowledge of how to operate department stores. They loaned money at interest rates that exceeded 17 percent. No matter that some of the deals didn't make sense: Investment bankers are like bird dogs; they will hunt with anyone who has a gun.

The failures stemmed primarily from investment mistakes, not the department store concept. There was too much money available. I believed at the time that the industry would survive and return to sound footing, although my retailing colleagues would be fewer in number owing to consolidations. The big guys would get bigger, and the little guys would disappear.

Thus, our need to grow.

We began talks with May Company in late 1987 for five stores, known as May-Cohen, which May had bought from the Virginia-based Cohen Brothers in 1959. Four of the stores were in Jacksonville and one in Daytona Beach. They would complement our other ten Florida stores nicely and give us a highly coveted location in downtown Jacksonville. May, however, wasn't interested in selling.

Six months later, the situation changed. May purchased Foley's (of Houston) and Filene's (of Boston) department stores from Federated at a cost of $1.6 billion. May needed to pay down some of its debt and offered to sell us the five May-Cohen stores. We were interested. The additional properties would give us a presence in both central and northeast Florida. And with our Robinson's operation up and running, there would be no additional corporate overhead.

(May's official public line was that Maison Blanche

contacted May. Just the opposite occurred this second time. May-Cohen was the smallest division in the May department store fleet, and the parent company felt it consumed more management attention than it was worth.)

The Jacksonville operation was most like Baton Rouge, and Jacksonville became our most profitable Florida city. The Daytona Beach store, located near the NASCAR race track, was the least successful. Daytona was a middle-class resort community where residents and tourists overwhelmingly embraced a casual dress style, which wasn't Maison Blanche's forte.

The approximately $62 million base sale price provided that May formally hand over the stores to Maison Blanche on August 1, 1988 (although the operation oversight of the credit accounts would not come until the middle of the following January). The purchase gave us a total of fifteen stores in Florida and boosted our volume to $440 million annually.

We had done it! With a stroke of the pen (not to mention millions of dollars), Maison Blanche became the largest family-owned department store chain in the nation—and we still had under construction two stores that would contribute to our annual volume. Runner-up with $344 million in annual volume was McRae's, based in Jackson, Mississippi.

One of the May-Cohen stores was turning only $4 million in annual sales. We knew from the start it would have to be closed. May Company had been hesitant to do so because it served an African American section of the city. We were equally sensitive, but the difference was we were too small to carry the burden of an anemic unit. Our Florida team met with the city's black leaders and explained the problem. They understood, and we closed the branch without incident. All of the store's employees were offered jobs in other MB stores.

Jacksonville was abuzz at the prospect of a new, upscale department store. "Where May Florida was known as corporate cool," noted *The Jacksonville Times Union* in a July 1988 article, "Maison Blanche has the peculiarities of a mom-and-pop operation. Known as an aggressive, innovative merchandiser, Maison Blanche offers interest-free charge accounts, designer merchandise, and an old-fashioned style of retailing where customer service reigns."

The chatter centered on the fact that Maison Blanche was bringing to Jacksonville fine jewelry and furs, Ferragamo shoes, and other designer apparel. The down side for the city was that prior to our signing papers, May-Cohen closed its corporate office in Jacksonville, laying off 325 employees, and shuttered its distribution center. We kept all 975 employees at the four branches and 20 people from management.

Converting the four May-Cohen units to Maison Blanche was smooth. We had learned lessons from our takeover of the St. Petersburg-based Robinson's. First, we replaced the merchandise much faster and without depleting inventories. The store's name was changed to Maison Blanche within two months. We now were familiar with the clothing requirements of Floridians, which, in Jacksonville, were closer to what we were used to in Baton Rouge. (In 1990, we built our twenty-fourth store— at the Mall of the Avenues in Jacksonville. It was a magnificent facility with more than 181,000 square feet chock full of fashionable merchandise.) To underscore that we meant business and were there to stay, Maison Blanche budgeted $7 million to $9 million per store for renovations and face-lifts.

All this activity, however, was creating a sizable debt burden. It had risen to $200 million and was rapidly increasing. We had expected to pay off the two purchases of the Florida stores in five years. After all, it had taken us less than three years to eliminate the debt on the Maison Blanche purchase owing to the healthy boost in sales that followed. This time, however, that sort of return did not materialize. Thus, in January 1988, I was forced to meet with Manufacturers Hanover Bank of New York City and Republic Bank of Dallas to explore long-term financing.

It was a mistake to bring them together. To my chagrin, I watched the two financial institutions decide how they were going to maximize their profits. Had we kept them apart, we would have been able to pit one against the other. Still, I was not overly concerned. Business was good. It took two years for the Florida stores to kick in, but by 1990 our 24 stores were churning close to a half billion dollars in sales. The boom in Florida was helping us weather a somewhat depressed Louisiana.

We were one of the most productive department store chains in America, even though our Florida stores originally pulled us from a sales volume of $260 per square foot down to $192. We had 8,000 full- and part-time employees (nearly 9,000 during the Christmas season) and were the thirty-ninth-largest department store operation in the nation. As Josef would tell people, "I think we have enough to say grace over."

One unnamed business executive was quoted in a business publication as saying Goudchaux's/Maison Blanche was "one of the premier operations in the country, in profitability, productivity, and management. They don't like being second to anybody."

Black ink notwithstanding, we initiated a fallback position that Josef and I had discussed many times: going public. Our business plan projected such a move would not be necessary. We hoped and believed that would be correct. If it didn't happen that way, we were prudently putting in place the things needed for issuing stock to the public. The infrastructure for going public would be created as a parachute in case raising additional capital became necessary.

My feeling was that after a business reaches a certain size, opening it for public investment could become attractive. Josef wasn't keen on the idea, but he was resigned to it. We both knew that our children were not old enough to run the business. I told *New Orleans City Business* in 1989 that Maison Blanche would attempt to go public "some day, no question about it, but it might be ten years from now." It ended up being more like ten months.

Our nation headed off to a Middle East war, interest rates moved upward, and a national recession loomed on the horizon like a perfect Gulf storm as 1990 progressed. In late December, I also lost my business partner of thirty years.

11 STORM CLOUDS

AS CHARLES DICKENS WOULD have put it, 1990 was the best of years and the worst of years. We reached the apex of our now reasonably large, family-owned business with the opening of newly constructed stores in Slidell and Jacksonville, the twenty-third and twenty-fourth in the chain. It was, however, also the year in which debt began to suffocate us. Nevertheless, the potential infusion of cash from an initial public offering (IPO)—which we conservatively figured at somewhat less than $100 million— would be sufficient to see us through tough times. The nation, unfortunately, was afflicted with a stealth recession, an economic downturn that hit retailing the hardest but would not be formally recognized for another year.

From a merchandising and operations standpoint, purchasing the May-Cohen chain was a healthy fit for Maison Blanche, more so than the earlier Robinson's stores. However, the added layer of debt incurred in buying and operating those stores, including what was needed for construction of the Lakeland store, strained our finances. Contrary to popular belief, banks normally will lend you more money than you ought to borrow. We previously paid lip service to a limit on debt, even though for several years we ignored our own dictum: Debt should not exceed 60 percent of the company's net worth. (After Maison Blanche, that became inviolate Sternberg law. We carefully plan cash flow.) The May-Cohen purchase exacerbated an already-surpassed debt limit.

In late 1989, I contacted a former Princeton classmate, Richard Fisher, then CEO of Morgan Stanley, one of Wall Street's two leading investment-banking firms, for assistance in launching an initial public offering (IPO) in the spring of 1990. Our business, per se, wasn't so much the issue. We were approaching a half billion dollars in annual sales—a sufficient sum for the time had the other legs of the stool solidly been in place.

Josef and I believed Maison Blanche could reach one billion dollars in sales without our buying more stores. But *servicing* our debt became a major hurdle. What kept us from doing that may well have been a frustrating inability to adequately infuse the Maison Blanche corporate culture and efficiencies into our Florida operations, which amounted to the majority of MB's overall business. Unacceptable costs were eroding critical earnings. The profits of the Louisiana stores were unable to staunch the Florida bleeding. Furthermore, sales at the eight Robinson's stores in the southwest part of the state began to lag behind our computer models.

I intensified Maison Blanche's traditional controls in order to maximize profits, but those efforts bore little fruit. Going public would have relieved the financial pressure had we launched the IPO in May 1990, as originally planned. Morgan Stanley's preparations for an IPO ran behind schedule, primarily because of a lack of urgency on the part of our accounting firm, Deloitte Touche. The

IPO would not be ready, Fisher warned, until September. That tardiness turned out to be a mortal blow.

On August 2, 1990, Saddam Hussein virtually ended any company's attempt to go public during that immediate time period. His Iraqi army invaded and occupied Kuwait on the pretext that its neighbor was tapping into Iraqi oil fields (which was true to some extent). There were other issues: Kuwait, according to Hussein, was a natural part of Iraq and, probably more relevant, the latter owed its smaller neighbor money it could not repay.

In the modern era, one nation simply does not invade another without world reaction, especially if the invaded nation is a critical oil supplier. The United Nations quickly approved a United States–led offensive, initially named Desert Shield, to free Kuwait. Five months later, after deploying a staggering number of troops to Saudi Arabia in an attempt to protect another of our big oil suppliers from expanded Iraqi aggression, the United States and its Allies were ready to pounce.

Desert Shield morphed into Desert Storm when coalition troops launched a devastating counter-attack on Iraqi troops in Kuwait in January 1991. They drove Saddam's relatively ineffective army back into Iraq. That Middle East action exacerbated a Wall Street slump, which, according to Dow Jones, became known as "Saddam Hussein's bear market."

The fighting was over in a month, but the stock market had declined 20 percent, and IPOs were out of the question. Our carefully designed parachute had collapsed. By the time an IPO was again attractive, it would be too late.

The United States was mired in a major recession, but the Middle East conflict temporarily diverted the nation's attention away from domestic issues. As the downturn intensified, the public stopped spending. Soon every department store in America felt the pinch. The government and news media wouldn't figure it out until the recession was almost over. (Louisianian James Carville, then Bill Clinton's campaign strategist, wrote and underlined for emphasis the now-famous line on a campaign-headquarters blackboard in 1991: "It's the economy, stupid." Punctuating the economic situation and capitalizing on its ramifications helped send Clinton to the White House.)

In April 1990, we looked outside the family for management expertise. We recruited former Federated Department Stores executive John Irvin, president and CEO of the Dallas Market Center, and hired him as president of MB. In the end (which wasn't that far away), he became more of a problem than a help. By the fall of 1990, financial strain regrettably forced the layoffs of several top management people, including Don Bell, senior vice president of stores, and Tom Cagley, a senior general merchandise manager. It was a decision of necessity, not of choice. Both were trusted lieutenants who had been Josef's and my right and left hands for more than a decade.

With sales in a decline and little or no chance of Wall Street relief, we considered our options and decided to sell some of the MB properties. Experiencing healthy Christmas sales would make Maison Blanche more tempting to buyers, but we didn't wait. We had to pump up revenues and cut our losses. Maison Blanche had a chain-wide blowout sale in October 1990. It produced a sales explosion, but one that would come back to haunt us.

Overall, Christmas 1990 was disappointing. Our customers were not in a buying mood. Holiday business, however, would pale in comparison to the other loss I experienced that December.

Josef had had his first heart attack in 1966 at the age of thirty-seven, two years before he married Mary Ann. In 1990, the stress of keeping our business afloat was taking a severe toll on his health.

Both he and I carried multi-million-dollar life insurance policies, premiums paid by the company with the store and families as beneficiaries. The face value of my coverage totaled $37 million; Josef's total was $19 million ($5 million of that went to the store when he died). Because of Josef's heart problems, his premiums were twice as high as mine for half the protection, and that bothered him. From almost the beginning, we had paid each other equally. In the late 1980s Josef wanted to reduce the value of his policies so that our premiums would be equal. I talked him out of it.

Although he seldom spoke of it, Josef worried about providing for Mary Ann and their children should he die.

Tom Cagley, who spent fifteen years as a member of Maison Blanche's executive committee, kept a daily journal. He wanted it for his children to read when they were grown. He shared several entries with me when he learned I was writing this book. One particular passage had to do with a conversation Tom had with Josef while flying back to Baton Rouge during a buying trip in the late 1980s.

Cagley, who thought of Josef as someone possessing "a subtle, unspoken understanding that tomorrow would certainly come and it would inevitably be better," related that while he was making the day's entry during the flight Josef walked down the aisle to Tom's row and sat in an adjacent seat. Josef asked what he was doing and, when told, inquired as to how many years Tom would continue making entries.

"Until my son, Nick, is twenty-one, leaves home, or I die," Tom responded.

"Do you think about things like that . . . dying?" Josef asked. "About leaving your children behind before they're grown?"

"A lot, do you?"

"All the time, every day," my brother reflected. "When you have children late in life, like you and I did, it seems natural. Not much we can do, though, except think about it and try to stay healthy and live long enough to get them started on their way, maybe to know that they're okay."

Tom responded that Josef and he were going "to go" first. "It's just our luck," he noted. "Our wives will have to carry the load. Mine is ready."

"Mary Ann is," Josef agreed. "It is one of the reasons I married her. She may not know that—I probably never said it to her that way—but I knew back then, from the very beginning, that she'd be strong enough. She's stronger than I am."

"Josef!" he challenged.

"No, Mr. Cagley, she is. Really."

At that point, having had his fill of morose conversations, Josef slapped both hands on his knees (as he typically did), smiled, stood up, and returned to his own seat.

Josef was aware of his heart condition, and he religiously maintained a low-cholesterol diet, even before that regimen became popular. He hated taking medicines, however, and refused the cholesterol drugs then available. In May 1990, when his cardiologist told him he had to have heart surgery, Josef underwent a triple bypass. (It was supposed to have been *quadruple*, but one of the four arteries was so damaged that no amount of repair would have helped.) He went home to convalesce.

Bypass surgery is supposed to be followed by a long rest, but the mounting financial pressure on Maison Blanche worried Josef so much that he could not take it easy. Even though we had hired John Irvin that spring to direct our storewide merchandising, Josef's self-imposed standards would not permit him to disengage. He remained occupied with the store almost from the day he came home from the hospital.

Stress, caused primarily by pressure from our bankers to maintain our sales and profit targets, continued to mount. We had personally guaranteed some of our credit lines (a mistake the family no longer makes). One Premier Bank officer, in particular, hounded Josef relentlessly. That caused Josef, a sensitive person, great distress, which he was supposed to avoid during recuperation. I believe to this day that this emotional burden from that bank caused his death.

On December 23, Mary Ann and Josef were taking a Sunday walk along the live oak–lined streets of their Baton Rouge neighborhood. At 4:30 p.m., he suddenly collapsed in her arms and died almost instantly. Lowering him to the ground, she yelled for help. An ambulance came. Josef's doctor, who happened to live nearby, rode with him to the nearby Baton Rouge General Hospital, futilely attempting to revive his heart.

Lea, Insa, the children, Donna, and I rushed to the hospital to be with Mary Ann. Lea had steeled herself for this, but Mary Ann was devastated. She recalled later that she was numb for a year.

Josef was buried in the B'nai Israel Cemetery on December 25. The number of mourners testified to the love affair the city had had with him. He had known so many of the people who had entered the front doors of Goudchaux's during the last four decades. Mighty or lowly, rich or poor, it mattered little to him. They each were extended warmth and a genuine greeting.

You didn't have to enter Goudchaux's, though, to know Josef. He had been active in the Chamber of Commerce, headed foundations, patronized the arts, served on gubernatorial committees, and volunteered to help local organizations from the United Way to the Boy Scouts.

The Roman Catholic bishop of the Diocese of Baton Rouge, Stanley Ott, led the sizable contingent of non-Jewish attendees who took time from their Christmas Day, one of the holiest times in the Christian calendar, to pay final tribute to their friend and professional colleague. Writing the eulogies for Josef was not hard. Those who knew him used the same descriptives: charm, warmth, kindness. He paid attention to people and took time to listen to them. He possessed courtly manners and a soft, reassuring voice. In all that, he was like his father.

Josef also had confidence in his abilities and the courage to follow through. His oft-stated philosophy hung in the air on the stark winter day of his funeral service: "We do things our own way. We are fiercely independent. It makes life very simple."

With their children—Joanna, twenty-one; Katie, twenty; and Jay, eighteen—at her side, Mary Ann recounted in her eulogy that her husband was a man who loved his family, his work, his religion, and his community, a man who saw something good in almost everyone. Her description of her husband was one in which everyone concurred: Josef was a gift, and "we who loved him are thankful that he was here."

Josef Sternberg, age sixty-two, was buried close to our father. *Shalom, bruder.*

Returning to work, I was now alone in our unadorned office at the Main Street headquarters. Over the ensuing months, I was unable to summon the emotional rush that had always enveloped me in the day-to-day bustle of retailing. The feeling had dissipated; directing our company wasn't as much fun without Josef. But too much was at stake in 1991 to wallow in self-pity.

An IPO remained too iffy to launch. Anyway, the situation was deteriorating to the point an IPO might not have mattered. The goal now was selling off properties, but not the entire chain. I decided to divest the company of Maison Blanche's No. 1 problem, the Robinson's stores in Florida. That would rid us of underachieving units and hopefully produce the cash to see us through the recession. I sold eight of the Robinson's stores to Dillard's in June 1991, a bit less than four years after we brought them into the MB family. We retained the three Orlando units, along with the Florida distribution center, as well as the Jacksonville properties.

I actually thought I had sold those units to Mercantile Department Stores, a large national operation founded in 1914 and operating 118 stores, but I hadn't reckoned on wily Bill Dillard II. This would have been Mercantile's first purchase since 1951. CEO and President David Hahn signed a letter of intent with me in Atlanta in the summer of 1991, stating that Mercantile would purchase the eight southwest Florida stores for $70 million plus inventory, less minor deductions for asbestos and other environmental concerns.

The Mercantile board approved the letter of intent, and we negotiated for six weeks before settling on a final contract. The day the Mercantile board was to sign the contract, I got a call from Hahn informing me that his board had reneged and the sale was off. I was flabbergasted. I had taken the phone call in the presence of a crowd of employees, who had joined me to hear the good news. It was devastating. Hahn offered no explanation and would, within days, step down as Mercantile's president and CEO.

As if on cue, Dillard jumped in from stage left and accepted the deal I had negotiated with Mercantile. Actually, he wanted an accommodation for a tax issue and for that would pay $200,000 more than what Mercantile had offered.

During the negotiations, I learned why Mercantile backed down. Chortling, Dillard told me he had called Mercantile's Roger Milliken, chairman and CEO of Milliken & Company, parent company of Mercantile, to "warn" Roger he was paying too much for the Robinson's stores.

Milliken trusted Dillard and forced his board at the last minute to back away from a contract that had been meticulously negotiated, drawn up, and sealed by a handshake. The papers were signed, subject only to board approval—normally a formality—but it was not to be.

(I later told Milliken about the apparent deception, adding that Bill Dillard actually paid more than Mercantile had offered. Milliken, not a person to treat lightly or to deliberately mislead, was humiliated by Dillard's chicanery. Seven years later, he would turn the tables on Dillard.)

Cash from the sale of the Robinson's stores to Dillard's left MB in relatively good shape by August 1991. We once again were in the vendors' good graces, receiving first-line merchandise on a timely basis. Even the lending institutions were smiling, although still wary of us. In early September, however, CFO Steve Tisdell noticed a budgeting technicality that was going to put us back in the financial soup. The previous October, we pulled off that gigantic chainwide sale. Sales volume for the month was out of sight. Somehow that bloated figure got cranked into the 1991 budget, making it impossible to hit our numbers for October 1991. Our lenders were receiving monthly MB statements. When they saw we missed sales projections, credit would again tighten. With that situation looming, we ordered as much Christmas merchandise as possible while the vendors were still smiling.

Steve withheld sending the October financials as long as he legitimately could, but dispatched them the first week of December. When October's numbers reached the banks, showing we missed budget and badly, they all but shut us off. Red flags were sent to our suppliers, who again balked at supplying us with adequate merchandise. In addition, the business press and industry analysts were talking, and it wasn't complimentary.

To make matters worse, our Christmas sales were dismal. That was not for lack of effort or imagination. We put on the mother of all Christmas promotions. From the tried-and-true boxes of Cracker Jacks with a diamond ring hidden in one of them to "scratch-off" secret discounts similar to lottery tickets, we tried nearly every gimmick in our promotional arsenal—for naught. Maybe our customers weren't in the buying mood, or maybe they sensed that this no longer was their parents' Goudchaux's.

As early as October, I had determined that there were three acceptable solutions to our financial quagmire: raise equity, borrow more money, or sell the company. We also had the option of filing for bankruptcy, but that was a dreadful choice and I was dead set against it. Option 1 was viable because, although an IPO was no longer in the cards, there were other ways to raise equity, such as selling a piece of the company or through a joint venture. Option 2 could work because we still were able to arrange a credit line. The company wasn't broken. Our debt structure was the problem, and various timelines on the loans were a complication. We still had a positive EBITDA (earnings before interest, taxes, depreciation, and amortization). In a good credit environment, we could have financed our way out of the immediate problem.

The environment, unfortunately, was anything but good. The national economy was a mess. The savings and loan crisis lingered fresh in every banker's mind. Of the six banks with which we dealt, four were themselves in trouble. Manufacturers Hanover almost failed and merged with Chemical; Republic Bank of Texas, in even deeper trouble, was taken over by Interfirst Bank; and Premier Bank of Baton Rouge and Hibernia of New Orleans were under severe financial strain of their own. Premier, for example, reported a quarterly loss of more than $100 million. It granted Bank One, based in Ohio, an option to purchase it, which Bank One later exercised. Only Sun Bank of Florida and First NBC of New Orleans remained healthy.

By December 1991, when the infamous October statement hit, the creditors and suppliers were baying at the doors of our sixteen stores. Some suppliers were not allowing us the normal 30-to 60-day period to pay for our merchandise. The Credit Exchange, a New York company that compiles credit reports on various industries, including department stores, issued negative reports on us.

In the fall of 1991, Tisdell gave the executive committee

the task of planning for a possible Chapter 11 filing. The planning was necessary strategy, even though I never seriously thought we would find that necessary. We engaged Weil, Gotshal & Manges, a New York City law firm that specialized in bankruptcy. It would prepare the legal outline for a Chapter 11, which provides a company with protection from creditors while it works out a plan to repay its debt. We also made a special arrangement with the Deloitte Touche accounting firm to help with such a transition.

Despite my optimism about a sale, it was prudent to prepare for bankruptcy as well. All possibilities, including those I considered remote, were covered. I stayed out of the planning because Chapter 11 was anathema to me. I knew it would have only prolonged the agony. Such action also produces a stigma among vendors and customers, no matter how seamless the transition in and out of bankruptcy.

To the average person, Chapter 11 may sound benign, but commercial bankruptcy is ugly and mean—and, ironically, it costs a lot of money. I was determined to sell Maison Blanche outright. It was a matter of finding a buyer and getting a fair price. I initiated two overtures in November 1991: the first to Bill Dillard, the other to Roger Milliken. When the smoke cleared, I had actually "sold" the stores to both of them.

< Progression of Goudchaux's/Maison Blanche logos, 1935–1992

12 LOWERING THE FLAG

IN RETROSPECT, I CAN say the sale of Maison Blanche was my finest act of brinkmanship negotiating. Our MB team met with the Dillards, father and son, early in December 1991. I chose to meet with them first rather than Mercantile because they seemed the more likely players. The Dillards were buying stores every six months, or so it seemed. Mercantile, on the other hand, had not made a major purchase in forty years.

We met at the New Orleans Centre, an Ed DeBartolo mall near the Superdome that housed Macy's and Lord & Taylor. (DeBartolo, widely considered the father of American shopping malls, was not only a giant in the mall development business but also somewhat of a character. He prided himself on getting only four hours of sleep a night. And when he arrived for work in the morning, rumor had it he also would set on his desk a large glass of bourbon and Coke, which he nursed all day.) DeBartolo himself was on hand for this meeting because the deal would require his relinquishing mall leases.

Dillard the elder made an initial offer of $31 million, assumption of the MB debt, and $5 million for real estate holdings—a $36 million package. We shook hands, but, in typical Dillard fashion, the price quickly was unilaterally chiseled to $25 million for the stores along with $5 million for real estate. My bargaining position was not strong enough for me to resist. We shook hands, this time for an overall total of $30 million.

Bill Dillard and Bill II headed a small team representing Dillard's. With me were CFO Tisdell, New York City attorney Herb Rosedale, and Dick Hanor, our real estate consultant from Florida, who had assisted us on our purchase of the Florida stores. (Dick's help was especially valuable, and he got paid just shy of $1 million for it.)

Having agreed in principle, we retired to a late lunch at Galatoire's, a New Orleans culinary icon. Tisdell, Rosedale, and Dillard's representative Jim Darr remained behind to draft a memorandum of understanding. An hour later, they joined us at Galatoire's. As the group was working its way through an array of five-star appetizers, the memo summarizing the deal was distributed to each of us at the table. I thought it was precisely what had been agreed to, but the elder Dillard bellowed, "This isn't the deal!"

He apparently decided he had been too generous and began chipping away on the agreed-upon price. I lost $10 million between the appetizers and coffee. The deal blew up, and the meeting deteriorated to the point of bickering over who would pay for the appetizers. I was surprised I didn't throw up. I was mad as hell but didn't have much recourse. I sat alone at the table after the others left, just shaking my head.

The problem with the Dillards was they never stopped negotiating. They kept trying to cut a better deal, even though they had a fabulous one. Bill and Bill II knew that, but in the MB case, they erroneously thought I had no option and got greedy. The Dillards believed we had to sell—and at any price.

Wrong. We had alternatives, which would become painfully clear to the Dillards the next time we met. The sharks were in the water, but this fish escaped. The deal with Dillard's was in turmoil, but I had a backup suitor—Mercantile Stores.

A week later, the MB forces split. CFO Steve Tisdell and Herb Rosedale met with the Dillards for Round 2. New York attorney Mike Shef and I huddled with Roger Milliken and Mercantile executives. No one else, other than my family, knew what was going on.

Tisdell made clear to the Dillards our second alternative: We had more than sufficient funds—some $30 million in ready cash—with which to file for bankruptcy and would do so if forced. Any thought the Dillards might have had of a blue-light special because of our stressed condition evaporated when Steve put the Chapter 11 prospect on the table. Our weakness was turned into strength. Bankruptcy, Steve underscored, could delay an acquisition indefinitely, and the creditors would be the primary owners and operators. Any suitor would be sidelined, probably for good. The Dillards got the message and were prepared to deal, but as it turned out, they were a day late and $10 million short.

Milliken, who remembered how he had been manipulated in the Robinson's stores negotiation, was not going to be snookered again. Milliken and his team had flown in his private jet to Baton Rouge, where Donna, I, and our son Erich met him at the airport for an escorted tour of the Louisiana stores. (He already had visited their Florida counterparts.) Completing his personal inspection of all sixteen stores at about the same time Tisdell was talking to the Dillards, Milliken and I began final negotiations in late December. It took only a day and a half to cut the deal.

The teams met for breakfast but were sitting at separate tables. Roger came over to me and said, as bluntly as this is written, that he would pay $10 million more than Dillard's had offered earlier that month. He then asked how much Dillard's had offered. I said $30 million. He instantly replied: That makes the price $40 million (plus assumption of the $230 million debt and another $6 mil-

lion for additional considerations, such as real estate).

Roger never once asked me to prove my numbers (which I could have done) or to check the books. By this time, Maison Blanche was down to $360 million in annual volume from its sixteen stores. Our employment roster in January was around 4,200, nearly half of the total at our high-water mark two years before.

Roger and I shook hands. It was the strangest deal I ever made. Dillard's essentially set the purchase price for Mercantile.

Roger Milliken and I signed an agreement in principle to sell the stores on Monday, January 20, 1992, in New Orleans, a little more than a half century after my father entered into an agreement with Bennie Goudchaux to buy the original Main Street store. The transaction closed three weeks later.

I called the senior Dillard to say I had accepted a better deal with Mercantile. He was not happy. (A few years earlier, Buddy Lipsey, a department store colleague from Alexandria, was standing near Dillard and heard him describe me to several of his colleagues as "a mean, f——ing Jew." At that time, I accepted it as high praise, but I always have wondered how he described me after my phone call.)

I had kept the family abreast of the negotiations throughout our dealings with Dillard's and Mercantile. Immediately after Roger Milliken and I shook hands, I called the family and told them to gather at Lea's home for a meeting. I returned to Baton Rouge late in the afternoon on that crisp December day, Donna beside me and son Erich at the wheel, to relate with finality the events of the day. I was relieved; the experience was wrenching. The entire scenario was the toughest of my life.

We gathered around Lea's kitchen table, the one she and my father had brought from Germany, to discuss the bittersweet news: We had sold Goudchaux's/Maison Blanche to Mercantile for $277 million, more than 2,500 times what my father had paid for the original store. The family would receive $47 million for the stores and holdings, with Mercantile also assuming the debt. In addition, I negotiated $7.2 million in severance for MB employees who would be losing their jobs, although some jumped ship and didn't wait the time required to qualify.

Mother was outwardly calm, but I wondered if she was as stoic after we left. The kitchen scene at times was strained, as you can imagine. That said, all of us were of one mind: Sale was our best choice.

In addition to their share of the sales proceeds based on stock holdings, the deal called for Donna and Mary Ann to receive payments of $80,000 over two years and Insa $25,000 over the same period. Lea, who was eighty-eight at the time of the sale, was to be retained with a life-time contract providing $36,000 a year. I would be given a million dollars over five years as a "paid consultant" to Mercantile. No work or time commitment was required. The sum going to me was in effect an annual payment to keep me from competing with Mercantile. (Two years later, Mercantile used the clause to force me off the board of Goody's Department Store in Tennessee, one of their competitors. Flattering, I suppose.)

Incredibly, Bill Dillard still had not reconciled himself to the fact that the game was over. On January 17, at a party given by Ashton Phelps Jr., publisher of *The New Orleans Times-Picayune*, in honor of Edwin Edwards' gubernatorial victory over the neo-Nazi David Duke, Ed DeBartolo urged me to reconsider Dillard's as a buyer. While we had an agreement in principle with Mercantile, we would not be signing binding papers for three days. No doubt Ed was put up to this by Bill Dillard II, who also was at the party and who would just happen to be available should I want to negotiate an eleventh-hour deal.

I refused to enter any conversation with the younger Dillard, even a "hello" or a handshake, and disclosed to Ed that Mercantile had paid $10 million more than Dillard had offered. He was the first non–family member with whom I shared that information, and when he heard it, DeBartolo backed off.

The morning of the Phelps party, *The Morning Advocate* had published a front-page story quoting our CFO Tisdell as saying that Maison Blanche had secured a revolving line of credit with six banks through May 15. It quoted two executives of credit exchanges as saying we were sixty days in arrears with some of our suppliers, and describing our situation as "very serious." Asked if MB was in financial difficulties, Tisdell said only, "It depends on how you look at it."

Because we still had not signed final documents, I kept the news of the pending sale under tight wraps. I wanted no false alarms, no problems like what occurred with the sale of the Robinson's stores, no leaks to the press, no interference on something this big.

Few believed we would ever sell Maison Blanche, at least its Louisiana stores. That feeling was especially strong among members of the MB executive committee, who still thought we were headed toward Chapter 11. They knew my feelings and that I was exploring a sale, but my success was unanticipated and considered remote. Committee members had no clue a sale had been consummated. When the news finally broke, there was shock and disbelief at what many thought was impossible.

I had told the executive committee after I returned from New Orleans on January 20, where I had signed the letter of intent to sell, that I wanted a meeting early the next morning. The group had been unofficially preparing detailed contingency plans in case of a Chapter 11 filing. Committee members thought my meeting might have something to do with that. They wanted us to be able to open our doors Wednesday morning without a hitch. It was prudent strategy, but what the committee didn't know was that, with two financially strong potential buyers, it was a remote possibility.

The meeting was heart-wrenching for me and a shock to the committee. Whatever the reactions, the situation was now out of everyone's hands but Mercantile's. When I arrived in the Main Street headquarters' conference room, I cut to the chase: MB had been sold to Mercantile Stores. The executive committee's collective mouth dropped open. (It wasn't good news for those assembled, since most of them would lose their jobs.)

I then met with mid-management and the buyers. Most likely, they would be losing their positions as well. I discussed the ample severance possibilities with them as I had with the executive committee. Finally, I walked downstairs to the main floor, where the sales staff awaited. And for the third time, I outlined what had transpired with

Mercantile. Branch store managers and salespeople would be retained, I said. (In fact, Mercantile probably would be adding sales staff to replace those positions we had allowed to go vacant through attrition during the prior year.) It was an emotional scene, to say the least. Some of these employees had been with Goudchaux's since my father's early days.

Every employee knew MB was in turmoil, but few expected this. I faxed a statement to store managers at the fifteen branches in Louisiana and Florida. They, in turn, read my words to the assembled employees.

As you can imagine, word we had sold to Mercantile spread like wildfire through Baton Rouge. As I walked out the door of the store later in the day, I faced a throng of reporters and a battery of cameras. I looked haggard as I read a prepared statement: Gayfer's, one of Mercantile's divisions, headquartered in Mobile, Alabama, would operate the Maison Blanche stores. The Main Street and Cortana Mall buildings would keep the dual Goudchaux's/Maison Blanche logo. The other Louisiana stores would continue to be called Maison Blanche, but the Florida properties would carry Gayfer's name.

Having delivered the news, I took no questions and left. I never granted an interview to discuss the sale. It was not something I wanted to talk about, and to this day it continues to be a tough topic for me. Two years after the sale, Lea did discuss it in an interview with the *Baton Rouge Business Report*. She handled it with admirable strength and pragmatism, declaring, "It was very sad, but I am a businesswoman. It was the right decision."

The Morning Advocate devoted nearly half of the front page and all of an inside page to the sale, including accompanying stories quoting longtime customers lamenting the loss of a dear friend. Under new owners, went the refrain, "It will never be the same." I could relate to that.

Everything considered, the outcome was reasonably good for most people, certainly better than the alternative. Family-owned department stores were going the way of neighborhood grocery stores and dime stores of two decades previous. Five years earlier, in a healthier national-

retail climate, we perhaps could have gotten twice what we did for the stores; but if we had *waited* another five years to sell, as department stores became even more obsolete, we might have received half that amount.

After the sale officially was completed three weeks later, on February 10, I left the store for the last time. I drove away from 1500 Main Street with a lot to think about. The past thirteen months had been emotionally draining. My brother and the company were gone. The next day Mercantile cut off the MB direct phone line to our house and told me I had thirty days to vacate my office and the premises. Milliken had given me the impression he wanted me to play a role in the larger Mercantile operation, but the Mercantile management made clear it did not want me hanging around. I could understand that. They need not have bothered. Mentally and emotionally, I was already gone.

Mercantile did agree to let the family keep our life insurance company and insurance agency. Actually, Mercantile was relieved when I inquired about retaining those insurance operations, both separately incorporated subsidiaries of Maison Blanche. Mercantile had no appetite for the insurance business and didn't want the liability. As I recall, ownership as part of the larger transaction was without an additional exchange of funds. I, on the other hand, was determined to make it the next chapter in Donna's and my careers.

Baton Rouge, meanwhile, was rightfully concerned about the sale of Goudchaux's/Maison Blanche. Other cities would lose little, if any, in the way of store personnel —a manager, perhaps—but Baton Rouge was different because of the presence of our corporate headquarters. From high executive salaries to civic contributions to lost business for local suppliers, the impact of the departure of a large headquarters on a city's economy and civic structure can be substantial. More than five hundred white-collar jobs (management, marketing, receiving, and clerical staffs)—with an annual payroll in the millions—departed for Mobile.

As it turned out, Mercantile soon would scrap its own corporate credit operations and fold it in with our former

I remember how sad we were when the Sternbergs sold [the store]. We still went there and we still called it Goudchaux's most of the time, but now the store felt slick and impersonal. . . . The last time I was in the building, I looked around at what it had become. People waited in line to try on boxes of reduced clothing. The huge, elegant dressing rooms, with mirrors all around, and racks of beautiful wedding gowns . . . had been stripped of their beautiful wallpaper. It reminded me of scenes in Dr. Zhivago.

—MICHELLE ODOM NESBIT

operation in Baton Rouge. Indeed, Mercantile was so impressed with the department that it asked Charles Unfried, our senior VP who managed it, to retain that position with its company. Mercantile had a corporate culture similar to ours, said Charles, but its executives liked MB's better and tried to maintain it. That is a difficult thing to do, and Mercantile had a hard time swallowing the MB stores.

In retrospect, I can say that the sale of Goudchaux's/Maison Blanche resulted from being too aggressive and slipping too deeply into debt. Some analysts at the time of the sale said we ought not to have expanded into Florida. That view has the benefit of hindsight. Our expansion strategy when we executed it seemed reasonable. It was progress and our best opportunity to achieve major successes. We were ready for a national profile. But ambitious strategies carry risks. We tried to do in four years what should have taken ten.

What we ought to have done was temporarily slowed our expansion after the purchase of the Robinson's stores until we had worked out the kinks with our Florida merchandise. At the same time, we needed to wait for the lending institutions to return to an even keel and the nation to get over its economic downturn.

The Jacksonville May-Cohen units were a better fit for Maison Blanche, but the additional debt load in purchasing those stores pushed us to the brink. Debt-to-equity ratio reached 5 to 1, which was not prudent, no matter what our "conservative" projections showed. Lesson learned:

Don't depend on your bank to tell you when to stop borrowing. The debt exposed us, and we were unable to cope with the continued double-digit unemployment, national banking distress and a severe retail recession. We also were unprepared for Wall Street's being unavailable for an IPO, which came as a total surprise.

Our computer models on the May-Cohen acquisition made a solid case that we would be clear of debt in five years, that our risk was rational, and that the only challenge was bringing the new stores reasonably close to the productivity of our Louisiana properties. The latter proviso, however, proved more difficult than we imagined.

We didn't like to admit it, but we never totally connected our merchandising mix with Florida customers in the relatively short period we owned the stores. May and Robinson's had featured moderately priced merchandise. We worked hard at selling more upscale goods than the Florida market was used to in those facilities. Doing so initially confused customers and challenged employees. We would have succeeded if given the time, but time ran out.

We learned that Floridians, at least in the western part of the state where most of our stores were located, are casual dressers. Tom Cagley, who left MB some fifteen months before we sold, described the Florida market to the *Baton Rouge Business Report* thus: "It [had] a different clientele . . . casual beyond belief. You have to live there and be among them to survive as a retailer."

I should note that Florida sales weren't *all* tank tops and cutoffs. One of our Orlando stores, for instance, would frequently see customers from South America buy furs by the suitcase-load and take them home to sell at a markup. In one two-week period, we sold a quarter of a million dollars in merchandise to a Saudi princess visiting Orlando. The family would only shop after hours, accompanied by a phalanx of gun-toting bodyguards.

It also is true that the entire nation was beginning to take a more relaxed approach to clothing, even professional apparel. Suits were becoming the exception in the white-collar work force, save in the largest eastern cities. Professional women were looking for comfortable wear, not high fashion. Except for some foreign customers, furs slowly moved out of favor in an ever-greening society. The Wal-Marts were in; higher-end department stores were out.

To exacerbate Maison Blanche's problem, retailing had soured nationally and credit had become tight. Bankers panicked, some banks failed. The feds had been closing savings & loans at a wholesale rate. Foreign debt was weighing negatively on the balance sheets of major world lenders as big debtor nations began defaulting.

Over a period of years, department stores were decimated. Macy's went bankrupt, carrying with it I. Magnin. Federated and Allied merged, then went bankrupt—dragging down such vaunted stores as Bullock's, Burdines in Florida, Rich's of Atlanta, Foley's, and Bloomingdale's. Saks Fifth Avenue lost $400 million in nineteen months and survived only because Arab oil money kept it afloat. Sage-Allen of Hartford and Garfinckel's of Washington, D.C., were additional casualties. Bergner's (which included Carson Pirie Scott and Donaldson's, among others) went belly-up financially. D. H. Holmes of New Orleans and Baton Rouge avoided severe problems by selling to Dillard's.

Then it was Chapter 11 time for Carter Hawley Hale, which included Weinstock's, Thalheimer's, and others, and for Zale's, the world's largest jewelry retailer. Dayton Hudson rescued Marshall Field's by purchasing it. Seattle's Frederick & Nelson, a landmark, closed following a Chapter 7 bankruptcy filing (which is a liquidation proceeding unlike Chapter 11, which allows a business to continue in order to pay its debts). During this period, more than 40 percent of the traditional fashion retailers were mired in financial difficulty. It looked as if the age of the department store was ending, although the survivors have since staged uninspiring revivals.

For the Sternbergs, the merchant line definitively had been broken. Not having department stores, in a way, seemed odd. Yet, in another sense, it felt invigorating. I was free, unencumbered with ongoing, traditional operations, able to travel a different road.

My merchant genes, refined by four to five generations of Sternbergs and Knurrs, made it clear in every mental, emotional and physical sense that taking my share of the sale money and cruising the Caribbean was not an option. My father used to say, "Don't take off your clothes until you are ready to go to bed." And I was—and still am—far from ready to slow down. I had another plan: developing and growing the insurance company. And that's what I did.

Six years after buying MB, Mercantile sold the stores to Dillard's. That 1998 transaction gave Roger Milliken the opportunity to avenge Bill Dillard's trickery in 1990 concerning the west Florida Robinson's stores. It was payback time.

In 1998, when Milliken and his board decided to sell the Mercantile chain, he assigned the project to the Wall Street firm of Goldman Sachs, with the condition that it could offer the chain to anyone except Dillard's. Mercantile had more than 100 stores in 17 states, operating under 13 names. Sales exceeded $3 billion. May Company, Federated, and others bid.

Dillard heard about it and called Goldman Sachs, only to be told he was the odd man out and could not be a player. Dillard countered with a huge preemptive offer of $2.9 billion, much of it in Dillard's stock. It was $500 million more than the next highest bidder. Milliken considered the offer, a sweet deal by any measure, but said if stock was involved he wanted 10 percent of the seats at Dillard's board of directors' table. Dillard refused, so Milliken said $2.9 billion was okay—so long as it was in cold, hard cash.

It is not easy, even for a company the size of Dillard's, to come up with nearly $3 billion in currency. But Bill

Dillard didn't have a choice. He was forced to go into the market and borrow it. That debt burden was onerous, draining Dillard's for several years.

In spite of her years, my mother continued to be active civically. In 1994, Lea and Erich (posthumously) were inducted into the *Baton Rouge Business Report*'s Hall of Fame in recognition of their "lifetime achievement and significant contribution to the local economy." Upon receiving the award, Lea said she was grateful to America for allowing her to come here. "I never forgot President Roosevelt, [who] gave permission for so many Jews to come to this country. And I was one of them."

In many ways, Lea Sternberg was as much Goudchaux's as my father. Besides being a director, co-owner, floor impresario, buyer, and one-person *tour de force* in sales, she was the unofficial store greeter.

Approaching her ninety-fourth birthday in 1998, Lea suffered a heart attack. Actually, it was several attacks. She was rushed to the hospital, where a breathing machine continued to keep her alive. The doctors recommended we take her off life support. Insa and I were not ready to give her up, and we refused to agree. To the doctors' surprise, Mom made a recovery and was sent home in the care of her nurse, Ruth Titus, who had been an employee at Goudchaux's before she changed professions. Lea's personality wasn't quite the same during the six months she remained with us, although visits from her nine grandchildren helped. While she wasn't as engaged as she once was, she continued to have strong opinions until the end.

And the end came on a Thursday morning, July 23, 1998. She suffered a brain aneurism and collapsed at her home. Ruth found her unconscious. The EMTs were summoned, but Lea Knurr Sternberg had already left us. Perhaps the strongest willed of all the Sternbergs, an indefatigable fixture at Goudchaux's, and the parent whom I probably most take after, she was gone. An era was over.

Lea, a fervent Jew, was memorialized the following day and lowered into the ground of the nearby Jewish cemetery, next to her beloved Erich. Her four grandsons were pallbearers. The line of mourners seemed endless. *The Advocate*'s David Manship generously published a tribute to Lea, written by the family, the following day. It read in part:

Yesterday, we lost Lea Sternberg, age 94. She lived a very complete life, with more than its share of vagaries . . . Lea and her husband, Erich . . . planted deep roots, worked hard and were successful. Their careers touched many lives. The company they developed . . . became the largest family-owned department store chain in the country, at one time employing eight thousand. She matched business commitment with philanthropy, and strived to be a civic minded, good citizen.

Our mother was eternally grateful to the community for the warmth and hospitality which greeted her and her family when they arrived and which supported them for the many years they lived here. She would want us to express, as we now do, the heart-felt thanks she constantly voiced for the many kindnesses and friendships which were a daily part of her life.

We will remember Lea at the head of her kitchen table, offering us stories and advice as she served an endless supply of hot tea and cookies. Always active, at 92 she learned to use the computer, entertaining herself with games and sending e-mail. We were fortunate that, to the end, her mind was sharp, her opinions strong, and her heart full.

. . . For Lea Sternberg, this was a land like none other, a country of generosity and greatness of spirit which could hardly be adequately appreciated. For "Ms. Lea," her favorite city would always be Baton Rouge, her favorite song would always be "God Bless America."

The Advocate reported Mother's death on the front page of the July 24 edition. The account of her wondrous life was continued on page 6. Ironically, between the front page and page 6 were three full-page Maison Blanche ads, announcing big summer sale specials. Lea would have liked that.

Whatever remorse I experienced over losing The Store to corporate outsiders has been mitigated over the years by reminders of what the family accomplished with Goudchaux's and Maison Blanche, certainly in Baton Rouge and, to a degree, in Lafayette and New Orleans.

The stores became an integral part of the lives of tens upon tens of thousands, who were saddened by its passing. We were a high-quality part of each community we entered.

To this day, former customers talk of the stores nostalgically, almost as if they still existed, their loyalty rooted in pleasant experiences. They remember fondly the Santa Claus and Mr. Bingle. They talk about Erich and Lea and the Sternberg boys. They share stories and "Goudchaux's (or Maison Blanche) Moments," memories of days past when a trip to either store was an adventure. (Some of these memories have appeared in these pages. More can be found in Appendix 3.)

When a corporate department store chain is bought by another chain and ceases to exist, its name is forgotten within a year. That has not happened with Goudchaux's or Maison Blanche. Those names still resonate for many. Nothing is forever, but family-owned stores like Goudchaux's and Maison Blanche have longer lives than most, even when physical evidence of their existence is gone.

The Sternbergs and the Knurrs were merchants, and they made a difference. Let what happened over the last two centuries bear witness to the importance of principles in our individual lives; to the importance of being aware of and making a positive impact on communities; to the importance of living one's traditions and beliefs. It is this legacy that has prompted me to share this story.

World War II–era billboard for Goudchaux's

Architect A. Hays Town's rendering of Goudchaux's on Main Street, 1964

EPILOGUE

WITH LEA'S DEATH, I became the last of a two-century-long line of Sternberg/Knurr merchants. That legacy prompted many emotions and undoubtedly was the spark that ignited a new adventure.

At fifty-seven, after selling Maison Blanche and having The Store's "dowry" to invest, I was, to a degree, in a position similar to that of my father in the mid 1930s. One only needs a dream, ambition, and capital, after all, and in 1992 I had all three. Not only that, I had a well-planned foundation of a company on which to build.

The transition from selling clothes and household goods to "manufacturing" and selling insurance went smoothly. Each pursuit requires skills in marketing, strategic planning, and ensuring high-quality service. While I may no longer be a retailing merchant, I view this venture, at least in a general sense, as a continuation of the Sternberg-Knurr business legacy. Starmount Life didn't magically appear in 1992 following the sale of Maison Blanche to Mercantile Stores. It was the result of an eighteen-year process. Goudchaux's Insurance began in 1974, as an agency selling life and accident insurance on a limited basis to charge-account customers. Its creation I owe, indirectly, to Utah Mormons.

ZCMI (Zion's Cooperative Mercantile Institution) Department Store was operating primarily in Utah, Idaho, and Arizona, with headquarters in Salt Lake City. It was the oldest department store west of the Mississippi River, having been founded in 1868 by the pioneering Mormon prophet Brigham Young. It continued to be operated by the Church of Jesus Christ of Latter-day Saints (LDS) until 1999, when it was sold to May Company. Like Goudchaux's, ZCMI was a creative, upscale, fashion-forward regional retailer. We belonged to the same national group (Mutual Buying) and conferred regularly.

Joe Anderson, ZCMI's president in 1974, told me that Beneficial Standard Life Insurance Company, also owned by the LDS church, marketed life insurance policies through the charge accounts of companies like ours. He gave the program a strong recommendation. I was intrigued, and we worked closely with Beneficial to get started.

With two Baton Rouge stores at the time, our charge accounts numbered only about 100,000. Into those billing statements we inserted, four times a year, insurance advertisements provided by Beneficial. From that base, in 1983, we started a "real" insurance company whose creation was prompted by Louisiana insurance magnate E. J. Ourso's abrupt reversal of permission to sell his funeral policies—because, as I related earlier, his agents deemed our size a competitive threat. Thus, we began creating and selling our own products.

Freeman Edgerton, president of State National Life and who sat with me as a director of WLCS Radio, interceded with the state insurance commissioner to grant a certificate of authority allowing us to operate with capital and surplus requirements of only $400,000. The certificate of authority was approved the same day it was filed.

Initially, Goudchaux's/Maison Blanche issued $1,000 life insurance policies for $18 a year; the annual premium on $2,000 was $26. Some of those customers remain on our books today.

Following the sale of Maison Blanche to Mercantile in 1992, I bought what would have been Josef's share of the insurance business from his family. Over years, the enterprise's name morphed from Goudchaux's Life Insurance Company to Starmount Life.

Starmount Life is celebrating its twenty-sixth anniversary as this book is published. It has grown from $700,000 in gross sales in 1992 to more than $60 million in 2008, with 2009 projected at approximately $70 million (the total for Starmount and AlwaysCare, our affiliate). As the next generation assumes leadership, we are expanding rapidly, doing business in forty-seven states (soon to be forty-nine), and have a new, 24,000-square-foot building under construction.

Starmount took off after it emerged from the department store umbrella where retailing demands absorbed our energy and resources. Over time, as the business proved itself, Donna and I invested $5.6 million, and an outside investor provided an additional $1 million. Today, Starmount is self-sustaining, with capital increases coming solely from retained earnings. We pay no dividends and maintain many of Goudchaux's business and management practices. For example, selectivity in hiring continues, with an average of nine candidates being interviewed for each one to whom we make an offer. Over 90 percent of those accept. Stock ownership is controlled by the same type of agreement that was in place at Goudchaux's.

In 2006, the *Baton Rouge Business Report* named Starmount "Company of the Year (under 100 employees)." In 2007, *Inc.* magazine recognized us as one of the nation's 5,000 fastest-growing private companies. In 2008, we received a Torch Award for Ethics in Business from the Better Business Bureau.

Donna joined me from the beginning as executive vice president, and she continues to handle life marketing. In 1998, son Erich and, subsequently, daughter Deborah became part of Starmount management, the former as president, the latter as senior vice president. Watching them develop, grow, and take charge is pure pleasure . . . most of the time. Our daughter Julie is an attorney and an author; son Marc is principal of a Gates Foundation supported public high school for at-risk students in the Bronx. Not one of Lea and Erich's nine grandchildren chose to be a merchant.

So it would appear that I am the last of five generations of merchants in the "shopkeeper" or "retailer" sense of the word. I am at peace with that. Two verses from the Hebrew Bible seem appropriate:

> Everything has an appointed season,
> and there is a time for every matter under
> the heaven.

And:

> . . . I saw that there is nothing better
> than that man rejoice in his deeds,
> for that is his portion, for who will bring him
> to see what will be after him?

Dayenu.

APPENDIX 1

The Negotiating Rules We Played by When Buying and Selling Stores

1. Merger and acquisition attorneys and accountants are critical to your success. They are specialists, and you must recruit the best. Your general counsel and traditional accountant support them.

2. Create with the other side an atmosphere of openness, sincerity, and trust. There is a role for aggression, anger, shouts, and table pounding. Use them sparingly, however, only for cause and without warning. Don't appear cold and calculating. Offer information about your feelings and provide personal insight. This should help build trust between the two sides.

3. Avoid irritating phrases, such as "a generous offer," "this is fair," or "we are reasonable." They often come across as just the opposite.

4. Be sensitive to the timing and labeling of counter-proposals. Discuss the other side's first offer, showing where it causes problems. Then offer a solution (which is, in fact, your counter-proposal). This is critical. Presenting your demands as the other side presents its position causes confrontation and sets the stage for deadlock or break-up.

5. Don't over-rationalize your viewpoint by verbalizing too many reasons. In negotiations, your argument fails with its weakest point. Stick to the one or two best ones.

6. Communicate clearly. Avoid making statements that can be misinterpreted.

7. Never negotiate with people on lower levels of authority than your own. (Herb Rosedale once stopped me in the middle of a three-way telephone conversation with a City Stores attorney. Herb abruptly announced the call over and told everyone to hang up. He called me back and told me why. The attorney for City Stores could only say, "No." I, on the other hand could say, "Yes," and be held accountable for it. It was not a balanced discussion. I should have been talking only to the other side's CEO and letting the two attorneys talk to each other.)

8. Test both sides' understanding, and summarize points to help eliminate misunderstandings. Make certain the other side is clear regarding the nuances of the deal to which it is agreeing. Misunderstandings are one of the main causes of break-ups and lawsuits. Remember, you don't just want a deal. You want a deal that works.

9. Ask questions. A good negotiator asks three times as many questions as an average one. Questions help persuade; reasons and statements do not. Questions move people toward you—and they give you breathing space.

10. Never accept the first offer. Employ deadlines judiciously. Offer only small concessions. Have a high level of personal expectation, and be perceived as somewhat unyielding. Information means power. Concede slowly; call a concession a concession.

11. Understand that any business which claims to be "breaking even" is losing money. Any business that says it is losing money is losing more than it says it is.

12. Have your attorney write the purchase agreement. It increases your legal bill exponentially, but it will save much time and agony, and there will be fewer surprises. In mergers there are no pleasant surprises. If there were, the property would not be for sale in the first place.

APPENDIX 2

Instructions to the Family on How to Deal with the Business in Case of the Death of Josef and Hans (originally written mid-1980s)

1. Reopen the stores as quickly as propriety permits. Wait no more than a day, and plan a major promotion. Rush sale ads through, and increase the advertising budget to quicken the momentum. Personnel mustn't be idle.

2. Your top priority is maintaining stability within the organization. Write a letter to all 3,800 employees pledging continuity. Avoid promises you can't keep, so write nothing about selling or not selling.

3. Inevitably, there will be management defections. Try to prevent them, but don't wring your hands publicly. Perceptions are important. Act as if you can handle anything.

4. The toughest part will be finding replacements for corporate staff. Top candidates will be reluctant to work for a company perceived to be in transition. Use overpayments and bonuses to lure them aboard, perhaps as high as 50 percent of their annual salary, payable after they remain a year. Promote from within. Pay your own key people the same kind of "stay" bonuses. Remember, however, that every special contract encumbers the company and reduces the selling price, so be prudent about such things.

5. Josef and I believe senior managers should be offered contracts. Those executives and perhaps five to ten other mid-managers should be given three-year agreements at their present compensation. Use stay bonuses where necessary. Hopefully, this will keep most of your top personnel with you.

6. Name a committee of outsiders to act as your advisers; include attorney Herb Rosedale in New York City.

7. Select one family member to be spokesperson. Disagree in private, but speak publicly with one voice. In the case of disputes, a majority decides, and all should honor that decision.

8. The chairman should be Don Bell, Wayne Hussey, Tom Cagley, or Skip Chustz.

9. Arrange meetings quickly in New York with Manufacturers Hanover Bank and in Dallas with Republic Bank to explain your plans for a sale of the company. Then seek out Morgan Stanley, Goldman Sachs, or First Bank of Boston to assist you in obtaining bids and in negotiations. Rosedale should be your negotiator, along with the investment banker. Until you select, always be speaking with two investment houses and play one against the other. The fee should be a percent of the sale price, giving the banking house the incentive to get a higher offer. Herb should also outline how he will charge. (It will be by the hour and thus finite, but you will discover that billable hours are infinite. There is not much you can do about that, but try. For example, require biweekly billing.)

10. Attempt to complete the sale within six to nine months.

11. Sell for cash only, and protect the personnel who work for you. Negotiate a reasonable severance package for those who will not be retained.

12. If more than one company is bidding, the winner, naturally, should be the high bidder—but remember your obligation to our Goudchaux's/Maison Blanche associ-

ates. The management should be protected through employment agreements or fair severances. The company at this time is worth between $60 million and $100 million. Whoever pays that much will demand freedom to run the stores as they see fit, but they will respect and accommodate your strong mandate to negotiate in favor of personnel.

13. Avoid selling for stock. Arrange for several bidders (even if you have to "invent" one). Remember, in a private transaction, buyers legally can conspire against the seller and make a side deal. Try to keep them apart; if possible, keep them from even knowing the names of the other potential purchasers.

14. There will be inheritance taxes. Arrange early to have the best inheritance-tax attorney and the best accounting firm help with this problem. Agree to a fixed cost for the attorneys. The draconian formula they will try to foist on you for their payment is written by attorneys for attorneys. There is no rationale—other than greed—for lawyers to be paid a percentage of the estate, although they always try. Don't accept it. The CPA will charge by the hour. Negotiate a "not to exceed" amount.

APPENDIX 3
More Goudchaux's Moments

As a student worker at LSU, we would pile into a car at lunch, go to the drive-thru window at McDonald's on State Street, and then head to Goudchaux's to shop on our lunch break. Little did I know that after graduating, I would be working there. My mother saw an ad in the paper for a buyer training program at Goudchaux's. I applied and was accepted. It truly was a good place to work; everyone was like family. On my last day, I cried all day. Hans called me in to his office and tried to talk me into staying, but the one thing I wanted he could not give me: Saturdays off.

—ROSE MARY (TERRITO) WILHELM

As a child, I hated shopping for shoes. I had long, narrow, hard-to-fit feet. My mom could never find shoes I liked in my size. One trip to Goudchaux's proved to be an exception. Two women waited on me that day, one being an older lady who was very helpful and seemed to appreciate my dilemma in finding shoes that were trendy for my young age. When I left the store, I told my mom that the "gray-haired worker lady was really nice." My mom corrected me, saying, "Honey, that wasn't an employee, that was Mrs. Sternberg, one of the owners." I felt like royalty.

—DAPHNE

I do miss the Sternbergs and their store so very much. Their family really cared for people.

—J. J. JUDGE

During some tragic years in the early 1970s, when my younger sister and my father died, my mom learned the caring, empathetic side of the Sternberg family, who supported her and gave her encouragement as she took on the role of mom to my sister's three children, aged three, four, and five.

—MARGO MURPHY

I was raised in the north Baton Rouge neighborhood called Dixie. When I was in high school, the Sternbergs gave me a job on Saturdays. I began in gift wrapping and was later promoted to sales. When I married James "Jimmy" Lieux Sr., I selected my china, silver, and crystal at Goudchaux's. The Sternbergs gave us a beautiful sterling silver tray for our wedding gift—an expensive gift at that time. Mr. Sternberg also helped me pick out my wedding dress. On the day of my wedding, he sent Miss Vi, an employee, to help me dress and get ready for the wedding. Throughout the years, the Sternbergs were always very kind and generous to me and my family. I'll always remember them and how they touched my lives.

—LULU LANGLOIS LIEUX

As a child in the fifties, I was always excited about a shopping trip to Goudchaux's. I would tag along with my mother as she shopped. As we made our way through the store, I watched for Mr. Sternberg as he would give me a nickel to buy a Coke. This made the whole ordeal worthwhile.

—C. J. SOILEAU

My youngest daughter, Janie, had beautiful blue eyes. One Sunday morning when she was three or four while we were at church, a lady came up to us and asked Janie, "Where did you get those pretty blue eyes?" And Janie replied, "At Goudchaux's."

—TELEDA WHITTINGTON

Many fond memories of the Main Street Goudchaux store were made when I worked downtown. Most of the girls had our 30-minute break down to a fine art with bonus time at the cosmetic counters and the helpful ladies there. We could call in our orders and they were always ready.

—DIANE REYNOLDS

We would bring our report cards to Goudchaux's, which would reward good grades with money. It was a nickel for every "A," which was a lot to a young child back then. Maybe department stores today should do that as an incentive for children to make better grades.

—PATTY ROUNDS

One of the store detectives was my husband, Billie L. Wilson [of the Baton Rouge police department]. He worked part-time from 1958 to 1988. On September 1, 1966, our last daughter was born, and we had spent several days trying to match up a name for her. Billie said, "Up on the fifth floor, I ran into Hans, Josef, and Miss Insa." I asked, "Who is Miss Insa and how does she spell her name? You go back up there and find out." And so it was that we named our baby Insa Diane. To top it off, the day I went home, Federal Express delivered a package from Insa and Dr. Abraham. Inside was a beautiful light yellow baby dress, loaded with white lace.

—JEANETTE FINCH

When my daughter was little, she told me that girls come from Goudchaux's and boys from Sears. When I asked why, she said "because that's where the clothes are." I realized that I had purchased most of her clothes from Goudchaux's and her brother's clothes from Sears. It was a logical conclusion.

—BARBARA BROWN

About 1970, my late friend Pearl and I went to Goudchaux's with her grandmother to return a shirt that was a Christmas gift. Grandma stood about 4-foot-8. The sales person politely explained the shirt came from Sears. Grandma reverted to Italian as she became increasingly indignant. Pearl tried to reason with her, but she would not have any part of it. [Hans Sternberg] observed the ruckus and told the sales person that indeed she could exchange the shirt. They had met their match. The customer was always right at Goudchaux's.

—CONNIE LEONARD

INDEX

in, 66; Mel Sternberg family in, 17–18, 23, 28; papal visit to, 109; restaurants in, 18, 118; school integration in, 54; WDSU-TV in, 67; World's Fair, 92, 97–98. *See also* Maison Blanche Department Store

New Orleans Centre, 118

New Orleans City Park, 97

New York City, 35, 41, 101–2, 108–9

Newman, Charles, 85

Newman, Henry, 85

Newman, Isidore, 85

Nicaragua, 18

Nicholson, Jim, 82

Noland, John, 80

Nordstrom's, 3

Nuremberg Laws, 15

Ohio State University, 46

Olshan, Carole, 77

Olshan, Mort, 76–77, 89, 101–2

Olson, John, 103

Ott, Bishop Stanley, 115

Ourso, Clifford, 45–46

Ourso, E. J., 101

Parking, 35, 42, *42*, 75, 77, 92, 102, 104

Parks, Rosa, 53

Pearson, Ruby, 65

Pennington YWCA, 79

Petite, Pam, 77

Phares, Greg, 63

Phelps, Ashton, Jr., 92, 120

Philadelphia, 16, 17

Plaisance, Don, 41

Politicians, 43, 80–82

Prayer service at Goudchaux's, 66

Premier Bank, 114, 116

Princeton University, 46–48

Pugh, Camilla, 80

Pugh, Gordon, 80

"Purchase with purchase" promotions, 72

Race relations, 50–57, *55*, 80–82, 110

Rarick, John, 80, 81–82

Rat farm, 101

Rath, Ernst von, 29

Refund policy, 65

Republic Bank of Texas, 110–11, 116

Reynolds, Diane, 74, 133

Rhea, Carolyn, 61

Ribbentrop, Joachim von, 37

Richard, Bettye Pearson, 37

Rich's Department Store, 46, 101, 123

Rike's Department Store (Dayton, Ohio), 85

Ripley's Believe It or Not, 4, 68, 104, *105*

Robinson's Department Stores, 105–7, 109, 110, 112, 115, 119, 120, 122

Roemer, Buddy, 103

Roosevelt, Franklin, 28, 124

Rosedale, Herb, 89, 118, 119

Rosenfield's, 39, 55, 62

Rosenthal, Ethel. *See* Sternberg, Ethel Rosenthal

Rounds, Patty, 134

Rubenstein's Department Stores, 74, 86

Sabagh, Monie, 61

Sachse, Victor, Jr., 20, 75

Sage-Allen (Hartford), 123

Saks Fifth Avenue, 3, 92, 103, 109, 123

Sales associates, 60–62, 77, 92, 107, 121

Sales statistics, 19, 50, 56, 62, 71, 77, 82, 85, 102, 104, 106, 110–12, 116

Saudi Arabia, 79–80, 115

Scott, Raymond, 52

Screen, Pat, 108–9

Sears Roebuck, 42, 55, 56, 62, 76, 82, 100

Security Industrial Insurance, 101

Security staff, 42–43, 54, 63–64, 66, 103–4

Segregation, 51–54

Shala, Noha Abou, 61

Shef, Mike, 119

Shoplifters, 63–64

Shopper's Fair, 55

Shopping malls. *See specific malls*

Siegel, Mimi, 61

Simmons, Lamar, 52

Six-Day War, 67–68

Sklar, Jerry, 89

Slidell mall, 104, 112

Smith, Rev. Charles, 56

Smith, Dan, 82

Smith, Mike, 64

Soileau, C. J., 133

A South Louisiana Bride's Notebook (Sternberg), 84

Southern Baptist Convention, 52

Southern Christian Leadership Conference, 52

Southern University, 54

Stahl, Joy, 61

Standard Oil Refinery, 43

Starmount companies, 60, 101

Starmount Life Insurance, 101, 127–28

Stein, Röschen. *See* Sternberg, Röschen Stein

Steinberg, Dick, 77

Steinberg's Sporting Goods, 81

Sternberg, Alfred, 8, *9*, 10, 17

Sternberg, Anna Lichtenfeld, 10

Sternberg, Bruno, 8, 10

Sternberg, Cecilia, 8

Sternberg, Deborah, 128

Sternberg, Donna Gail Weintraub: and brother-in-law Josef's death, 114; children of, 66–67, *78*, 99, *99*, 128; courtship and marriage of, 60, 66–67; and fund-raising events, 68, 80; at Goudchaux's, 62, 67, 76; and insurance company, 128; in Junior League, 45; overseas buying trips by, 76, 77; photographs of, *70*, *78*, *99*; and sale of Maison Blanche, 119–20

Sternberg, Emelia, 8

Sternberg, Erich: automobile owned by, 28, 38, 40; Baton Rouge homes of, 25–27, 37, *38*; birth of, 8; childhood of, 9–10; children of, 13, 15, *17*, *26*, *27*, *38*, 40; courtship and marriage of, 12–13; in Cuba, 17–18; education of, 9; emigration of, to America, 15–16, 24; finances of, 13, 15–16, 18, *19*, 33; and fund-raising events, 68; and gadgets, 41; health problems of, 10–11, 58; and heart attacks, 58; in Jackson, Mississippi, 17; Jacob Sternberg's living with, in Baton Rouge, 26, 29, 37, 44; on Nazi Germany, 15, 37; in New Orleans, 17–18; in Philadelphia, 16, 17; photographs of, *9*, *26*, *38*, *42*, *49*, *50*; physical appearance of, 11; and politics, 82; posthumous award for, 124; purchase of Goudchaux's by, 8, 18–20, *20*, 33; reading interests and mathematical skills of, 40–41; reparations for, from Germany, 45; and sense of humor, 41; sponsorships of Jews' emigration by, 30; and Sternberg store in Aurich, 11, 15; Sunday outings and trips by, 28, 37; U.S. citizenship for, 38–39; and WLCS radio station, 52, 127. *See also* Goudchaux's Department Store

Sternberg, Erich (Hans J.'s son), *78*, 82, 128

Sternberg, Esther, 8

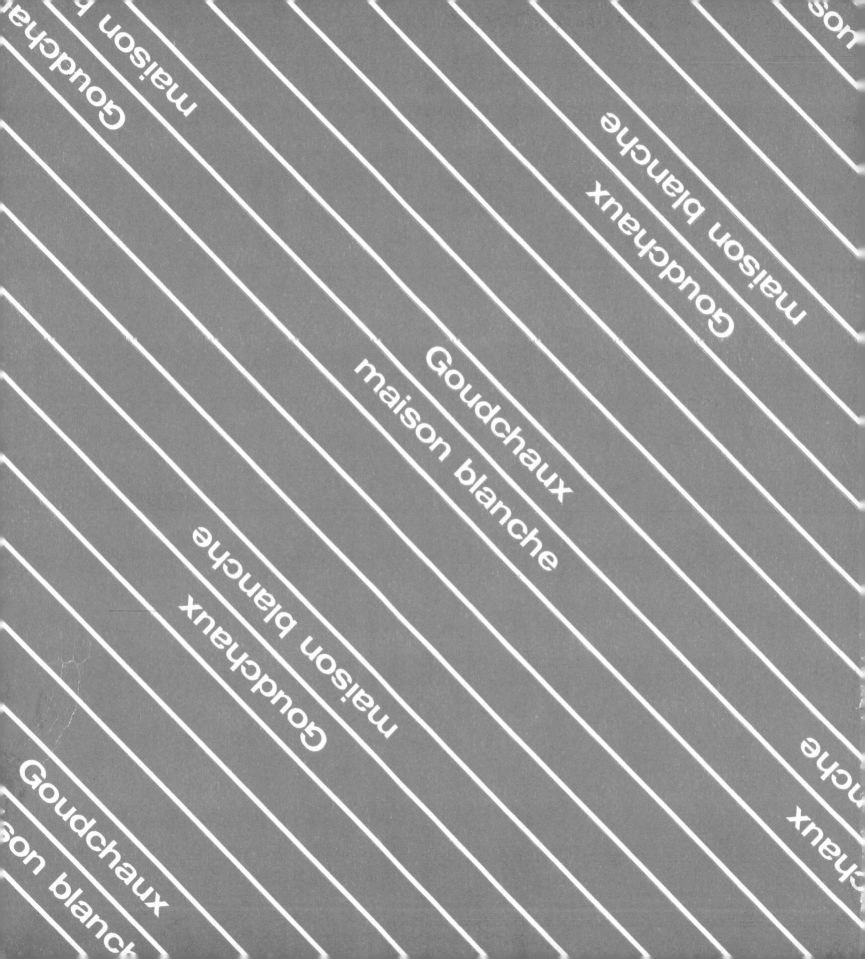